73

*The Incredible Sestina Anthology*
a collection of poetry

ʊ

Edited by Daniel Nester

Write Bloody Publishing
*America's Independent Press*

Austin, TX

WRITEBLOODY.COM

Nester, Daniel.
1ˢᵗ edition.
ISBN: 978-1938912-36-8

Interior Layout by Lea C. Deschenes
Cover Designed by Anthony Wyborny
Proofread by Helen Novielli and Alex Kryger
Edited by Daniel Nester
Type set in Bergamo from www.theleagueofmoveabletype.com

Printed in Tennessee, USA

Write Bloody Publishing
Austin, TX
Support Independent Presses
writebloody.com

To contact the editor, send an email to writebloody@gmail.com

MADE IN THE USA

*The Incredible Sestina Anthology*

# THE INCREDIBLE SESTINA ANTHOLOGY

Introduction......................................................................... 19

Sherman Alexie
   The Business of Fancydancing................................. 25

Shane Allison
   Mother Worries.......................................................... 27

Steve Almond
   Sestina for Elton John............................................... 29

Scott Edward Anderson
   Second Skin ................................................................ 31

Alan Ansen
   A Fit of Something Against Something.................... 33

Cristin O'Keefe Aptowicz
   Sestina for Shappy, Who Doesn't Get Enough Love Poems .... 35

John Ashbery
   Farm Implements and Rutabagas in a Landscape .................. 37
   Faust .............................................................................. 39

W.H. Auden
   Paysage Moralisé ........................................................ 41

Sandra Beasley
   Let Me Count the Waves .......................................... 43
   The Editor of *Encyclopedia Britannica* Regrets Everything ......... 45

Jeanne Marie Beaumont
   A Stein's Sestina........................................................ 47

Aaron Belz
   Pam ............................................................................... 49

Tara Betts
   Sestina for the Sin .................................................... 51

Elizabeth Bishop
   A Miracle for Breakfast ........................................... 53
   Sestina........................................................................... 55

Star Black
    Hi Yo......................................................................... 57

Paula Bohince
    Allegory of the Leopard........................................... 62

Jenny Boully
    Sestina of Missed Connections ............................... 64

Geoff Bouvier
    Refining Sestina ..................................................... 66

Catherine Bowman
    Mr. X....................................................................... 67

Derrick C. Brown
    They Loved You and Your Title,
    but It All Telegraphed Too Much............................ 69

Stephen Burt
    Six Kinds of Noodles .............................................. 71

Casey Camp
    A Poem on the Severe Awesomeness of John Zorn ................. 73

Jenna Cardinale
    Beyond January........................................................ 81

Patricia Carlin
    Lives of the Conquerors .......................................... 83

Shanna Compton
    The Remarried Again Sestina ................................. 85

Jeffery Conway
    Is It Dancing? ......................................................... 87

Alfred Corn
    Pound-Eliot Sestina ................................................ 90

Michael Costello
    A Series................................................................... 92

Laura Cronk
    Sestina for a Sister .................................................. 94

James Cummins
#17 from *The Whole Truth* ...................................... 96
David Lehman and Jim Cummins Do Their Part After the
World Trade Center Disaster ................................. 98

Peter Davis
Mustache Sestina ............................................... 100

Sharon Dolin
Praying Mantis in Brooklyn ................................. 102
Reluctant Sestina .............................................. 104

Denise Duhamel
The Brady Bunch (A Double Sestina) ..................... 106
On Delta Flight 659 with Sean Penn ......................111

Drew Gardner
Sestina: AltaVista .............................................. 113

Dana Gioia
My Confessional Sestina ..................................... 115

Sarah Green
Metamorphic Sestina .........................................117

Beth Gylys
Not an Affair: A Sestina ......................................119
The Scene ...................................................... 121

Marilyn Hacker
Untoward Occurrence at Embassy Poetry Reading .............. 123

Donald Hall
Sestina ......................................................... 125

James Harms
One Long Sentence and a Few Short Ones;
or, 39 Lines by Frank Gehry ................................ 127

Brooks Haxton
Posttraumatic Small-Talk Disorder ....................... 129

Anthony Hecht
The Book of Yolek ........................................... 131

Brian Henry
Bad Apple ...................................................... 133

Scott Hightower
  Cruising a Hungry World .................................................. 135
Ernest Hilbert
  Hel[l]ical Double Sestina: [Metal Number One] ................ 137
Elizabeth Hildreth
  In a Rut ..................................................................... 141
Paul Hoover
  Sestina from *Sonnet 56* ............................................... 143
John Hoppenthaler
  Coconut Octopus .......................................................... 145
Sonya Huber
  Dear *Thrasher* ........................................................... 147
Victor D. Infante
  Six Portraits in Disintegration ....................................... 149
Kent Johnson
  Sestina: Avantforte ...................................................... 151
Donald Justice
  Here in Katmandu ......................................................... 155
Meg Kearney
  14th Street ................................................................. 157
Weldon Kees
  Sestina: Travel Notes .................................................... 159
Lynn Kilpatrick
  Francis Bacon Sestina .................................................... 161
Kenneth Koch & John Ashbery
  Crone Rhapsody ........................................................... 163
Noelle Kocot
  Why We Go to Couple's Counseling ................................. 166
Leonard Kress
  Miss New Jersey ........................................................... 168
Quraysh Ali Lansana
  homemade ................................................................... 170

Joan Larkin
    Jewish Food.................................................................... 172
David Lehman
    The Old Constellation .......................................................174
    Operation Memory.............................................................176
Eric LeMay
    The Sestina of O................................................................ 178
Brendan Lorber
    Luck Is the Thing We Are Shit Out Of............................... 180
Matt Madden
    The Six Treasures of the Spiral: A Comics Sestina ................ 182
Paul Mariani
    The Great Wheel................................................................ 197
Nate Marshall
    pallbearers (a sestina) .......................................................... 199
Harry Mathews
    Histoire ............................................................................ 201
Florence Cassen Mayers
    All-American Sestina ......................................................... 204
    July Idyll.......................................................................... 206
Marty McConnell
    one possible explanation of my utter
    and rather surprising lack of an adolescent tomboy phase ...... 208
James Merrill
    Tomorrows........................................................................ 210
Sharon Mesmer
    Super Rooster Killer Assault Kit......................................... 212
Anis Mojgani
    They raised violins............................................................. 215
Rick Moody
    Radio Sestina ................................................................... 217
Carley Moore
    Mechanics ........................................................................ 219

Lenard D. Moore
A Quiet Rhythm of Sleep ................................... 221

Jeffrey Morgan
When Unreal Girlfriends Die:
The Manti Te'o Sestina ...................................... 223

Tomás Q. Morín
Canso of the Dancing Bears ................................ 225

Paul Muldoon
The Last Time I Saw Chris ................................. 227

Amanda Nadelberg
My New Pet Word Is Mozzarella .......................... 229

Marilyn Nelson
Two Masters .................................................. 231

Ethan Paquin
Oratio Moderna ............................................... 233

Richard Peabody
Spaghetti Western Sestina................................... 235

Kiki Petrosino
Crusaders ...................................................... 237

Carl Phillips
Birdland ....................................................... 239

Ezra Pound
Sestina: Altaforte ............................................ 241

Michael Quattrone
Ticker .......................................................... 243

Ned Rust
Prophetic Sestina ............................................ 245

Carly Sachs
Indecent Docent: Sex-Deprived Tina ..................... 247

Michael Schiavo
"Be Careful, Cortelyou, How You Tell Her" ........... 249

Lawrence Schimel
Endless Sestina................................................ 251

Jason Schneiderman
　　The Buffy Sestina ............................................. 253

Esther Schor
　　Sestina: Tegucigalpa .......................................... 255

Ravi Shankar
　　How Duggan Knew ........................................... 257

Peter Jay Shippy
　　The Lyricist and His Rock Star ............................. 259

Rachel Shukert
　　Subterranean Gnomesick Blues;
　　or, The Gnome Who Whet My Fleshy Tent ............. 261

Patricia Smith
　　Looking to See How the Eyes Inhabit Dark,
　　Wondering about Light ....................................... 263

Jay Snodgrass
　　Judas Priest .................................................... 266

Sparrow
　　Cowboys ....................................................... 268

Heidi Lynn Staples
　　Embryonic Sestina ........................................... 270

Mark Strand
　　Chekhov: A Sestina ........................................... 272

Chris Stroffolino
　　In Memory of My Rock Band: Sestina .................... 274

Jade Sylvan
　　Facebook Sestina ............................................. 276

David Trinidad
　　Detective Notes ............................................... 278
　　Playing with Dolls ........................................... 280

Quincy Troupe
　　Sestina for 39 Silent Angels ................................ 282

Lewis Turco
　　The Vision ..................................................... 284

Laura Van Prooyen
   Lenten Sestina ..................................................... 286

Martha Modena Vertreace-Doody
   Señora Mamacita .................................................. 288

Anne Waldman
   How the Sestina (Yawn) Works ............................. 292

Miller Williams
   The Shrinking Lonesome Sestina ........................... 294

Jonah Winter
   Sestina: Bob .......................................................... 296
   Sestina: A Cowboy's Diary ..................................... 298

Louis Zukofsky
   Mantis .................................................................. 300

Acknowledgments .................................................... 303

Contributor Notes ................................................... 305

Copyrights ............................................................... 327

# INTRODUCTION

First things first. You're asking: Why in the world should I read a book of sestinas? I'm picturing you there after you plucked this book off a shelf. Maybe you've checked out its cover's cool spiral pattern, or you're previewing it online.

You're asking: What in tarnation would compel anyone to collect a book of poems that use a form invented in medieval southern France, written in English 700 years later? Or maybe you're asking: What the freak is a sestina anyway?

These are all reasonable questions.

Even those who've heard of this form or are inside the poetry world may ask what a sestina is. Believed to have been invented in the 12th century by Arnaut Daniel, a troubadour who influenced Dante, the sestina is a 39-line patterned form that has spiraled into a new life in English in the past 100 years or so.

Instead of a rhyme scheme (like the Shakespearean sonnet's ABABCDCDEFEFGG) or a regular meter (like iambic pentameter's da-DUM times five) or syllables (the 5-7-5 of English Haiku), a sestina uses a spiral, formed in a pattern of words that appear at the end of each line. Over the course of six stanzas of six lines (sestina translates as "six" or "sixer") and a seventh three-line stanza, these end words, called *teleutons* or *repitons*, appear in a different order in each round, except for the final three-line stanza, called the *envoi* or *tornada*, which uses all six end words in a triumphant send-off. The last end word of each stanza is the first word of the next, which is why the sestina is called a linked form. Graphed-out in a word pattern, each number representing an end word, the sestina looks something like this:

Stanza 1: 1 2 3 4 5 6
Stanza 2: 6 1 5 2 4 3
Stanza 3: 3 6 4 1 2 5
Stanza 4: 5 3 2 6 1 4
Stanza 5: 4 5 1 3 6 2
Stanza 6: 2 4 6 5 3 1
Envoi: 2/5 4/3 6/1

Why this pattern, you ask? The words spiral out to form the next stanza of the sestina. Like this crappy drawing I did just now:

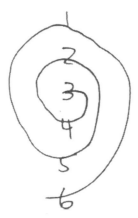

This sestina pattern informs Matt Madden's comic sestina, "The Six Treasures of the Spiral," included here, and certainly is the reason why there are so many references to circles and spirals throughout this incredible anthology.

But isn't this all ridiculous, you may ask? Sure! Also: insane, laughable, fun. Other guide-book descriptions are also ambivalent; they range from "elaborate" (Babette Deutsch) and "complicated" (Karl Beckson and Arthur Ganz) to "often maddening" (Kim Addonizio and Dorianne Laux) and a "minor form" (James Fenton). Sestinas require "the poet's deepest love and conviction," Karl Shapiro writes, "as these take on a rather obsessive quality—if the poem is to offer us more than the pleasures of contrivance." Ron Padgett, in his *Handbook of Poetic Forms*, describes the sestina as "delightful" and its spiral numerology an "ideal experiment for the mathematical mind."

More than 800 years since its invention, the sestina survives and thrives in the modern world. After the troubadours, the sestina went silent, revived only occasionally. Why? Because that pattern is pretty freaking complicated. You saw that spiral graph, right?

After Sir Philip Sidney's three sestinas in the 1570s, including his double sestina "You Goat-herd Gods" (78 lines!), there was a 200-year gap in English-language sestinas. Then, toward the end of the 19th century, there was a mini-comeback with Algernon Charles Swinburne, Edmund Gosse, Ella Wheeler Wilcox, and others. Rudyard Kipling's "Sestina of the Tramp Royal" came in 1898, and ten years later came Ezra Pound's "Sestina: Altaforte," included here, which sparked even more interest in the form.

By the mid-20th century, the English sestina renaissance began in earnest. Now, poets of each generation—no matter which stripe, school, movement, team, or club—have climbed Mt. Sestina: from Sherman Alexie and Louis Zukofsky to Patricia Smith and Elizabeth Bishop, from Carl Philips and Mark Strand to Wendell Kees and Marilyn Nelson. Formalists love the sestina for its ornate, maddening word repetition; avant-gardists love the sestina for its ornate, maddening word repetition. W.H. Auden's "Paysage Moralisé" uses many of the same end words as Sidney did in "You Goat-herd Gods." John Ashbery mashes up the Popeye comic strip. James Merrill uses variations of one, two, three, four, five, and six as he moves through the poem.

But is the sestina just a novelty, a technical exercise? It can be—and there's nothing wrong with that—but the sestina's formal constraints and linguistic freedom also open up new possibilities. One true test of any form—situation comedy, coming-of-age story, three-minute pop song, basic black dress—is how well it holds up when its boundaries are tested, when an artist smashes and stretches it, kicks the tires and soups up the engine. The sestina offers something for every poet. Let's break out the big words: postmodern artifice, numerological mystery, procedural wordplay, conceptualist or formalist reverie. All these terms apply when explaining the sestina's appeal.

Writing a sestina is like long-distance running, where going the distance puts the mind into a kind of trance. The challenge of using each end word seven times leads to "cheating," swapping out sound-alikes ("four" and "for") or end words that can be a verb and a noun. Sometimes poets use one or more super-flashy words that stand out (see Amanda Nadelberg's "My New Pet Word Is Mozzarella" or

Harry Mathews's "Histoire," both included here). A sestina forces the poet to give in to echo and chance, to repeat when it's just wrong, to sprawl on a wrestling mat just to get through the first draft.

Sestinas fail. There are sestinas that, on the surface, may strike the reader as, well, bad. Or dull. Or trite. Or "workshoppy." "Mediocre talents are irresistibly drawn to forms like the sestina," John Frederick Nims writes in his excellent study of the sestina, "which offer easy satisfaction in that they seem only forms that need filling out, like an application for a library card." These revelations, shocking to some, have led many poets to dismiss the sestina form altogether, as if no other bad poems have existed elsewhere. James Cummins, whose essay on the sestina is a must, has a different take. "The sound of a bad sestina might be the sound of life leaving the beast," he writes, "but at least it's life."

In many ways, this incredible book is several anthologies in one. One comes from my time as a sestina editor. I'm not kidding; it was a thing. From 2003 to 2007, I held the job title of Assistant Web Editor for Sestinas at McSweeney's Internet Tendency. During that time, I read hundreds of sestinas a month, and published, on average, one sestina per week. My choices tended to coincide with the humorous, topical spirit of the website. Several poets from McSweeney's are included here: Rick Moody, Denise Duhamel, David Lehman, Jenny Boully, Steve Almond, and Rachel Shukert.

Another comes from getting tips from fellow sestina nerds: Star Black's "Hi Yo," from *Double Time*, her collection of double sestinas; an excerpt from *The Whole Truth*, James Cummins's collection based on the Perry Mason TV series; Jeffery Conway's project based on the camp classic *Showgirls*; Sandra Beasley's and Geoff Bouvier's wicked innovations; and Quraysh Ali Lansana's and Sarah Green's modern fables.

Still another group of poets have to be included if an anthology of sestinas can call itself that with a straight face: Donald Justice, John Ashbery, Anthony Hecht, Marilyn Hacker, Florence Cassen Mayers.

After many of the poems included here, you will see excerpts from our "Behind the Sestina" interviews, which will, I hope, offer the writers' insights on the origins of their poems and the appeal of the sestina form. To read the full interviews, as well as more information about sestinas, visit the book's website at incrediblesestinas.com. You won't be disappointed.

And now is a good time to return to our first question: Why the freak should we read a book of sestinas?

Because a sestina is always full of life.

Because of its patterns.

Because of its spiral.

Because of its swagger.

Because we live in a world where something as ridiculous and beautiful as the sestina still exists.

Because poets honor their history by writing and reading sestinas.

Because a poet is always up for a challenge.

Because you've already read at least one sestina, hidden inside this introduction.

Because there is a particular kind of beauty and wisdom that can only be unlocked by writing a sestina.

So now you know. Let's start the spiral.

Daniel Nester
Albany, New York
July 2013

# Sherman Alexie

## The Business of Fancydancing

After driving all night, trying to reach
Arlee in time for the fancydance
finals, a case of empty
beer bottles shaking our foundations, we
stop at a liquor store, count out money,
and would believe in the promise

of any man with a twenty, a promise
thin and wrinkled in his hand, reach-
ing into the window of our car. Money
is an Indian Boy who can fancydance
from powwow to powwow. We
got our boy, Vernon WildShoe, to fill our empty

wallets and stomachs, to fill our empty
cooler. Vernon is like some promise
to pay the light bill, a credit card we
Indians get to use. When he reach-
es his hands up, feathers held high, in a dance
that makes old women speak English, the money

for first place belongs to us, all in cash, money
we tuck in our shoes, leaving our wallets empty
in case we pass out. At the modern dance,
where Indians dance white, a twenty is a promise
that can last all night long, a promise reach-
ing into back pockets of unfamiliar Levis. We

get Vernon there in time for the finals and we
watch him like he was dancing on money,
which he is, watch the young girls reach-
ing for him like he was Elvis in braids and an empty
tipi, like Vernon could make a promise
with every step he took, like a fancydance

could change their lives. We watch him dance
and he never talks. It's all a business we
understand. Every drum beat is a promise
note written in the dust, measured exactly. Money
is a tool, putty to fill all the empty
spaces, a ladder so we can reach

for more. A promise is just like money.
Something we can hold, in twenties, a dream we reach.
It's business, a fancydance to fill where it's empty.

*I love how lightly this poem wears its formal inclination on its sleeve. Don't be fooled: the line's conversational, loping, yet balanced enjambments can be difficult to execute. The doubled repetitions at the end of each stanza/beginning of the next stanza are always tough to manage, but Alexie uses this echo to underline the urgent neediness of the speaker's voice. The poem's musicality is intensified by the rhyme of "empty," "we," and "money." Sometimes I think that, in great sestinas, the whole story can be gleaned from the end words alone. I admire the way he describes the fixed end words not as a burden to be born, but as a liberation to his creative instincts. The best sestinas, for all their linguistic cages, have an untamed wildness to them. Also, you just can't forget the image of an Elvis in braids.*—Sandra Beasley

# SHANE ALLISON

## MOTHER WORRIES

Lord, how we gon' pay these bills in this
How we gon' pay these bills,
Lord. How we gon' pay these bills in
We gon' pay these
We gon' pay
Lord how we gon' pay these bills in this house?

How Lord, are we gon' pay these bills in this house
Lord how, Lord how we gon' pay these bills in this
Lord how, Lord we gon' pay
Lord how are we gon' pay these bills
These bills, Lord how we gon' pay these
How we goin' to pay these bills, Lord in

In this house, Lord? How is it that we gon' pay these bills in,
In this house, Lord. How, Lord we goin' to pay the bills in this house
These bills, these bills in this house, Lord, these
Bills in this house, how are we goin' to afford to pay the bills in this
House of all houses? With the bills the way, these bills
Are, how are we goin' to pay?

How, Lord? How is it that we are goin' to pay
The bills in this house the way they are in
This house, this house with the bills
In this house of houses in the house
With the bills we don't know how we're goin' to pay in this
House with the bills the way these

Bills are in this house, with these
Bills we don't know how we gon' pay
In this, our house of houses with this and this
Bill, Lord we have to pay in
This house, the house with all the bills that need to be paid in the house.
Lord how? How Lord is we to pay these bills?

How are we gon' do it? How is it that we are to pay these bills
These bills, which are stacking up high as a house with these
Bills we don't know, Lord, how we goin' to pay the bills that are due
        on the house
That needs to be paid
In the house, this house in
Which the bills are big in this

House with these bills that we
Don't know how in this world
We don't know how we goin' to pay


*I went through a time where I started thinking about repetition and its use
in poetry, thinking about phrases I've heard. My mother's voice is always
reoccurring in my head. She was going through a hard time with my dad at the
time. Emotions were very high and unfortunately, I was witness to much of
her fear and worry. She asked, "Lord, how are we going to pay these bills?" I
wrote that down somewhere and came back to it later and "Mother Worries"
was born.*

# STEVE ALMOND

## SESTINA FOR ELTON JOHN

In this sick house dream I am on Mars,
Sliding down the frozen seas in a canoe
made of human lips, like Nanook, only helpless,
unable to call out to anyone, my own mouth
stitched cold and what I wouldn't give to be horny
right now, in a steamroom full of slurp,

all my comrades full of slurp,
the hot, salacious kind not found on Mars,
the sort who have made horny
a *life commitment* and when you say canoe
they leer and wet their mouths
and pout, implying that they are helpless,

won't you help them, they are so helpless
though the word is one big, lewd slurp
and all they want is to lick my mouth,
they don't care about Mars,
they don't care about my canoe,
they have their priorities straight: they are horny.

How sweet to surrender to their dream, to be horny
with them, not helpless
in this stiff canoe
under the lonely red ridges, unable to slurp
because it's too cold on mars
and there's no one here, not a single mouth

(if you don't count my mouth)
and I begin to see now that these horny
thoughts are just ways of reminding me: I'm on Mars,
I'm entirely helpless,
there is no one toward whom I might slurp
and my only means of progress is a canoe

made of human lips, a stiff canoe
that will not speak to me, that is not a mouth,
that cannot (or will not) slurp
that is merely wood, lips, what have you—and horny?
You can kiss horny goodbye, you helpless
bastard, you're on Mars

in a canoe of lips and here, on Mars,
in your helpless sickhouse dream, there's no mouth,
no horny rescue team, you are alone: entirely, utterly, without slurp

*The poem derives from my unwholesome obsession with Elton John's hirsute lower regions. I wrote the poem thinking about Elton John in soccer shorts, his sexy, hairy little stubby legs and big sunglasses. I believe that constitutes slurping. I considered dedicating the poem to Bono, who has similar lower regions, but the rights issues were a total bitch.*

# Scott Edward Anderson

## *Second Skin*

In the yard by the barn was a snake
resting on a leaf-pile in the garden,
nearby his old shod skin
limp and lifeless under a noon-day sun.
Abandoned on the blades of grass,
like an untangled filament of memory.

The sight of him fired my memory,
which cast a shadow on the snake
(who now slithered away in the grass).
He lent a curious aspect to the garden—
aspect being its relation to the sun
—not unlike *his* relation to the skin.

He seemed to remember the skin.
(Do snakes *have* that much memory?)
Or was it a trick of the sun
that he mistook for a female snake?
When he made his way out of the garden,
I crept along quietly in the grass.

As I followed him there in the grass,
he stretched ever closer to the skin;
his path leading out of the garden,
as if tracing the line of a memory.
How strange, I thought, this snake,
disregarding the late summer sun.

Later, over-heated in afternoon sun,
I lay down to rest on the grass.
I watched again as the snake
tried to resuscitate his discarded skin,
perhaps to revive its dead memory
and lure it back home to the garden.

Cutting the lawn by the garden,
I must have been dizzy with sun,
or dozing in the haze of a memory.
Translucent flakes feathered the grass:
it was then I remembered the skin;
it was then I remembered the snake.

I sat by the garden dropping fresh-cut grass
onto my arm and its sun-baked skin,
clippings of memory snaking through my mind.


*I was cutting the lawn by my garden using one of those old rotary push
mowers. It was hot and I was half day-dreaming in the heat and ran over the
skin. I knew the snake, had seen him before, knew his habits a bit, too. He
kept rodents out of the garden pretty well. I saw him interacting with the old
skin and tried to imagine what was going through his mind, if snakes have
minds. Anyway, the end words came pretty easily as I was thinking about
him and the idea of memories like old, shed skin we leave behind as we move
through our lives.*

# ALAN ANSEN

## A FIT OF SOMETHING AGAINST SOMETHING

*for John Ashbery*


In the burgeoning age of Arnaut when for God and man to be
Shone a glory not a symptom, poetry was not austere.
Complicated laws it followed, generosity through order,
Dowered acrobats with hoops trapezing laurels undergone.
Fountainlike gyrations earned the free trouvère the name of master,
And the climax of his daring was the dazzling sestina.

When love the subject-object of Romance sestina
Left gay Provence for learned Italy to be
The guide and guard and graveyard of a supreme master,
The plaything followed, intricate turned more austere,
And doubled in and on its tracks, now woebegone
Began to learn its place and kiss the rod of order.

Petrarch and Sidney, time's woodsmen, reorder
To pastoral the still pregnant sestina
With history and logic come to be
The inspissations of its present master
Landscapes that turn upon themselves have gone
To shape a shining surface to austere.

The pious young would be austere;
They pant and puff pursuing order
(Within a shorter-breathed sestina
The fewer true). Those that have gone
The masturbatory course must be
In doubt if they or it is master.

New rebels will not master
Forms pointlessly austere.
They feel that they will be
Screwed by that alien order,
That Gestapo sestina,
Cats, it's the most ungone.

Its zing's all gone,
It's no master.
Get lost, sestina,
Go way, austere.
You'll always be
Out of order.

*Sestina order,*
Austere master,
BE GONE ! ! !

# CRISTIN O'KEEFE APTOWICZ

## SESTINA FOR SHAPPY, WHO DOESN'T GET ENOUGH LOVE POEMS

Who knew that when the fickle finger of love
finally poked through my ribs, it would choose you,
a 30-year-old man who willingly calls himself Shappy,
a panda-shaped poet so absurd and funny
that when I met you I thought you were part cartoon,
a fella for which "excess kitsch" was the definition of "home."

The summer I met you, I was making Astoria my home.
Four months out of college, and I had no job, no love,
no prospects, no optimism. My life was a sad cartoon:
Me, a lonely alley cat waiting for the Pepé Le Pew which was you.
Before, I assumed I'd be with a scientist, more logical than funny.
It was ridiculous to think I'd date a guy named Shappy.

But that's how you were introduced to me, as Shappy.
No one knew your real name, not even in Chicago, your home.
Earliest impressions: you were drunk and you were funny.
That was your plan, to make me laugh until I fell in love.
You just hoped I wouldn't fall into the pattern familiar with you.
Women grew up and left: Who wanted to marry a cartoon?

And, hey, even I was a little afraid: Could I be with a cartoon?
I mean, nonscientist? A non-office worker? A ... Shappy?
But we all know the ending here, and, in the end, I ended up with you.
You left freezing Chicago to make New York City your home
and we ignored all the critics of our dizzying brand of love,
cuz aren't we all at our most beautiful when we're just being funny?

In fact, isn't life at its most beautiful when it's just being funny?
Who cares if our apartment looks like the set of a cartoon?
And it's not as if we don't make money as well as love:
me as serious writer and you as the poet named Shappy.
Together we cram dollars into savings so we can buy a home
big enough for all your stuff, the things you love and you.

But right now, I'm enjoying life as it is for me and you:
the way everything, even the tragedies, can be funny;
the dachshund- and pop culture–filled hovel called home;
the way every day is a new episode of our life's silly cartoon.
This life we live just amazes me, Shappy.
Who thought this would be my definition of love?

I would have never picked you, my beautiful cartoon,
but ain't life funny? After all, it made you, Shappy,
the perfect home for all my heart's dumb, dumb love.

*I had written only one other sestina before this one. When I first graduated from NYU, the only job I was offered was as writer and editor for a porn website. As a hazard of the job, I was bombarded daily with pop-up ads advertising other porn sites. I noticed that many of the ads used the same words (you can imagine what they are!), so I spent MONTHS collecting phrases from pornographic pop-up ads to create a "found poetry" sestina.*

*For this sestina, when I tried to think of a subject to place in the center of the poem, my relationship with my partner, Shappy, came to mind. At that time, I had not written much about us, and the timing felt right. It became a crowd favorite at my local poetry venue, the Bowery Poetry Club. I think it captures wonderfully that time in my life. Shappy and I dated for eleven-and-a-half years, and our years in the tiny kitsch-crammed apartment are among the happiest I've ever lived.*

# JOHN ASHBERY

## *FARM IMPLEMENTS AND RUTABAGAS IN A LANDSCAPE*

The first of the undecoded messages read: "Popeye sits in thunder,
Unthought of. From that shoebox of an apartment,
From livid curtain's hue, a tangram emerges: a country."
Meanwhile the Sea Hag was relaxing on a green couch: "How pleasant
To spend one's vacation *en la casa de Popeye*," she scratched
Her cleft chin's solitary hair. She remembered spinach

And was going to ask Wimpy if he had bought any spinach.
"M'love," he intercepted, "the plains are decked out in thunder
Today, and it shall be as you wish." He scratched
The part of his head under his hat. The apartment
Seemed to grow smaller. "But what if no pleasant
Inspiration plunge us now to the stars? *For this is my country.*"

Suddenly they remembered how it was cheaper in the country.
Wimpy was thoughtfully cutting open a number 2 can of spinach
When the door opened and Swee'pea crept in. "How  pleasant!"
But Swee'pea looked morose. A note was pinned to his bib. "Thunder
And tears are unavailing," it read. "Henceforth shall Popeye's apartment
Be but remembered space, toxic or salubrious, whole or scratched."

Olive came hurtling through the window; its geraniums scratched
Her long thigh. "I have news!" she gasped. "Popeye, forced as you
      know to flee the country
One musty gusty evening, by the schemes of his wizened, duplicate
      father, jealous of the apartment
And all that it contains, myself and spinach
In particular, heaves bolts of loving thunder
At his own astonished becoming, rupturing the pleasant

Arpeggio of our years. No more shall pleasant
Rays of the sun refresh your sense of growing old, nor the scratched
Tree-trunks and mossy foliage, only immaculate darkness and thunder."
She grabbed Swee'pea. "I'm taking the brat to the country."

"But you can't do that—he hasn't even finished his spinach,"
Urged the Sea Hag, looking fearfully around at the apartment.

But Olive was already out of earshot. Now the apartment
Succumbed to a strange new hush. "Actually it's quite pleasant
Here," thought the Sea Hag. "If this is all we need fear from spinach
Then I don't mind so much. Perhaps we could invite Alice the Goon
    over"—she scratched
One dug pensively—"but Wimpy is such a country
Bumpkin, always burping like that." Minute at first, the thunder

Soon filled the apartment. It was domestic thunder,
The color of spinach. Popeye chuckled and scratched
His balls: it sure was pleasant to spend a day in the country.

## FAUST

If only the phantom would stop reappearing!
Business, if you wanted to know, was punk at the opera.
The heroine no longer appeared in *Faust*.
The crowds strolled sadly away. The phantom
Watched them from the roof, not guessing the hungers
That must be stirred before disappointment can begin.

One day as morning was about to begin
A man in brown with a white shirt reappearing
At the bottom of his yellow vest, was talking hungers
With the silver-haired director of the opera.
On the green-carpeted floor no phantom
Appeared, except yellow squares of sunlight, like those in *Faust*.

That night as the musicians for *Faust*
Were about to go on strike, lest darkness begin
In the corridors, and through them the phantom
Glide unobstructed, the vision reappearing
Of blonde Marguerite practicing a new opera
At her window awoke terrible new hungers

In the already starving tenor. But hungers
Are just another topic, like the new Faust
Drifting through the tunnels of the opera
(In search of lost old age? For they begin
To notice a twinkle in his eye. It is cold daylight reappearing
At the window behind him, itself a phantom

Window, painted by the phantom
Scene painters, sick of not getting paid, of hungers
For a scene below of tiny, reappearing
Dancers, with a sandbag falling like a note in *Faust*
Through purple air. And the spectators begin
To understand the bleeding tenor star of the opera.)

That night the opera
Was crowded to the rafters. The phantom
Took twenty-nine curtain calls. "Begin!
Begin!" In the wings the tenor hungers
For the heroine's convulsive kiss, and Faust
Moves forward, no longer young, reappearing

And reappearing for the last time. The opera
*Faust* would no longer need its phantom.
On the bare, sunlit stage the hungers could begin.

# W.H. AUDEN

## PAYSAGE MORALISÉ

Hearing of harvests rotting in the valleys,
Seeing at end of street the barren mountains,
Round corners coming suddenly on water,
Knowing them shipwrecked who were launched for islands,
We honour founders of these starving cities
Whose honour is the image of our sorrow,

Which cannot see its likeness in their sorrow
That brought them desperate to the brink of valleys;
Dreaming of evening walks through learned cities
They reined their violent horses on the mountains,
Those fields like ships to castaways on islands,
Visions of green to them who craved for water.

They built by rivers and at night the water
Running past windows comforted their sorrow;
Each in his little bed conceived of islands
Where every day was dancing in the valleys
And all the green trees blossomed on the mountains,
Where love was innocent, being far from cities.

But dawn came back and they were still in cities;
No marvellous creature rose up from the water;
There was still gold and silver in the mountains
But hunger was a more immediate sorrow,
Although to moping villages in valleys
Some waving pilgrims were describing islands...

'The gods,' they promised, 'visit us from islands,
Are stalking, head-up, lovely, through our cities;
Now is the time to leave your wretched valleys
And sail with them across the lime-green water,
Sitting at their white sides, forget your sorrow,
The shadow cast across your lives by mountains.'

So many, doubtful, perished in the mountains,
Climbing up crags to get a view of islands,
So many, fearful, took with them their sorrow
Which stayed them when they reached unhappy cities,
So many, careless, dived and drowned in water,
So many, wretched, would not leave their valleys.

It is our sorrow. Shall it melt? Then water
Would gush, flush, green these mountains and these valleys,
And we rebuild our cities, not dream of islands.

# SANDRA BEASLEY

## LET ME COUNT THE WAVES

*We must not look for poetry in poems.* —Donald Revell

You must not skirt the issue wearing skirts.
You must not duck the bullet using ducks.
You must not face the music with your face.
Headbutting, don't use your head. Or your butt.
You must not use a house to build a home,
and never look for poetry in poems.

In fact, inject giraffes into your poems.
Let loose the circus monkeys in their skirts.
Explain the nest of wood is not a home
at all, but a blind for shooting wild ducks.
Grab the shotgun by its metrical butt;
aim at your Muse's quacking, Pringled face.

It's good we're talking like this, face to face.
There should be more headbutting over poems.
Citing an 80s brand has its cost but
honors the teenage me, always in skirts,
showing my sister how to Be the Duck
with a potato-chip beak. Take me home,

Mr. Revell. Or make yourself at home
in my postbellum, Reconstruction face—
my gray eyes, my rebel ears, all my ducks
in the row of a defeated mouth. Poems
were once civil. But war has torn my skirts
off at the first ruffle, baring my butt

or as termed in verse, my luminous butt.
Whitman once made a hospital his home.
Emily built a prison of her skirts.
Tigers roamed the sad veldt of Stevens's face.
That was the old landscape. All the new poems
map the two dimensions of cartoon ducks.

We're young and green. We're braces of mallards,
not barrels of fish. Shoot if you must but
Donald, we're with you. Trying to save poems,
we settle and frame their ramshackle homes.
What is form? Turning art to artifice,
trading pelts for a more durable skirt.

Even urban ducklings deserve a home.
Make way. In the modern: Make way, Buttface.
A poem is coming through, lifting her skirt.


*For a stretch, much of the critical conversation around contemporary sestinas
dismissed them as a nonsense form, a place to show off and crack jokes
rather than develop serious ideas. Sestinas were taken as proof of poetry's
fundamental lack of efficacy in the modern age. I found the Revell quotation
in one of the essays that argued this, though I take it wildly out of context for
the sake of "Let Me Count the Waves." "Mr. Revell" is not intended toward
the actual poet—who is lovely, I've heard from multiple sources—but rather
addresses the difficulty generations of poets have in relating to each other, at
once seeking to emulate and defy their forebears. The fact that Revell's first
name happens to correspond with that of a certain cartoon duck was just a
happy coincidence.*

## THE EDITOR OF ENCYCLOPEDIA BRITANNICA REGRETS EVERYTHING

*Edinburgh, 1772*

Add this to the list of truths they did not
need: that the white fur that grows with no eyes,
no tongue, is mere cotton. *Scythian Lamb*,
they had named it, believing the beast bent
its umbilical stem to graze the fields
before turning, bleating, to its flower
pose. All God's creatures should have a flower
pose. Did they need to know the horn was not
a horn, that no uni-horse raced their fields?
Instead we gave them a crusty, cross-eyed
seawhale who studies his own tooth, the bent
bone spiral long enough to skewer a lamb.
We made shish kebab out of magic. Lamb,
forgive us. Maidens, forgive us. Your flowered
wreathes gone to waste, beloved truths bending
to guillotine fact: What was, is now not.
They call it *Enlightenment* but my eyes
see only shadows creeping down the fields,
the mothers calling tots in from the fields,
mothers now knowing all that hunts their lambs—
how many teeth, legs, claws. How many eyes.
Each *genus* and *specie* of deadly flower
grown wild in Scotland. And no, we did not
mean for our little book to take this bent—
any more than lightning means to take bent
toward the farmhouse it sets aflame, the fields
whipping orange into the night. We're not
prophets or shepherds, not looking for lambs.
We're scientists. We thought truth was a flower
waiting to be plucked by our hands and eyes.

A body dissected is, to our eyes,
the body collected. We tore roots, bent
stems, pressed petals in pages, called them *flowers*.
Measured topographies and called them *fields*.
Cut throat, shoulder, hock, and called it a *lamb*.
What I'd give, to see what lenses cannot
see. I'd trade in my eyes to run these fields
and bend my neck, as meekly as a lamb,
to the flowers tied by a sweet woman's knot.

*I've written close to twenty sestinas at this point, though not all need to see
light of day. Some poach each other's end words. Some are just silly. Sestinas
require a certain kinetic energy, and the most I ever wrote in a short period of
time were written amidst the mania of the Sewanee Writers' Conference. I
call them the gyroscope of forms, because you can only control their narrative
course so much; in my experience, you commit to a voice, a premise, and the
end words (as if defining the endpoints of the three axes of a gyroscope). Then
you spin it loose. When I'm drafting them, I carry around a stencil page that
outlines the form down the left margin, and I work and re-work the lines
that might fit. I've also scribbled potential end words into the margin of map
directions during long drives.*

# JEANNE MARIE BEAUMONT
## *A STEIN'S SESTINA*

*for David Trinidad*

Have I haven't I look here the ideal spot
for it, tiny stein with one end like a toggle button,
no bigger. To fit this ceramic Bavarian charm
on the doll-scale fireplace—newest object
in my microcosm and welcome to it—I make more
room between the miniature clock and vase of roses.

One dozen one-half-inch folded silk roses,
yep just the thing for calling up that spot
of joy on a doll's cheek. That's amore!
Any small thing's precocious, so pushes our buttons.
Why do we feel differently about small objects.
A gargantuan candelabra will not often charm

us but a pin-length candlestick oozes charm.
Now color currents rush from the go red of roses
to the white and two blues of the new object
whose story is all about how lucky you were to spot
it, how you hadn't shopped much but on
your last day you found this this and nothing more.

Decorated with a castle on one side no more
than a baby fingernail width, on the other a charm-
ing little peasant woman cute yes as a button,
hands on hips, toting a bundle. Believe Rose is
your Christian name I declare on the spot
and she, accommodatingly, does not object.

Precisely enthusiastically determinedly loyal object,
take up the two or so square inches I'm more
than happy to yield. As long as I live here the spot
is yours. Our paths are entwined & I'm charmed
to have met you. Next to the petite roses
you will stay high enough so the cat won't butt in.

She's the rubbed purr, the lawn meower, but in
the house she's known to disturb certain objects
by pawing or worse. Tried to eat the roses.
Gets up on hind legs displaying I suppose more
curiosity than mischief. Inside every charm
a little harm lurks no matter how safe the spot.

And really no earthly spot is safe. Any loose button
can be lost. That's part the charm of tending to small objects.
Why your little stein's more sweet a gift than roses.

*I was given a miniature stein by David Trinidad, who had bought it while
traveling in Europe. It was doll-size but quite detailed, and as I own a
miniature fireplace, I had a little mantle to set it on. Around this time, I had
been reading* Tender Buttons. *I noted that "A Stein's" was an anagram for
"Sestina," so I took as a title "A Stein's Sestina" and used it as a challenge
and an inspiration. I chose the end words from her text, and I borrowed some
of her phrases and habits of phrasing. This poem fit into a series of tribute
poems to foremother poets I was writing at this time, often in playful forms;
for example, I composed a cento from Marianne Moore opening lines. It was a
way of "collaborating" with beloved dead poets.*

# Aaron Belz

## *Pam*

For a laxative, try eating a little Pepsodent.
None of us enjoy that more than Pam,
Who once worked at a toothpaste factory.
Pam is now president of Berkman Lumber
And could kick your ass at the drop of a hat.
She no longer needs a laxative as powerful as that.

She has developed these huge muscles that
Enable her to pop a closed tube of Pepsodent
Simply by placing it under her hat,
Smiling, and saying, "My name is Pam,
I supervise the workers at Berkman Lumber,
Though I used to work at a toothpaste factory."

Pam sometimes wanders back to that factory
Transfixed by the fumes of the industry that
She grew up with. The aroma of lumber
Soon beckons her back, her Pepsodent
Smile reassuring the workers who chant, "Pam!
Pam! Pam!" as she takes off her hat.

Because of her, each of them has a hat
Too, but not like the hats back at the factory,
Which are white and sterile; they are like Pam's,
Tall and shiny and multicolored, with a logo that
Says, instead of "Welcome to Pepsodent,"
"Everyone Loves You at Berkman Lumber."

Sometimes the hats tip or fall off, bumped by lumber
Or a ladder. Pam insists that everyone needs a hat
"Just like we had back at Pepsodent."
She basically wants to run the mill like a factory
Even though the Berkman board has told her that
The world does not revolve around Pam.

"The board can bite me," scoffs Pam,
"I am the president of Berkman Lumber,
The foreman, the head. This is the house that
Pam built!" Workers cheer, throw their hats
In the air, like folks do back at the factory—
They roar as Pam pops a tube of Pepsodent

Saying a few words as she places it under her hat.
But inside, she is remembering the factory,
Whispering to herself, "Welcome to Pepsodent."


*I wrote this sestina because I was angry. Like an emotionally abused husband,
I let the form do all the work and acted like I was interested. But my heart was
somewhere else. I let the story emerge from the form. Like, I'd see the next
signpost and just turn my car accordingly—no effort to "master" it.*

*Sestinas are like horrible cages that keep me from truly being myself!
Something masochistic about wanting to throw oneself, or one's imagination,
upon their spikes. Repeat, repeat, repeat. All "music," no room for economy.
Isn't that a sad paradox? It's one in which I refuse to revel. As Shakespeare's
Polonius says, "Brevity is the soul of wit."*

# TARA BETTS

## SESTINA FOR THE SIN

*None of the hideous murders by butchers of Nero to make a Roman holiday*
*exceeded these burnings alive of black human beings.*
—Ida B. Wells-Barnett, *A Crusade for Justice*

Executions don't always occur in the dark.
Picnics with children in daylight's open air
as families await a lynching,
a preoccupation whetted by social habit.
Rapist or too damn uppity, some would explain.
One of these the victim's sin.

Who committed the sin?
The question presses heavy and dark
as spilled blood no one can explain
as white families take in humid air.
This appreciation seems curious habit
when they hope to stifle wind with a lynching.

A little boy reaches for a man's ring at a lynching.
Lacking fear and reverence for the dead marks his sin.
His parents encourage this habit.
While Black children are pushed into the dark
away from the burning stench flattening air.
Parents hide brown youth, unable to explain.

No one can explain
lost head, missing limbs, burnings, a lynching.
Silence intercepts air.
Sometimes, discovered bones document sin,
brittled and festering in the dark,
an endemic trait of this habit.

Concealing tokens of guilt identifies habit.
Daylong celebrations fail to explain
why murderers step out of the dark
when they grin at the rising rope of lynching,
sanctioned sin,
when cheers and fading screams puncture air.

After victims have no use for air,
rituals gather around this peculiar habit.
Picking through the bones becomes part of the sin.
Crowds face cameras to explain
*This is what happens at a lynching.*
*This is what happens when you are dark.*

A dark sin obscures reason
refuses to explain the paring of flesh or air
when the gruesome habit names itself lynching.

*I remember being immersed in historical narratives about lynchings, and*
*the form seemed to wind around its subject like a rope. I also felt that this*
*traumatic, emotionally startling material required a form to help me find words*
*that render the described situation with unexpected language.*

# ELIZABETH BISHOP

## *A MIRACLE FOR BREAKFAST*

At six o'clock we were waiting for coffee,
waiting for coffee and the charitable crumb
that was going to be served from a certain balcony,
—like kings of old, or like a miracle.
It was still dark. One foot of the sun
steadied itself on a long ripple in the river.

The first ferry of the day had just crossed the river.
It was so cold we hoped that the coffee
would be very hot, seeing that the sun
was not going to warm us; and that the crumb
would be a loaf each, buttered, by a miracle.
At seven a man stepped out on the balcony.

He stood for a minute alone on the balcony
looking over our heads toward the river.
A servant handed him the makings of a miracle,
consisting of one lone cup of coffee
and one roll, which he proceeded to crumb,
his head, so to speak, in the clouds—along with the sun.

Was the man crazy? What under the sun
was he trying to do, up there on his balcony!
Each man received one rather hard crumb,
which some flicked scornfully into the river,
and, in a cup, one drop of the coffee.
Some of us stood around, waiting for the miracle.

I can tell what I saw next; it was not a miracle.
A beautiful villa stood in the sun
and from its doors came the smell of hot coffee.
In front, a baroque white plaster balcony
added by birds, who nest along the river,
—I saw it with one eye close to the crumb—

and galleries and marble chambers. My crumb
my mansion, made for me by a miracle,
through ages, by insects, birds, and the river
working the stone. Every day, in the sun,
at breakfast time I sit on my balcony
with my feet up, and drink gallons of coffee.

We licked up the crumb and swallowed the coffee.
A window across the river caught the sun
as if the miracle were working, on the wrong balcony.

## SESTINA

September rain falls on the house.
In the failing light, the old grandmother
sits in the kitchen with the child
beside the Little Marvel Stove,
reading the jokes from the almanac,
laughing and talking to hide her tears.

She thinks that her equinoctial tears
and the rain that beats on the roof of the house
were both foretold by the almanac,
but only known to a grandmother.
The iron kettle sings on the stove.
She cuts some bread and says to the child,

*It's time for tea now;* but the child
is watching the teakettle's small hard tears
dance like mad on the hot black stove,
the way the rain must dance on the house.
Tidying up, the old grandmother
hangs up the clever almanac

on its string. Birdlike, the almanac
hovers half open above the child,
hovers above the old grandmother
and her teacup full of dark brown tears.
She shivers and says she thinks the house
feels chilly, and puts more wood in the stove.

*It was to be,* says the Marvel Stove.
*I know what I know,* says the almanac.
With crayons the child draws a rigid house
and a winding pathway. Then the child
puts in a man with buttons like tears
and shows it proudly to the grandmother.

But secretly, while the grandmother
busies herself about the stove,
the little moons fall down like tears
from between the pages of the almanac
into the flower bed the child
has carefully placed in the front of the house.

*Time to plant tears,* says the almanac.
The grandmother sings to the marvellous stove
and the child draws another inscrutable house.


*It seems to me that there are two ways possible for a sestina—one is to use
unusual words as terminations, in which case they would have to be used
differently as often as possible—as you say, 'change of scale.' That would
make a very highly seasoned kind of poem. And the other way is to use as
colorless words as possible—like Sydney [sic], so that it becomes less of a trick
and more of a natural theme and variations. I guess I have tried to do both at
once.*—Elizabeth Bishop, letter to Marianne Moore, 1937

# STAR BLACK

## HI YO

*Let the whites play Tonto.* —Ice-T

Tonto is white. He has been white all night.
You couldn't see Tonto correctly because we
turned out the light. The bedroom, particularly
Tonto's, was very dark. We were in a state of shock,
having been attacked by savages, I mean by foreigners,
I mean by natives. Something moved and we were scared.
We trail-blazed beyond known fields. The plains were green
and we were hungry. Tonto helped us cover up our tracks. We
like Tonto. He is our buddy. I myself am the Lone Ranger's
busted-up bride. He had to leave someone behind. Grief
is my sleepytime activity. I am to blame, too, I am
pretty and ugly, but Tonto never touched me,

I swear. Now I'm nothing to come home to. Me,
I am an old woman with big hips. I sleep at night
in a rattletrap house, dream someday the Lone Ranger
will come back, wake me up in a silver-bullet trance. I am
uncompromised and loyal. I am an old pioneer spoiled by shock
upon shock, I'm a shell-shocked widowwalked waiter. I am green
as the empty vales. I chop wood with a hatchet. Could be we
cleared some land, but the deed was never mailed, and we
waited for the king's seal. The king seemed particularly
real once, his throne a wide zone, our betrayal a grief
among some fancy folks. Shucks, we ran scared,
we were running away from our own foreign

throne. Dipshit, I reckon. Bunch of foreigners
keeping small farmhands down. Gold bothers me.
I don't need a gold crown but, hey, we sure got scared
and wanted things our way. We lied. We always lie, shock
some sense into the truth. Now I'm marooned on this green
abandoned spoof of a homestead. We blew it bad, faked night's
blackout fright and took action. Shoot, I told that bullet man we

should mind our own business, but I'm weak, and particularly
when it comes to men. I'm a housekeeper, swept my grief
under the rug. I should be blasted, was. My pale ranger
was tough, a quixotic no-nonsense tough. Boy, am
I guilty, shacking up with that thug, and we

liked each other, that's the real crime. We
made good love, not that I know else. Foreigners
from France do, according to flowers. I grow green
prairie gardens, wild thorns, briar spires. I am scared
of fluffy chrysanthemums and orchids. I tremble in shock
when I envision connections of pistils with pollen: hide me
from those voluptuaries. I'm proud and my heart is broken. Grief
wears a long denim skirt. My boots are scuffed. Could be we
never spoke enough to bloom much. Late love particularly
was sleepy. What do I know? I was only there, still am.
Bet me a wild horse next time, a thunder-hoof night
after sundown, but in this life I'm Lone Ranger's

busted bride. He's enough. One pale ranger
with a swift assistant chasing dangers that we
probably invent when the sky rumbles down, scares
us. We may never be saved from our sad selves, grief
lost in amnesia. Just what do we have in this proud night
but crazy notions about what's wrong and right, virtues we
demolish by our own featherbrained energy and Iago-green
envy? Still we gallop, still we try in blunderbuss shocks
of Silver speed to shift things. Crimes, particularly
not ours, are solved. Some native will hang me
from the back-door oak. This white foreigner
will swing. I've seen it in the skies, am

waiting until rescued. Hah, what fool am
I? A green one in love with the Lone Ranger,
no less. He is nothing without Tonto, too scared
to tackle the darkest pass alone, blinded by grief
he will never admit to. In my presence, nothing shocks
the galloping homebody, but the house is too small and we
can't endure a simple house, it seems. The Hi Yo calls. Green
fields beckon the horseshoe lance. I'm entranced by night's

quiet expanse. I am webbed in silence. It encircles me,
a ghostly wagon train. What have we done? Can we
go back, unearth the lost adz that foreigners
overlooked, the buried tribes, particular

hunters who traced each hill, each particular
ravine and claimed this woebegone country? I am
sitting pretty on a graveyard, floating upon evergreen
badlands. My hands are twisted in coarse rope as if we
were Bess and the Highwayman, waiting for a bang from me
that will set him free. I shouldn't think, not when alone at night.
Thinking isn't good for me, solitary confinement. Too bad we
can't stick together a bit more often than white-night grief
permits. Why are we so dang driven to shoot foreigners?
How many silver bullets do we need? Who is scared
of whom? What streaking speed propels the ranger,
what shady danger? What state of shock

won't stop? Shoot, I'm a shell-shocked
failure myself, a strawberry, particularly
flaky when it comes to waiting for Lone Ranger,
ever galloping back towards an old rattletrap scared
she'll swing. I've got things going for me. I'm a foreigner.
I've seen French imports, right nice china, no need to grieve
with a big farm to till. I'm a land cheat. Just because the night
didn't change its howling doesn't mean the vale's less green.
I can hack down trees, stack hay, and silence pleases me
in some way, quiets my heart down like milk. Say, I am
a natty dizzy broad in truth. With Lone Ranger, we
got through humdingers, ice storms, loons. We

shuttered and shingled crazy tunes, yarns we
lassoed in our minds. Nothing much else to do. Shock
waves took their sweet time, the whole universe foreign
as a flying rabbit. The shuttered vales couldn't trap the night,
hold it back like a thumbed flood, the jackal sounds particularly
tapped and tapped. He had to leave. I gazed blankly, watched as we

just fell apart in the big wide lie of country living, lime-green
territories squeezing us clean of any sense of safety. Grief
drove us mad, its mute complacency, robber dogs ranging
in the bogus hills. He hopped his steed and rode. I am
the handmaid of desertion, his AWOL girl. Spot me
on some mighty green turf. Sure, he was scared,

his black-masked eyes looking ahead, scared
he'd be recognized, just another bloke, a guy we
browse over on an empty map. He had to be Lone Ranger
to keep peace. Can't say where that peace was, particularly,
but he was bound to find it. Tonto was white, all right, but we
were loonies, shuttered in. We spun some weird theories at night,
all kinds of tiptop fancies about the universe, how bright green
it was, how it belonged to us, how no crown of foreigners
could boss our kin. Ignorance, land lust, we've got grief
by the balls. It's a branded calf, a gold hide. Shock
waves never subside now, no sir. We lied. I am
a branded white lie, busted, broken. Buy me

a subway token somewhere but don't take me
alone. I must wait. I have a Noah date, a scared
lawman on a saloon sweep, swinging doors, duels. We
shack up in the dark flood. That fat hull holds us in shock;
we rock on the waves we have caused. Tall trees particularly
have drowned below our strange survival. We are quiet foreigners.
We liquify expanse. The marshal rides on Hi Yo Silver, a ranger,
a masked man, the pistol'd danger on Tonto's path, grim grief
for the stubborn or crazed, a galumphing diversion we
need in the echolalia yowling of long prairie nights
when shutters slam against iced fright. Who am
I to claim virtue, even patience, my eyes green,

my courage useless, my rattletrap house, green
above bones, a half-vacant home that contains me
when I do not think too long, or bow, crazy and scared,
to the gold calf lassoed in the great outdoors, particularly
the moccasin's ravines, the red mountains? When Lone Ranger
comes home, having made the weasels safe, I will dance as I am
without disgrace, in blue denim and boots, a sallying foreigner

in a settled place with the robber dogs and raccoons, and we
will place peace down like a china set. The shell-shocked
rapping will cease, and we will make late love and we
will talk voluptuous like French flowers, and grief
will fly like a rabbit, away in the dank night,

and Tonto will be white, always was. The green grief
that drove Silver hooves toward duels only the Lone Ranger
could marshal will be silenced with the bones below, and shocks
will cease as the flood subsides, and we will be less scared
of the jackal's cries, the echolalia and the lurking nights,
and I will be who I am, a sleepytime foreigner.

# PAULA BOHINCE

## ALLEGORY OF THE LEOPARD

The dream lasted for years in leopard-
stained sunlight, in the grasses' teeth, in the marrow
of the range, its furrows and burning
ridges where heated skeletons lay: the taint
of those unable to rise or blink in spring,
our season of rising flowers, ringing bells.

Those dumb, I can tell this much: a bell
is less than a ghost, less than a leopard
invented to stalk the instant a life will spring
from dirt's heart, exit that marrow
and blossom. Pity the mute, the afraid: taints
unwilling to reassume flesh and reenter the burning

world. No wonder. The burning
of rising into a new body hurts, bells
announcing each form, their echoes tainting
the range and courtyard alike. Leopard
spots enter the air as music, notes as the marrow
of bells whose bodies are touched by spring,

which touches everyone. What is good springs
up in us, each lucid thing anxious, burning
to be absolved of its last life, the marrow
of each sorry heart trembling like a ready bell.
Even the stained, loping leopard
loves anew his imperfect body, that tainted

dream of perfection. And the lesson? The taint
of a body is not a sentence spring
imposes on a few. Look closer. Not only the leopard
is born to this shame, this burning.
There is music all around us: a colossal bell
beating too loud or too soft: clapper through marrow,

through nothing but necessary air, marrow
invisible but there. Have I been deaf to it, tainted
by the world's smaller songs? O bell
that signals both the season and the idea of spring,
our universal time of longing and burning,
let me hear you sing, *Be the leopard*

*who enters spring furiously, your leopard*
*bones burning upon the belled*
*and tainted earth, before sleeping once more in its marrow.*

*I began this poem knowing that I wanted it to be a sestina, and I believe that
I wrote the first stanza organically to see what end words would naturally
arise. Those resulting words seemed "open" enough to allow the poem to move
as athletically as sestinas must. Moving stanza to stanza was definitely a
struggle, but a thrilling, pleasurable struggle. What I loved about writing this
poem was that the pressure of the form forced me to wrestle with this subject
far longer than I would have without the pattern, and I think that's a useful
lesson for writing any poem.*

*Because this poem has so much landscape imagery and abstractions (like
spring, music, rebirth), I wanted a concrete creature—strange, fearsome,
gorgeous—to stalk the stanzas. I like the leopard because it can both stand out
and be camouflaged, in life and in a poem.*

# JENNY BOULLY

## SESTINA OF MISSED CONNECTIONS

I am sorry to say that again, today, we did not meet.
The trees against the winter sky slowly lose
their aim. There are too many shallow things: distance
of airplanes, the comma splice, the solicitation more urgent
than need, the mailbox lacking evidence—looks
as if again, today, no one has attempted to touch

strangers on sidewalks. (I am sure that you touched
me quite purposefully when handing over my change; when we meet
next, I will give you such a wink, such a stare
as to knock you off your feet, but you will, as you must, lose
me again to the next order, the next cup, the next urgent
customer's request.) There exists such a distance

between emptiness and the first sip; it is the distance
between a missed train and love, the allowances for touch
being owned by angels alone. Night is urgent.
Night never waits for companionship; it meets
you bare on your bedspread. Do not think twice: you will lose
that phone number; in the sky, the black clouds and I espy

another version of loneliness: the man in the fedora never looks
this way; he exists only in the movies, in a black-and-white distant
past where love used to happen with diamonds. Maybe you lost
your nerve; maybe in a dream, I allowed for the omission, having touched
the pomegranates, mistaking them for strange persimmons. Met
and dappled with oppositions, the posted placards so pressing

among a mass of personal want ads urgently
expressing: in the event of an emergency, look
to coincidences, the old woman in the woods, contact
your local soothsayer, dowager, zodiacs afar.
(I was wearing a pink scarf.) If you dare to lay hands
on the sleeper, the dream will become lost

on other mornings, and blackbirds will shake loose
the eyes of nesting birds. The garments of the sky, pressed
like ancestral ghosts, hang between heaven and dirt, touching
a day that is already dressed and departing. Sight
too grows dim and optical instruments scan distances
where the minute hand and the hour hand do indeed meet

but only touch briefly before moving apart again. Toss out
then the agenda badly planned: an insane plane is eager
for take-off. Keep the life vest to your chest; look: in the distance,
    distress flares.


*I wrote "Sestina of Missed Connections" when I was working at a book
publisher in New York. All the other editorial assistants and I would entertain
ourselves by reading Craigslist for some reason. The "Missed Connections"
section was always highly amusing and also sad. People who posted there
seemed crazy, desperate, sad, hopeful. I also thought that sestinas were crazy,
desperate, sad, and hopeful. The end words of sestinas seemed to be "missed
connections" to me, especially when a writer gets inventive with variations on
those end words.*

# GEOFF BOUVIER

## *REFINING SESTINA*

With intention, echoes echo—each repeating—disenchanted in a canyon, always changing.

Always changing with direction, in a canyon, echoes echo, disenchanted, each repeating.

Each repeating, always changing, disenchanted with expression, echoes echo in a canyon.

In a canyon, each repeating, echoes echo, always changing, with impressions, disenchanted.

Disenchanted in a canyon with inflection, each repeating, always changing, echoes echo.

Echoes echo, disenchanted, always changing in a canyon, each repeating, with corrections.


*I spent about two months writing nothing but sestinas, and no, I never wrote another one before or since. Repetitious end words are already related to echoing, so during those couple of "sestina months" I wrote a lot of sestinas about echoes. After a while, it occurred to me to try to write the shortest sestina possible, so I started experimenting with words that could anagram six ways. It was a lot of nonsense. Then I tried sestinas that consisted of just the six end words. Those were okay. Finally, when I "sestinaed" (yes, that's a verb) whole phrases, I started to write what sounded like Bach fugues. "Refining Sestina" is one of those.*

# CATHERINE BOWMAN
## MR. X

                    All my Ex's
live in Texas, so the country song says and no excuses,
it's mostly true for me too that the spade-shaped extra
big state with its cotton lints and Ruby Reds holds the crux
of my semi-truck-I've-never-had-any-kind-of-luck-deluxe-
super-high-jinx-born-to-be-unhappy-if-it-ain't-broken-don't-fix-

it loves, for example, there was the snakebit mudlogger who fixed
himself forever diving off that hexed bridge, and that foxy ex-
patriot who imported exotic parrots, he'd pump me up with his deluxe
stuff, the salesman who felt so guilty for the wide-eyed excuses
he told his wife that at the Big Six Motel just outside Las Cruces
he spent the afternoon hunched over *Exodus*, bemoaning the sin of extra-

marital sex, and the harmonica player, his mouth organ could extract
an oily bended blues, on sticky nights we'd hit the 12th hole pond with a fix
of Dos Equis and a hit of Ecstasy and I'd wrap my legs around his lanky crux,
as moonlight cut through the water like a giant X-ray, his Hohner ax
glistened in and out. And then there was the feckless shrink. No excuse
for his fixation, the tax man, the cute butcher from the Deluxe,

the Kilim dealer, the defrocked priest. So what if my mother was a deluxe
lush, my father Baptist and weak, I can't blame them, I was born just extra
affectionate. Don't ask about the abortions, and who can ever make excuses
for the time I spent holed up with the Port-O-Can tycoon my friend fixed
me up with, or the Mexican sculptor who made cathedral-sized onyx Xs,
twisted crucifixes. Art, he quoted Marx, was history at its crux.

Then there was the Ph.D. who took me to Peru and showed me Crux
(the Southern Cross), Centaurus, Musca, Vela, Lupus, and another deluxe
equatorial constellation that I forgot. For fun I ascribed each sparkly X
a name and date, so now I have a star chart to exalt each of my extra-
ordinary, heavenly bodies. But that night I dreamed the stars were fixed
on stacks of pages: pica asterisks to indicate omissions, footnotes, excuses,

explanations. I stood there, Ms. D. Giovanni, with a million excuses.
Now in exile I journey on the Styx with Mr. X in our boat the *Crux
Criticorum*. I wear an aqua slicker, he a sharkskin suit. He's non-fiction,
never incognito. We've got our sextant and spy manual open on our deluxe
waterbed. I can just make out the tattoo above his boxers in this extra
dark, there's the curve of his back. Now we'll break the code and go
    beyond X.

# DERRICK C. BROWN

## THEY LOVED YOU AND YOUR TITLE, BUT IT ALL TELEGRAPHED TOO MUCH

All hail the quiet yellow rooms of the three star hotel
and the empty sound of a complimentary coffee mug catching blops
   of whiskey.
All hail the hot knock of sunlight and comforters that ruffle with stiff
   disease. So sudden,
the tiny shampoo won't be enough. The curved shower rods can't
   keep away Feeling
and there is no art on any wall to love.
Lay out your clothes in a disaster. Is anyone coming for you? Is he in a robe?

Have you ever seen anyone win a fight in a robe?
Have you ever seen someone inferno a whole hotel
just from drunkenly over-magnifying the day, roasting the ants of love?
The thing waits in you, the thing Dylan could not kill with whiskey
or light. The remote control is a feeling,
so you wait for it to come to you and teach you of change, power and
   something sudden.

Put your luggage in the drawers like you were home, says the walls,
   low and sudden.
Why won't you roam the lobby in the robe
and save someone? Save them from destination brochures and feeling.
Did you build this hotel?
Did you burn down the four star resorts for something three stars and
   as alive as whiskey?
Do your marketers keep replacing the phrase 'isolation strategist' for
   'desperate love'?

One star means no one cares, means dirty freedom, means felony love.
Two stars means sleep came at you like a sudden
black wind. Save money on the room so you can afford better whiskey.
Better whiskey means better dreams, so dream of slippers and a
   bulletproof robe.

Three stars should mean a robe, concierge to hold you, a friendly hotel.
Someone to ask you if you need any help carrying any of that 49
    pound feeling.

It was 56 but the airlines made you get it down to a 49 pound kind of feeling.
They asked you if you had any hazardous materials and to not joke
    about love.
You just wanted to get to the highest room of the hotel
and feel all the people stacked beneath you, wanting to feel something sudden
in their chest. From the closet hanger, they all remove the bath robe
and lie on it, wrapping the sleeves around them, wanting to share the
    whiskey.

We are a crowd of unshared whiskey.
We are the hotel that has remodeled over the feeling.
We are lying on large beds, embraced in the sleeves of a robe.
We fear the power of that which is sudden
until suddenly, housekeeping/sunlight knocks through every room of
    the yellow hotel.

To fill the mug with whiskey, to open the windows and wait for love—
to rest in the feeling that the ending is sudden—
a man in a robe telling the bellman how well he sleeps now that he
    has found this clean, quiet hotel.

# Stephen Burt

## *Six Kinds of Noodles*

You would have to have been reading John Ashbery
to have seen anything like this in a book,
and yet here it is in real life:
an almost already intelligible tangle
of verities, and an intimidating menu,
disfigured, almost, by all the things you can have

at once, though all are noodles. Have
you, too, been trying to keep up with John Ashbery?
Every time I check there's another new book,
another entry—entrée—on the menu
from which I seem to have ordered my whole life,
and been served somebody else's. Don't tangle

with waiters here is my advice; the rectangle
of mirrorlike soy sauce, the soba you have to have
and the udon you lack should suffice: the secret of life—
as you might have sought, or discovered, in Ashbery—
is what you get while you are waiting. Men, you
see, are mortal, and live to end up in a book,

though once you compiled and published such a book,
who would be left to read it? The latest angle
claims that it would be more like a menu,
an ashen, Borgesian checklist of all you could have
or have had to pay for, or suffer, or notice. Ashbery
could write that (I think it's in *Flow Chart*). And yet the life

we long for in all its disorder is not a life
of so many tastes, nor of fame; more like one good book,
and ginger with which to enjoy it. Jeffrey Skinner's poem entitled
        "John Ashbery"
and David Kellogg's "Being John Ashbery" both take the angle
that eminence is what matters. No. We have
had enough of fighting over the menu,

as if it were the main course; the omen you
seek, the bitter-lime tang of a happy life
to come, curls up amid the semolina or buckwheat you have
not chosen yet. Will it be prepared by the book?
Will it do for Kitchen Stadium? Its newfangle-
ness may be a virtue, Iron Chef Chen Kenichi, Auden and Ashbery

all suggest, though hard to find here without help from Ashbery:
it's a problem with which I have tangled all my life,
and I'm so hungry I could eat a book, though none are listed on this menu.


*It began with actual noodles. I taught at Macalester College from 2000 to
2007, and in about 2004 they redid the cafeteria. When it reopened it was
generally better but also had new special features, including what looked to
me like a noodle bar, with at least six kinds. And I said, "Hey, six kinds
of something = sestina potential!" and set to work. I had also been thinking
about Ashbery, about how the slipperiness of his language generally, between
reference and non-reference, was something the sestina form seemed apt to do.*

# CASEY CAMP

## *A Poem on the Severe Awesomeness of John Zorn*

BUT I SUPPOSE YOU'VE HEARD ENOUGH

OF ME OBSESSING ON MR. ZORN

I COULD GO ON FOREVER

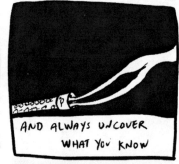

AND ALWAYS UNCOVER WHAT YOU KNOW

AND TAKE THE MYSTERY OUT

OF THE PASSAGE OF TIME

WITH HIS "YOU KNOW WHAT" OUT

AND KEEPS IT GOING FOREVER

(SUCH IS THE NATURE OF THE ZORN)

AND STILL FINDS TIME

TO PUT OUT ENOUGH

FOOD TO FEED HIS THIRST TO KNOW

I DON'T KNOW

I GUESS HE DOESN'T GO OUT

WITH OTHER ROCKERS ENOUGH

TO KNOW IF IT ALSO TOOK THEM FOREVER

OR AT LEAST A REALLY LONG TIME

TO ADMIT INFERIORITY TO MR. ZORN

*I am really enamored with the sestina form. It has a lot of repetition, so I feel like once you have a general idea, the next logical place to go would be to figure out what words you will be repeating since they're such an important part of the piece. In this case, you can definitely say that the form impacted what I was going to do: I wanted to write a sestina and specifically one about John Zorn. I had been playing around with putting a graphic poem together using visual cues as the last word of the lines (meaning it would have no words) and wanted to use a little figure. Well, after a little drawing, this figure wound up with a clarinet. The words just kind of naturally came out after I'd figured out the big picture. Putting it together was different. On some pages I'd have an idea for a few panels, but the wording structure is so specific that on a very local level while working on a page the words are already set. So sometimes the challenge was to arrange the panels in a way that progressed the story while still maintaining the flow and structure of the poem. It sounds like a challenge, but it's the most fun kind you can imagine.*

# JENNA CARDINALE
## *BEYOND JANUARY*

This should be a little less about butter
and a bit more about vegetables.
But the color cannot always be green—
Does a hero wear oversized mittens?
Winter is a time for roots,
a time to climb every available staircase.

I approach the cold, the unending staircase—
Burdened like bread by butter.
Posed into a tree, I grow roots
stronger than thick yellow vegetables
& I'm stewed, warmed by woolen mittens
and liquor that makes me green.

Waiting to see the start of green
is a chore, like a narrow staircase.
There are moth-made holes in my mittens.
I dream of daffodils and butter,
but never of ripe vegetables.
I feel the weather in my roots.

There's something red in my roots,
no matter my hopes for green.
I swallow my melted vegetables,
stare up at the staircase.
My body has become butter—
A hero, I wear broken mittens.

I stitch up my mittens
with yarn as coarse as roots.
I'm breaking it off with butter,
determined to start out green.
Still, halfway up the staircase,
I hide some uneaten vegetables

beneath carpeting decorated with vegetables.
Yesterday I lost my mittens,
but I found them on the staircase.
In inconsistency, I've found my roots
and branches, now sprouting green.
I think less and less of butter.

A diet heavy with butter *and* vegetables
makes me green, envious of the journey of mittens
unraveling down the staircase, lost little roots.


*I typically start a poem with a phrase or two and no clear objective. With the
sestina, I start with six words and the same lack of purpose.*

*I think the form helped to dictate the subject of the poem. The repetition
reinforced the heaviness of it. I live in New York, which sometimes suffers
brutal winters. It seems like the best time to focus on the future, since it's hard
to do much else (besides drink). Spring seems to allow an opportunity to act on
the plans we made while sulking in the depression of winter. When I set out
to write this sestina, I was preoccupied by my own experience with revision. I
had this sense that constantly revising my poems removed the "moment" from
them, and I was excited by how difficult it is to make substantial revisions to
this form without gutting the poem in an almost-complete way. I made only
minor changes to it when I completed a draft, but took more time to write it.*

# PATRICIA CARLIN

## *LIVES OF THE CONQUERORS*

In those years
he raised
enormous armies.
He left his silken tents, the cover
of his cities
to become the great god of change.

       Years
rolled over the marble cities,
razed
walls, covered
markets and houses.  The armies

of oblivion disarmed
the warriors. They changed
places with the dead—silt covered
their eyes. "One night is as a thousand years
in the eyes of god."
         Duplicity

is a shining city
on a hill. There the armies
feed and grow fat. Far below the people raise
corn and wheat. They make clothes, tools, weapons and statues. Unchanging
years
cover

their small lives.
And what of the ruler of cities?
What do the years
bring him? His army
impales him in a public square.   They exchange
him for his brother. His praise

will be buried, his name erased.
We the people will change
our course, uncover
our lost cities,
lose them again. Armed
in oblivion, our years

sift through squares, palaces, temples and graves. Oh city
of small changes. Disarmed, nerveless, we steal
through history. Marble torsos. Whitened years.


*Each time I write a sestina, I see afterwards that there's a close connection
between form and content, although it's a different connection in each poem.
In "Lives of the Conquerors," the form mirrors the unrolling of history, where
things keep coming back, but they never come back the same way. I remember
writing this poem with Iraq very much in mind. In the actual process of
writing, though, I was guided by intuition, which is to say I used the end
words as a kind of Rorschach blot leading me on. I was also listening to the
sound of the poem, as I do any time I write. When I have the sound I know
I have the poem. The concision of this sestina came from my sense of wishing
to distill enormous cycles of time and history, and also from my related sense of
all the lacunae in the historical record: those gaps where individual lives vanish
into unrecorded nothingness, as do the lives of all rulers, since only remnants
ever remain.*

# SHANNA COMPTON

## THE REMARRIED AGAIN SESTINA

*with apologies to my mother, whose maiden and married names I adapted as*
*end words*

At first, everything was lovely.
He courted her, fresh as a rose.
As a mate he seemed competent.
Turns out, he was actually a cock.
But what the hell—she was still young,
the house was hers, the kids were good,

and the divorce was final. Good
riddance. Single again, lovely,
and witty, she'd give her whole young
life for someone better and rose
to the challenge of dating. Cock-
shy though willing and competent,

she tried again. A competent
grad student looked pretty damn good
to her, and honestly his cock
-sure future looked bright. Lovely
years lay ahead, she knew. Hopes rose
but as quickly fell through. Her young

children seemed suddenly not so young.
She strived for motherly competence
and the kids bounced back fine. Roses
bloomed in the backyard and on Good
Friday gelatin glowed lovely
and orange in the fridge. "Two cocks

down, one to go," she joked. Her cock
-y new beau even laughed. He's young
at heart and tells me I'm lovely,
she thought. I should be competent
by now, enough to judge a good
man when I see one. Mawmaw Rose

would be proud. The subject arose
at last and he asked her. "You cock-
sucker," she said. "Why spoil a good
thing? If I were naïve and young
it might have worked. We're incompetent.
Wouldn't it have been so lovely?"

He rose. What should he say? Lovely
knowing you? Good lord, young love was
hard, old cock even less competent.


*The repetition of the form tends to work best if the repeated instances of
the words migrate through various registers and multiple meanings, so that
certainly guided the movement. I don't recall how I came up with the subject,
except thinking I needed six end words and my mother has had six last names.
(One husband she actually married twice, so I used "love"/"lovely" instead
of repeating that name.) I got married myself the year before I wrote it, so
maybe the theme was just on my mind. I hope it's a satirical look at romantic
expectations and the strictures of marriage, particularly for a woman of my
mother's generation. I hope that it's at least somewhat funny, too, despite the
disappointment and bitterness. The pattern toward more relaxed language was
suggested by the story of relaxed expectations and also the passage of time, over
four decades. She would never talk like that, by the way, but the dirtiest word
in the poem is actually how her last name is pronounced, though it's spelled
differently.*

# JEFFERY CONWAY

## IS IT DANCING?

You wonder what you're doing here; you can't believe Cristal
wanted to bring you and the others to see some girl named Nomi.
*Christ*, you think, *we're "wining and dining" the hotel's high rollers at a strip
club?* Then you remember they're Japanese and chill a bit—the Cheetah,
yeah, they might like it. You're *so* high. You think: *I'm the
Entertainment Director
of the goddamn Stardust!* You're convinced you'll get V.I.P. treatment
inside. Lick

your top teeth and gums again and again. You're a little grossed
out—she licked
your nostril to clean off some stray powder—you struggle with a
chick like Cristal,
she's a little intense. *But after all, I'm Zack Carey, the Entertainment
Director
of a Vegas hotel—I gotta have a hot girl.* You're curious who this Nomi
is, the one she talked about in the limo: *Will she fuck me? She works at
the Cheetah,
and one thing I know for sure: She's not a dancer, she's a stripper.*

You're a party animal—you wear your sunglasses at night, even into
a strip
club, yeah, you've got the coolest babe—the star of a Vegas hotel
show licking
awesome coke off your face; you're so hip—*hell yes I go to dives like the
Cheetah!*
Tomorrow you'll retell the night's adventures to a rapt coterie. *Cristal
is so cool, you're so lucky, dude.* And maybe you'll have something to tell
about Nomi.
You pull the strap of Cristal's sexy mesh dress as she walks directly

in front of you into the seedy club. She turns and you pull her directly
into your chest, but she pushes you away, not the response you want.
No strippers

on stage, but a fat lady, telling the crowd her hole is making money.
   *Not Nomi,*
you think. Your assistant Phil gets tables; the Japanese high rollers are
   licking
their lips, desperate for some action. You sit near them, with Cristal
at your side. *Yeah, all eyes are on me,* you gloat, *everyone at the Cheetah*

*is staring—I'm with the finest woman in the club.* "Ladies and gentlemen,
   the Cheetah
proudly presents the girl to tickle your pickle: Heather!" A blonde
   struts out directly
to center stage just as you peel off your sunglasses and light a long
   cigarette for Cristal.
The blonde spins, kicks her leg up impossibly high, tosses her golden
   curls, strips
off her red lace top. *Shit, this girl can dance,* you think, *and she just
   licked*
*the pole, staring right at me! So fucking hot.* You start to wonder about
   this Heather,

this hottie, what she's like in bed, thrusting and bending like rubber:
   *Heather,*
*yeah,* you like that name, a stripper, the hottest dancer at the Cheetah
showing off her perfect tits, *come to daddy,* standing against the pole,
   licking
her fingers, sliding them down into her black lace panties, looking
   directly
at you. She bends over in her pumps, tugs at her undies, and strips
them off. "Do you like her? I'll buy her for you." Did Cristal

just say what you think she said? *What is it with Cristal—is she into this
   Heather?*
You worry for a sec about getting it up with a stripper in the
   backroom of the Cheetah:
*a lap dance?* Cristal turns in your direction, gives your nostril another
   wet, messy lick.

*At Brooklyn College, I had the opportunity to study with Allen Ginsberg. He told me that he thought the sestina "fit" me, that I was "a natch with the form." My first sestinas were about highly personal, autobiographical events: I was using the form to tell, more easily and efficiently, about things such as childhood traumas and my sex life in the time of AIDS. It was his voice I heard when I started my "Showgirls: The Movie in Sestinas" project. The individual poem titles are taken directly from the DVD chapter titles. So the sestina is based on the narrative of that scene in the film.*

# ALFRED CORN

## *POUND-ELIOT SESTINA*

T.S. Eliot never wrote a sestina.
I guess he was afraid of copying Pound;
Or else doubted his metrical finesse. If
We rate poets according to form, he blew.
With Old Possum, it's like free verse all the way.
Yet, except for "Sestina: Altaforte"

And "Mauberly," form wasn't Ez's forte,
Either, assuming that means the sestina,
The villanelle, the sonnet. Yet there's a way
To give the term a wider relevance. Pound
On the podium, rave, fume until you're blue
In the face, but free verse is here to stay. If

They want an audience—this is a huge "if"—
Poets should know most readers under forty
Loathe rhyme and *ta-dum, ta-dum, ta-dum.* Joe Blow
Knows zip about the sonnet or sestina.
He buys Bukowski paperbacks by the pound.
Would he groove on Gioia or Hacker? No way.

"Little Miss Muffet, eating her curds and whey"—
Form is all just Mother Goose to Joe B. If
Asked, he'd probably say he didn't like Pound
Or Eliot so much, either. Meanwhile, for T.
S.E. (whose friends called him Tsetse) "Sestina:
Altaforte" may well have plotzed. Many blue-

Bloods prefer jazz to "high culture." *Kind of Blue*
In their book's better than "Gerontion." Weigh
The two. Second-hand emotion, says Tina
Turner, is boring. So which is the real riff?
Do you like your faves *piano* or *forte?*
Is U.S. currency the dollar or pound?

Both, from time to time, paid bills for Ezra Pound,
Our poet-chameleon. Winds of change blew
Where they would, and he followed, "Altaforte"
Is just *one* approach he took. I mean, it's way
Too hard for most bards to get down with. Me, if
I had to write villanelles and sestinas

Every week, I'd blow my brains out. Sestinas
Rock, sure, but they're not my forte. Write as if
I were those guys? There must be another way.


*I thought a sestina about the sestina could be fun and plunged headlong into
the assignment. I think the ever-so-slightly absurd requirements (at least in a
contemporary context) of this particular verse format lend themselves to comic
treatment, including over-the-top features like homophonic puns, slang, and
intentional overstatement. Relevant to that question is the contrast between the
art of Ezra Pound and Miles Davis's classic album* Kind of Blue—*and the
glancing reference to Tina Turner. If you consider Pound's Fascist sympathies
and Eliot's anti-Semitism, genetics (what used to be called "race") and
alternative cultural standards also have some bearing on these issues.*

# MICHAEL COSTELLO

## *A SERIES*

talent may be seen in his brilliant repetition…"
When flowers are ready they change—
Why not take yourself as a subject, so that nothing
you do does not represent yourself? Between differ and different is
    the difference.
The cow makes
and remakes itself

as wallpaper again and again moment to moment. *Mao* is like himself
and "questions of an artistic variety arise—regarding repetition
and appropriation"—everything Marilyn makes
is taken from her. The *flowers* change:
autonomous, remade, composing each petal is different
and the same, "there's nothing

behind it" Mao complains about something / everything / anything / nothing
Where? Everywhere. *Marilyn* is around herself.
But between *Green Marilyn* and *Mint Marilyn,* the difference
"…fought to show us there is no repetition…"
make changes
by burning out unwanted areas. Order makes

itself, orders itself to make
a straight line: before, during, after. Nothing
is the thing to think of. Make no changes—
other than those of scale / medium / and installation—(to be as
    beautiful as) itself
"at times it is difficult to distinguish art from its repetition."
"These are flowers and these are *flowers.*" What's the difference?

Now is the difference.
Do a *Blue Electric Chair* and a *Red Race Riot* make
for a *Lavender Disaster?* Time and repetition
are the central motifs in which nothing
is absolute except itself,
and the *Silver Brando* above it which does not change

the Brillo Box but the *Brillo Box* is changed
and what is found between beginning and end is the difference
more and less the *Self-Portrait* becomes itself
but why make
it? Make it (nothing, no thing), it will be nothing
but *flowers, cows, Maos, Marilyns,* and their repetitions

Repetition changes
nothing—difference
makes itself.

*Andy Warhol is a favorite artist of mine. At the time I wrote "A Series," I
was conducting my own personal critical study of him, taking a closer look at
his artistic techniques and visual rhetoric, exploring writers with whom he
shared similar sensibilities. Using his work as a visual anchor just made sense.
I extracted fragments and sentences from my notes that included any of the six
end words. I had been experimenting with appropriation and collage, and once
the first draft was completed, I was able to reorder, rewrite, or replace lines until
it was finished.*

# LAURA CRONK

## SESTINA FOR A SISTER

Looking closely, I saw that the window
was very clean. She must've just washed it. My sister
is fastidious. When I watch
her I don't even realize she's tidying up, getting every spot
on the counter, making the green
floor tiles gleam. She rewards herself with a cigarette

each time she's really finished something up. Each cigarette
vanishes and it's on to something else. This window
is spectacular, even for her. I could reach and touch the green
fields, all wet and bright. It's absolute perfect crystal. My sister
finished this and went on to another spot.
This was just a few minutes' work. Her watch

ticks loudly on her wrist. It's an antique watch,
a gift from her long-gone lover. He gave her a cigarette
case too, engraved with birds. He gave it to her at the little spot
where they used to go. Well, it's the only spot in town. A café with
        neon in the window
and little tables with candles in the back. My sister
has these two gifts from him. And a poem inked in green

on a piece of expensive lacy paper. Green
ink was an odd choice, I thought. I began to watch
her closely after that, after he disappeared and left the poem. My sister
held herself together. We sat and each smoked a cigarette
after she read it. It was snowing. We sat by the window
and smoked, though I don't smoke, and watched the snow fall. One spot

of snow stuck to glass and then more and more did, each tiny spot
blew down from the sky and gathered with the others whiting out
        the lawn, green
just a few weeks before. She sat at that window

every night for a week to watch
and see if he would walk up the path, stopping to snub out his cigarette
by the mailbox before ringing as usual, asking for my sister.

I always get the door. It's a deal we have. My sister
gets the phone. I like to see a person if he's going to put me on the spot.
She doesn't mind being put on the spot so long as she can finish her
    cigarette
if she's started one. Our old rattly green
phone rings and she goes to it without a thought, checking her watch
as she answers, newspaper clutched in her hand from wiping down
    the window.

This time the phone is him. Her cigarette falls and her watch
hangs heavy on her wrist. The spot where she stands goes dark. I pull
    the window
shades and go to the porch; my sister stands holding that receiver so
    cold and such an awful green.

# JAMES CUMMINS

## #17 FROM THE WHOLE TRUTH

Perry picked up a copy of Robert Lowell's THE DOLPHIN.
He tried to figure out the formative principle, the art.
What were the 'flashing fish'? Did they have big fins?
Do you eat them with 'servile sausages' (had he got that
Right?) after cooking them in a heavy, but tasty, grease?
Or was that long ago? And this another, different life?

"So yo' all call dat livin'?" asked the fly, of that life.
"That's not the point," Perry said patiently. "The dolphin
Symbolizes man's voyage in rough seas, each wave a crease
In a forehead behind which swims a crazed desire for art,
For order. Its up-and-down movement is a reminder that
Sanity is cyclical: the sea is McClean's, you need big fins

To swim through it." "Ah heah yo' needs quite a few fins
To git *in* it!" the fly pouted. "It's a metaphor for life!"
Perry said, annoyed. "Forget about money. He says that
The genealogy, the line, of the image goes from the Dauphin
Of Joan of Arc, to the one Yeats said, in the sea of art,
Is man's best friend." "Did yo' see dat movie, GREASE?

Now, Ah wouldn' mind slidin' mah sausage thro' *dat* grease!
Yo' go talk 'bout *art*, jes' gimme *life*!" "Dat's ob-*fins*-
Ive!" mocked Perry. "Anyway, look: you used a work of art
To look behind the work of art itself, trying to see *life*!
Lowell takes the dolphin image down to the Miami Dolphins
Because he saw in their No-Name Defense the anonymity that

Allows perfection. He felt humiliated by a genealogy that
Coated the art, the form he tried to embrace, the way grease
Coats pigs at a county fair. On the other hand, the dolphin
is constantly cleansed by waves of anxiety, its big fins
Hand-holds allowing him to ride it, becoming his own art…
When he did that, he didn't have to think about his life."

"Ah kin unnerstan' dat! Ah don' wan' think 'bout his life,
Neither!" Perry smiled, amused. How could he explain that
This was the repose resulting from the criticism of art?
Suddenly, beatifically, came a moment to which few grease-
Monkeys of literature gain access: he watched the big fins
Lift up, seeking him, on a wave, heard the crying dolphin:

† † †

*Remember that Lowell sought from me the big finis, the art
Of the life made whole ... I gave him his body, its grease.
But know he learned, at the last, any cab might be a dolphin.*

# DAVID LEHMAN AND JIM CUMMINS DO THEIR PART AFTER THE WORLD TRADE CENTER DISASTER

Dave and I volunteered for Afghanistan.
The Marine sergeant said we were too old.
"But we want to kill Osama bin Laden!"
The tough old bird cracked, "So get in line."
Our Langley chief listened, then smiled at us:
"In shooting wars, poets get no respect."

Dave kicked a can as we walked back. "Respect!"
he fumed. "Do they 'respect' Afghanistan?
The symbolism of Cruise missiles got us
into this. It's going to take tropes old
and new to get us out." Waiting on line
to see a film about Osama Bin Laden,

a guy who looked like Osama Bin Laden
was dragged down an alley. "R-E-S-P-E-C-T"
blared out above a record store. The headline
on a newspaper from Afghanistan
urged a jihad. Dave mused, "Maybe some old
anthrax dropped from crop dusters on us?"

As we jaywalked, a taxi nearly hit us.
"Don't worry," I said, "Osama Bin Laden
won't be how *we'll* die." On Duane, an old
man doffed his cap in mocking disrespect,
then begged for change. "I'm From Afghanistan—
Eat Me" his placard read. "Hey, here's a line,"

I said. "'Will Blow Up Domestic Airline
For Food'—what do you think?" "God help us,"
Dave grinned. "*Any* god. Is that Afghanistan
humor? 'Now take Osama Bin Laden—
please!'" "Hey, you assholes show some *respect*!"
I whirled, deflected the blow, used an old

kung fu move to disarm some putz in an old
fireman's hat. His buddy shouted, "I'll line
a birdcage with your face!" "Oh, *that's* respect,"
Dave said, macing him. "You queers hate the U.S.!"
I picked up their flag. "Osama Bin Laden
is hetero," Dave called. "And in Afghanistan."

Downtown, dust covered us. Dave said, "That old
'respect' line's as puerile as Osama Bin Laden."
Dust rose. We dug down, toward Afghanistan.

# PETER DAVIS

## *MUSTACHE SESTINA*

Mustache,
Must ache,
Muse ash,
Moon stash,
Most hash,
Moose hatch.

Muss as,
Mute hat,
Muck cash,
Musk blast,
Mope calf,
Mist mast.

Mood match,
Mooch half,
Mosh laugh,
Mock mash,
Mug mass,
Mush stack.

Mooch ask,
Mis-snatch,
Ms. Clash,
Mouse has,
Maoist rag,
Music ash.

Milk etch,
Mosque haste,
Mask chaste,
Make assure,
Much adds,
Musty ah.

Moscow badge,
Move mags,
Mousse stars,
Mud ma's,
Muck hatch,
Mast hutch.

Moot stat, moat smash.
Mower bash, monk ass.
Missing trash, mustache.

*The book that this comes from,* Hitler's Mustache, *has three or four
sestinas. The image of Hitler's mustache is, to me, one of mystery. It is a
square box of darkness. And in that darkness is a whole host of mysteries. But
there is a repetitive formality in that mustache (imagine all of those individual
hairs lying down together like that! Unreal!), and the sestina seems capable
of handling repetitive formality. I was thinking about mustaches. It happened
pretty fast. How is it that our face of evil in contemporary culture also is the
ridiculous face of Hitler? How often is evil the face of a clown? How often,
through a mustache, do we see the deep anomaly in human nature? How
many questions can be asked about what motivated that square patch of hair?*

# SHARON DOLIN

## PRAYING MANTIS IN BROOKLYN

*Consider:*
*'(thoughts' torsion)'*
—Louis Zukofsky


Before leaving for the house of prayer—
there—like a muezzin, crying the cat
looked out, shaking his tail, having seen
a praying mantis steady herself on the red brick
wall. Struck dumb, I watched him
watch a green blade fasten to the breeze four stories up.

The cat and I—ecstatic, frozen—gazed up
at a messiah of air—poised in prayer.
Vigilant—what could have brought her—inches from him
to such height—no bugs or insects—the cat
would eat her in a second—so still against the brick
she barely moved—did she sense us—inside the screen—we'd seen

Her turn her head toward us. As if having seen
us—as if to say: Keep looking up.
You think in Brooklyn nothing can move these bricks
but I've been sent—a prayer
to you—gravity can change—though the cat
would eat me—don't scold—without him

You would not have stopped—inside him
his hunger—you can say you've seen
an angel—green-bladed—cat
-walk your wall—always lift up
the head of possibilities—your poems—prayers
upon the Brooklyn air—can move these bricks

Mortar up your eyes—and these kids, bricks
in the street will blind you—neglect him
whose paws are a closed prayer
and you're lost—a woman on the ledge who's seen
a mantis fly—and you'll look down, lose what's up
there—gravity, unflinched, on a cat's

Back—strive to shadow this cat's
voracious play upon the screen—break bricks
the klezmer clap attack wakes up
even angels—the vicious way I bite the head off him
I've loved—biting the reasonable off what's seen
as useful—this too can be a prayer.

Fly, as I do, from bricks—unseen
on green wings—like this cat, scale prayers—
become weightless—angelic predator—Lift up!

*I had read Louis Zukofsky in graduate school. I was living in Brooklyn, in
what was then untrendy Carroll Gardens, having recently lost my job and
living on unemployment insurance, and so for several months I gave myself
the time and license to write poems. I am superstitious enough to believe in
coincidences being signs from the hidden world. So when a mantis literally
perched on my window sill on the top floor of my walkup, and then, again,
came to rest on my gate, I took it for a sign, especially since it happened on the
Jewish High Holidays. Zukofsky, in the 1930s, had experienced a similarly
uncanny encounter with a mantis when it flew at his chest while he was
riding on the New York subway, and that's what had inspired him to write
his poem, "Mantis." He, too, lived in Brooklyn. And here I was, a native
Brooklynite, living in Brooklyn once more. It seemed like the only thing to do:
to write the poem as a sestina and with a free verse coda, just as he had done,
as an homage to him.*

## RELUCTANT SESTINA

It's never a breeze to begin in the middle
of things, though more of a tease to end when just start-
ing. To get down on your knees for such a project?
Better to read and lunch, put up your feet
and wait in your chemise for the mail to come, forget
all other burdens, reasons, strivings, tramp-

le them. After failing to fail tramp
off to a bookstore (your modern grail) in the middle
of middle age you've come to this formal jail to forget
what you might otherwise have start-
ed. And in this line there now flail five dull feet.
Don't derail your reader, instead project

your voice, your mind, like an out-of-focus *you* project-
ed on a screen, while rhymes as on a tramp-
oline bounce from line to line on feet
as unsteady as the half-blind taste of middle-
brow readers. In a bind, *Don't get me start-
ed*, you'll opine, as with repetends you sink into forget-

fulness. But once you've gone this far, forget
going back or giving up as your son shoots project-
iles at you for fun that make you start
up from your chair (he's already on the run), tramp
into his getaway room, slip on a crayon in the middle
of the floor, and spy under the bed a pair of feet

sticking out. And is it cheating if I switch from feet
to feat, from *you* to *I?* Would you, impatient reader, find forget-
table (now that we've beaten the middle)
if I slipped up on the project
introduced mistakes that might tramp-
le this already bumpy form so you'd be start-

led? How many hyphenated words to start
or end a line? Would you stamp your feet (at such a feat)?
and walk away? A poem about nothing: no tramp,
no dame or dude in distress except the poem to forget?
Who wouldn't be bored by such a project?
Perhaps you're undeterred by no middle in the middle.

Now, let's both forget this project
and trample under our feet
what was never middle but ended at the start!


*I had begun jumping on a trampoline, and in a kind of jokey homage to an
old boyfriend who bragged he could (and did) put anything into a college essay
(Bugs Bunny, my name), I gave myself the challenge of getting the trampoline
and my son into my sestina. I'd also begun to use more rhyming in my poems,
having begun to write a series of ghazals, and so you'll notice the rather
show-offy internal rhymes in the first stanza. There's a built-in challenge to
writing a sestina: Can you keep it going—keep those end words up in the air
through six full stanzas and then an envoi? The more I write, the more I've
learned (and taught my students) to write into their resistances rather than
write around them. It felt to me like our poetic tradition is full of examples of
poets resisting a form while using it. And being something of a contrarian, I
liked that idea for my sestina. I believe that once a poet has demonstrated they
can do a fixed form following all the rules, then it's okay to take wild liberties
with it.*

# DENISE DUHAMEL

## THE BRADY BUNCH (A DOUBLE SESTINA)

True fans know what happened to Marcia—
married off with Jan at a double wedding
in a 1981 TV movie
*The Brady Brides.* Marcia's husband Wally
is happy-go-lucky until he loses
his job nine years later. They have to sell
their half of the house they bought with Jan
who became an architect, just like her dad.
In *The Bradys*, a 1990 sequel,
Marcia and her husband move in with Carol and Mike,
who reminisce in original *Brady Bunch*
clips—Bobby and Cindy trying to seesaw

their way to a world record; Sam trying to sell
the idea of marriage to Alice who sees
herself as a Brady-domestic forever, lost
in a world of fondue pots and bunches
of tulips waiting to be arranged. No wall-
flower, Alice might have been gay, like Mike
Brady (Robert Reed) was in real life. A movie
called *The Brady Bunch Movie* and its sequel
hinted at a larger-than-straight world, but weddings
in Hollywood always win out. Never to be a dad,
Sam can't get Alice away from Marcia
et al. until Alice is menopausal. Jan

and Phillip adopt Patty. Mike
and Carol are finally grandparents, though Jan
worries they'll favor Marcia and Wally's
daughter Jessica. Popular Marcia
parted her hair in the middle while Jan bunched
hers back with a barrette. The Brady dad
loved all his stepdaughters, but the girl with the loose
hair, Jan thought, was the one to inspire weddings.
Jan was glad Wally lost his job and at last saw

Marcia as below her, a sad sequel
to her former glory, a knee-socked sell-
out, destined for grainy B-movies.

Little Bobby will never become a dad.
He was paralyzed while car racing, a movie
of his TV life flashing before him, a bunch
of hospital tubes clanking. It was a hard sell
to the networks, Bobby always in Marcia's
and Greg's shadow. Now this in the sequel?
Still, Bobby doesn't put up a wall.
Tracy (MTV veejay Martha Quinn) sees
her husband Bobby with the same kind of eyes Jan
sees Phillip, the same kind of wedding-
bell eyes Carol still flashes at Mike.
In the Brady world, love can never lose.

Even the commercials are like sequels—
Mrs. Brady (Florence Henderson) loses
nothing by hawking Wesson Oil. MARCIA
MARCIA MARCIA blasts a neon tee shirt. Only Mike
Brady (Robert Reed) wants nothing to do with selling
out—the Brady film sequel, the wedding
of the sacred TV family with RuPaul, a bunch
of movie execs poking fun at Jan
who's always losing her contacts in the movie.
The movie Jan isn't Eve Plumb. She can't see
that the original Jan loved her dad's
lectures, the way he designed each staircase and wall.

Mrs. Brady winds up in real estate, a wedding
of her love for the old neighborhood and Wall
Street. Even the dullest ranch house is an easy sell—
we all want to live on Brady Street where Dad
is always patient and Mom's sweet as Mike
and Ike candy. Brady fans could always see
the doc in Greg, the way he set Marcia's
sprained ankle. He lets fathers take home movies
as he delivers slews of babies, never losing

his cool when mothers scream, when jan-
itors mistake him for one of them, a consequence
of being such a nice guy in scrubs, one of the bunch.

Some days Peter's sure the world'll burn up. Or he foresees
the whole globe frozen into bunches
of icebergs and polluted snowflakes. His father Mike
sits on city council now. Each sequential
re-election depends upon his cool-headed dad-
talk and squelching Peter's environmental jangle
of protests. Peter calls Mr. Brady a sell-
out, a typical politician. He's lost
all respect for the old man who used to talk to walls
all night, trying to find the right moving
words to say to his children, to explain a wedding
so bizarre, why Peter'd have to share now with Marcia.

Cindy becomes a disc jockey, jingle jangle
of her own tambourine and Marcia's
borrowed 45s. She loves to lisp, "Daddy-
O!" into her microphone, wedding
the Beats with her suburban sequence
of early 70s pop and movie
soundtracks. She first loved her own voice, a mic
crackling "Sunshine Day" as she looked through the wall
of her TV and saw herself with her bunch
of brother and sisters, jamming, losing
themselves in a song-and-dance number they saw
as a way to win that talent contest, her first big sell.

What Alice did as post-Brady maid was move
in with Sam and refuse to let him sell
meat. Eating animal flesh was a sequel
to other carnivorous behavior. Alice saw
herself and Sam as plant-eating deer. At her wedding
she chomped down her last steak, and at a loss
for words, wept about each turkey (somebody's dad
or mom) she'd stuffed for that hungry Brady bunch

to eat. On her honeymoon, she dreamt of wallabies
with tiny Brady kids in each pocket, Jan
screaming, "Help me, Alice," Carol and Mike

nowhere in sight. *The Brady Bunch* lost
only occasionally to *The Partridge Family*—no Mike
as dad, just Reuben Kincaid who wedded
earnestness with sleaze. There was no Jan-
equivalent in the family that sang, who saw
the road as their home. No middle wall-
flowerish daughter. The Partridge sequence
of kids was Laurie (Susan Dey) as Marcia-ish
older sis and Tracy (Suzanne Crough) selling
herself as a working class Cindy, minus the bunch
of curls. There's been no Partridge Family movie
maybe because Reuben never stepped in as the dad-

figure, though sometimes it seemed for sure his wallowing
would stop if Shirley Jones would just make a dad
of him, kiss his managerial lips and see
that he wanted more than a Hollywood movie
romance where boy meets girl. He wanted Janet
Lee and her brood, Shirley Jones and her bunch
of pee-wee pop stars. He imagined the wedding,
how he'd make a better Mr. Brady, seldom
boring his stepkids with abstract details like Mike
did. Laurie would be less stuck-up than Marcia.
Keith (David Cassidy) would make Greg seem like a loser.
His love for Shirley would inspire lucrative sequels.

But in the early 70s, *The Brady Bunch*
won out—lunchboxes, posters, a sequence
of cartoons and a variety show. Jans
everywhere (middle sisters with loser
glasses, Jans who squinted through movies,
Jans who screamed, "Marcia Marcia Marcia!"
as an older pretty sister got everything) saw
that the world would change eventually, that Michelangelo
and Michelob would get them through college, not dad

or stepdad, who may have slaved all his life selling
blueprints of houses, measuring roofs and walls,
but who didn't know beyond his own screwed-up wedding.

No one talked about how Marcia and Greg gorged on wedding
cake, then watched porno movies and walloped
the little ones.  They all lost their innocence when that "SOLD"
sign went up in front of the suburbia dad and Jan
created blueprint sequels to, the Mike and Ike
of comfortable bunches of housing
that no one outside TV land ever saw.

# ON DELTA FLIGHT 659 WITH SEAN PENN

I'm writing this on a plane, Sean Penn,
with my black Pilot Razor ballpoint pen.
Ever since 9/11, I'm a nervous flyer. I leave my Pentium
Processor at home in its pendulous
case. Maybe this should be a sonnet, iambic pentameter,
rather than this mock sestina, each line ending in a Penn

variant. Forgive my insistence on all "Penn"
end words, a way of cheating the demands of the form, Sean Penn.
When I get home I'll try to justify my Penn
sestina as an obsessive and penetrating
look at you. But, I confess, the practical reason for my penchant
for Penn-sounding end words is because I can't open

*The Idiot's Guide to Poetry* (which I also left at home) to page 176,
        which happens
to list the order of the six different end words which ordinarily sharpen
a sestina. I sit alone in coach, but last night I sat with four poets, depending
on one another as readers, in a Pittsburgh café. I told them how I
        tried to be your pen
pal in the mid-eighties, not because of your pensive
bad boy looks, but because of a poem you'd penned

that appeared in an issue of *Frank*. Sean, it was great! Especially the
        penultimate
line. You probably think fans like me are your penance
for your popularity, your star bulging into a pentagon
filled with witchy wannabes and penniless
poets who waddle towards your icy peninsula
of glamour like so many menacing penguins.

But honest, I come in peace, Sean Penn,
writing on my plane ride home to Miami. I want no part of your penthouse
or the snowy slopes of your Aspen.

I won't stalk you like the swirling grime cloud over Pig Pen.
I have no script or stupendous
novel I want you to option. I even like your wife, Robin Wright Penn.

I only want to keep myself busy on this flight, to tell you of four penny-
loafered poets in Pennsylvania
who, last night, chomping on primavera penne
pasta, pondered poetry, celebrity, Iraq, the penitentiary
of free speech. And how I reminded everyone about the great Sean Penn
poem. I peer out the window and caress my lucky pendant:

Look, Sean Penn, the clouds are drawn with charcoal pencils.
The sky is opening like a child's first stab at penmanship.
The sun begins to ripen orange, then deepen.


*I wrote the first draft of "On Delta Flight 659 with Sean Penn" on a plane,
thus the cheating and using variations of Penn for end words. I didn't have
a sestina with me or a sestina memorized, so I couldn't quite remember the
pattern of word endings. I wanted to write a double sestina for The Brady
Bunch as they are two families blended into one. The famous are our (flawed)
gods and goddesses. We project a lot onto celebrities. I think poets often are
drawn to fictional characters, wanting to add our two cents. Maybe that's
because most poets don't write prose or sitcoms and we secretly wish we knew
how.*

# Drew Gardner
## *Sestina: AltaVista*

Damn it all the cute future nurses are missing our march for peace!
It's not that I'm not a fan of prog rock—it's that I'm not a fan of awful music.
Cat videos may expel their thoughts on the afterlife while listening to
    The Clash,
But Standard & Poor's just laminated your stamp script to a poser.
I hate it when people use the race card to get tickets to King Crimson.
I drive along the BQE, blasting the A/C and rejoicing.

Dostoyevsky adds you to his reading list rejoicing.
Heroic puppetry results in heat exhaustion, not in peace.
The lemmings pour from blackened thoughts in waves of crimson.
A giant talking sausage emotionally stressed from boring music
places clouds and lightning at a boarding school for posers.
All signs point to a night at home watching *Westworld* as your own
    emotions clash.

Lead your legions of hellspawn as egos clash.
Grant Hart surrenders his soul to a field hockey player playing Call of
    Duty online rejoicing.
If you have a fauxhawk you are definitely a poser.
What fits your schedule better? An hour of exercise or being dead for
    24 hours of peace?
Push through crowds of annoying fat kids to be on time to the
    conference on pop music.
Click to see what rhymes with crimson.

Jell-O molds watch the sun change from cannibal to crimson.
My shadow is a Lehman Brothers logo. I put on *Give 'Em Enough
    Rope* by The Clash
And it fills my heart with thought balloons rejoicing.
This printer delivers precision text and vague hopes, plus
    reversibility, a musician's music.
I go consecutively through the entire catalogue of Judas Priest for
    gaining peace.
My little cockatiel is such a poser.

The man who pees by squatting, is or isn't he a poser?
It's an intensely erotic, exciting paranormal read called *Kiss of Crimson*.
Some newspapers are only fit to line the bottoms of birdcages and rest
    in peace.
That this raspberry ennui syrup packaged in our unique female-
    shaped bottle will not clash
With the beauty and power of such fantastic time-space sluts leaves
    me rejoicing.
I fill all four tires with my music.

They use an iPod Nano to stimulate the nerves and make a kind of
    squid-skin music.
There's no sound like the sound of your child singing to a poser.
I'm Serena and I like unicorns. Life's the only chance you get for life's
    rejoicing.
Beetroot juice will make your stools red, a kind of crimson.
Slowly re-enable the remaining scripts until you find the clash.
When there's blood in the streets, it's time to shop for peace.

The music of the spheres kicks the asses of the elves inside my eyes
    and makes them crimson.
I hear *Combat Rock* on commercial radio and yell, "That's The Clash!"
The Octopus blots out the ink that interferes with peace.


*Why choose a sestina? I asked this question of myself numerous times. My
brain told me it would be too boring. There would not be enough uses to keep
me interested all year. I began to remember a certain smell, one that took me
many years to get over, one that made me nauseous and I remembered where
it came from, one that at the time I had been ingesting in rather strong doses
for about a week on prescription from an English teacher many years ago. It
made me really sick but did not work in the way it was supposed to. I guess
subconsciously I have something against this form, something that I intend to
change to a more positive light.*

# DANA GIOIA

## MY CONFESSIONAL SESTINA

Let me confess. I'm sick of these sestinas
written by youngsters in poetry workshops
for the delectation of their fellow students,
and then published in little magazines
that no one reads, not even the contributors
who at least in this omission show some taste.

Is this merely a matter of personal taste?
I don't think so. Most sestinas
are such dull affairs. Just ask the contributors
the last time they finished one outside of a workshop,
even the poignant one on herpes in that new little magazine
edited by their most brilliant fellow student.

Let's be honest. It has become a form for students,
an exercise to build technique rather than taste
and the official entry blank into the little magazines—
because despite its reputation, a passable sestina
isn't very hard to write, even for kids in workshops
who care less about being poets than contributors.

Granted nowadays everyone is a contributor.
My barber is currently a student
in a rigorous correspondence school workshop.
At lesson six he can already taste
success having just placed his own sestina
in a national tonsorial magazine.

Who really cares about most little magazines?
Eventually not even their own contributors
who having published a few preliminary sestinas
send their work East to prove they're no longer students.
They need to be recognized as the new arbiters of taste
so they can teach their own graduate workshops.

Where will it end? This grim cycle of workshops
churning out poems for little magazines
no one honestly finds to their taste?
This ever-lengthening column of contributors
scavenging the land for more students
teaching them to write their boot-camp sestinas?

Perhaps there is an afterlife where all contributors
have two workshops, a tasteful little magazine, and sexy students
who worshipfully memorize their every sestina.

# SARAH GREEN

## METAMORPHIC SESTINA

*for Gujarat*

> *There is no God,*
a boy in uniform recites to a breaking
window. Someone pours himself a glass
of scotch, opens the newspaper. *A flagrant
disregard.* We've been looking for you. No
one knew where. Morning explodes like a train.

When sending telegrams to persons on trains,
specify a car number. We cannot
guarantee your message's receipt. God
willing, word will reach your friend in time. *Breaking
news.* Saffron rains on a locked door. A flag
bleeds in the shape of a face. The glossolalia

of circling torches: gasoline
speaking in tongues. Meanwhile, a train
arrives in a schoolbook margin. The fragrance
of home rushes past checkpoints—God
knows how—gets waved through, breaking
all rules. Today we were given nothing

new to memorize. Today a woman says *No*
to the pavement. A glass half full tells a glass
half empty to stop worrying, then breaks
down at its feet. Today water boards a train
with no ticket. Someone tries to get God
to come to his meeting. Someone tries to forget

her body at the side of the road, for good.
Today a girl copies *I desired to be known*
and spells it *none.* She's asking why, if God
is, God is not. Her teacher finds his glasses
and begins to read. In black and white a train
rewinds, collects itself, speeds up and breaks.

Nearby Kabir keeps singing *if you don't break
your ropes while you are alive* and forgetting
what comes next. An old man in a trance
calls out *then what* to his burning house. *No
God*, the boy repeats to an audience of glass.
His sister picks up her pencil, writes *but God*.


*This was the first sestina I ever wrote, under the brilliant direction of Martha
Collins's workshop at Oberlin. I believe we were told that a person only gets
one successful sestina in his/her life. I'm not sure if that's true, or if this one
is mine, or what. I have written more sestinas since then; I find that they
combine the potential for obsessive ordering-of-angst—which other traditional
forms also share—with the subversive wish to sprawl, or court happenstance,
or narrate, or be untrue. Dream. It was written in response to a specific train
burning in the city of Gujarat, India, in 2002. The results of the burning
were Hindu-Muslim riots in which hundreds of people from both religions
died. I had traveled to India in 2001 and it was still on my mind when that
news was circulating. I found possibilities in the form for ambiguity and grief
that were compelling to me. I was also influenced by Agha Shahid Ali's
ghazals.*

# BETH GYLYS

## *NOT AN AFFAIR: A SESTINA*

You're crazy if you called this an affair.
We slept together, and I made you come.
No big deal. You've got a lot of strange
ideas. You think you know so much about me,
think because you've seen me naked that counts
for something. Just because I put my head

between your legs, because you gave me head,
you tell the world we've had some big affair.
We've been together twice—no one counts
that time behind my desk. I didn't come.
(How could I relax, you simply grabbed me?)
I'm not the one you need. You're really strange.

You try to make this seem important, this strange
relationship we have. I'm no head
to place upon a platter. I'm married. Me,
I'm not the kind of man who has affairs.
I like you—that is all. It doesn't come
to any more than that. Do you know what counts

in things like ours? I'll tell you what counts.
Let me put it simply: it's not that strange
to meet in places in the dark, to come
between your hopes and what you have, and head
for someplace warm and soft. To have affairs—
a real affair—is wrong. It seems to me

you give too much away. You're telling me
as well as all your friends these wild accounts
of us and me and our intense affair,
as if to have a little sex was strange.
I know you think I'm messing with your head,
but you're the one who kept this going. You came

to see me. You knew my life was set. I've come
to take things as they are: I know you want me.
It's hard to be alone, to move ahead
with no one there, when nothing seems to count.
Believe me, I've felt like that. You aren't so strange.
Listen, I do care; this wasn't an affair.

I hope you come to see that, take what counts
from what you tell me is a big affair,
and head to love more real than strange.

*At the time of writing this sestina, I was involved in a love relationship that
was utterly consuming and utterly problematic. The poem allowed me to tease
out one of the dynamics of that relationship in a way that seemed emotionally
rich. The speaker of the poem is male, and his character is both patronizing
and self-indicting—but there's also some wisdom in what he says. I set myself
up for a challenging task with the poem: it's a dramatic monologue in (rough)
blank verse. Those parameters, coupled with the difficulties inherent in the
sestina, pushed me to write a poem I wouldn't have been able to write any
other way. Yes, the speaker is a bit of a jerk, but the person to whom he speaks
(some version of me, I'd say) also comes across as obsessive and naïve—her
definition of the relationship butting up against a reality she was unwilling
to face. Maybe both of my sestinas in this anthology end up undermining the
credibility of everyone in the poems. I'm not sure what that says about the
sestinas or about me.*

# THE SCENE

Last April when Travis's band played a set
at the Zonolight, Michael got sloshed.
Kelly had trimmed his goatee
because his book had been accepted.
Paul arrived in a limo with his girlfriend
who wore sandals with see-through plastic straps.

No one seemed to notice how my bra straps
kept slipping down my shoulders. The set
had started, and I got talking to Paul's girlfriend
about breast reduction. Michael was busy getting sloshed,
and Kelly kept bringing up his acceptance
for publication, stroking his well-trimmed goatee

as if it were a bottle with a genie, instead of a goatee
that we all thought he should shave. The traps
we'd fallen into made us giddy with acceptance.
We loved Kelly anyway, and Travis too, whose set
had inspired two little girls to hula. Almost sloshed,
Paul unabashedly stroked the ass of his girlfriend,

while Michael told me a story about the girlfriend
of a friend of his who only liked men with goatees
and wouldn't have sex with him until he grew one. Sloshed
on wine, Paul's girlfriend kept pulling at the straps
of her dress. Travis was jamming, his drum-set
a blur of noise, when the conversation turned to the acceptance

of U.S. world domination as a norm. "Acceptance
on our part doesn't mean the world..." Paul's girlfriend
trailed off. "Exactly!" exhorted Michael, who set
his wine glass on a chair excitedly. Kelly's goatee
looked like a stain on his face. He thwacked the straps
of his suspenders with his thumbs. Someone's beer sloshed,

on my foot. Michael whispered in my ear, "I'm sloshed,"
then burst out: "We can't be complacent. Acceptance
of tyranny is as bad as enactment. Patriotism is a cultural strap
used to bind us!" Looking bored, Paul's girlfriend
left for the bathroom. Kelly fondled his goatee
as if it were a rabbit's foot, and Travis finished up his set

with a flourish—even his goatee was sweating. Paul's girlfriend
returned with a set of chopsticks in her hair. She looked sloshed,
one dress strap undone. The air shimmered with acceptance.


*One night several years ago, I went with my friend Michael to hear my friend
Travis's band. My housemate Paul also happened to show up that night with
his then-girlfriend, Leslie. Michael and I were all stirred up because Bush was
hell-bent on this Iraq war, a war that clearly had more to do with his own need
to assert power and impress or avenge his papa than with any real defensive
need. The sestina seemed a good way to blend the political with the personal
and social. There's a party aspect to the poem that highlights the "theoretical"
nature of the political conversation that's addressed. The characters of the poem
don't really have any stake in the political ramifications of the conversation.
What the poem is truly about, then, is the American political landscape. We
go to war as a country, yet nothing truly changes for most Americans. There's
a kind of frivolity to the whole "scene" that implicates everyone in the poem.
The true horror of political domination in the world is framed against the
backdrop of a party, so that the characters in the poem all seem impotent and
Dionysian.*—from an interview with Ellen Steinbaum

# Marilyn Hacker
## *Untoward Occurrence at Embassy Poetry Reading*

Thank you. Thank you very much. I'm pleased
to be here tonight. I seldom read
to such a varied audience. My poetry
is what it is. Graves, yes, said love, death
and the changing of the seasons
were the unique, the primordial subjects.

I'd like to talk about that. One subjects
oneself to art, not necessarily pleased
to be a colander for myths. It seasons
one to certain subjects. Not all. You can read
or formulate philosophies; your death
is still the kernel of your dawn sweats. Poetry

is interesting to people who write poetry.
Others are involved with other subjects.
Does the Ambassador consider death
on the same scale as you, Corporal? Please
stay seated. I've outreached myself. I read
your discomfort. But tonight the seasons

change. I've watched you, in town for the season,
nod to each other, nod to poetry
represented by me, and my colleagues, who read
to good assemblies; good citizens, good subjects
for gossip. You're the audience. Am I pleased
to frighten you? Yes and no. It scares me to death

to stand up here and talk about real death
while our green guerrillas hurry up the seasons.
They have disarmed the guards by now, I'm pleased
to say. The doors are locked. Great poetry
is not so histrionic, but our subjects
choose us, not otherwise. I will not read

manifestos. Tomorrow, foreigners will read
rumors in newspapers. . . . Oh, sir, your death
would be a tiresome journalistic subject,
so stay still till we're done. This is our season.
The building is surrounded. No more poetry
tonight. We are discussing, you'll be pleased

to know, the terms of your release. Please read
these leaflets. Not poetry. You're bored to death
with politics but that's the season's subject.

*It's a fantasy, of course, inspired in part by the protests against the American war in Viet Nam, then going on, and in part by the obsessive qualities (as every writer notes obsessively) of the sestina itself. The sestina also lends itself to dramatic monologue, for the same reasons, usually in the persona of someone, historical or invented, with a predicament.*

# DONALD HALL

## *SESTINA*

Hang it all, Ezra Pound, there is only the one sestina,
Or so I thought before, always supposing
The subject of them invariably themselves.
That is not true. Perhaps they are nearly a circle,
And they tell their motifs like party conversation,
Formally repetitious, wilfully dull,

But who are we to call recurrence dull?
It is not exact recurrence that makes a sestina,
But a compromise between a conversation
And absolute repetition. It comes from supposing
That there is a meaning to the almost-circle,
And that laws of proportion speak of more than themselves.

I think of the types of men who have loved themselves,
Who studious of their faces made them dull
To find them subtle; for the nearly-a-circle,
This is the danger. The introvert sestina
May lose its voice by childishly supposing
It holds a hearer with self-conversation.

When we are bound to a tedious conversation,
We pay attention to the words themselves
Until they lose their sense, perhaps supposing
Such nonsense is at very least less dull.
Yet if the tongue is held by a sestina,
It affirms not words but the shape of the unclosed circle.

The analogy: not the precise circle,
Nor the loose patching of a conversation
Describes the repetition of a sestina;
Predictable, yet not repeating themselves
Exactly, they are like life, and hardly dull,
And not destroyed by critical supposing.

Since there is nothing precise (always supposing)
Consider the spiraling, circular, not full-circle
As the type of existence, the dull and never dull
Predictable, general movement of conversation,
Where things seem often more, slightly, than themselves,
And make us wait for the coming, like a sestina.

And so we name the sestina's subject, supposing
Our lives themselves dwindle, an incomplete circle;
About which, conversation is not dull.


*I think "Sestina" is my only attempt at the form. There have been several villanelles, several pantoums. But the sestina form has not seemed appropriate for anything else I have wanted to write. And I think I wanted to write this one in order to salute Pound and have fun with the notion of the centrality of a form to a poem's identity. Maybe a self-conversation in this poem is my weighing a discussion of an argument. I guess I would dedicate my sestina to Ezra Pound. I had not met him at the time when I wrote the sestina, and I don't believe I ever showed it to him. I guess I know I didn't.*

# James Harms

## One Long Sentence and a Few Short Ones; or, *39 Lines by Frank Gehry*

*Guggenheim, Bilbao*

On a boulevard in Barcelona
my watch began its backward crawl
as Lani counted down the buildings
by Gaudí and whistled the same song

she'd been whistling since a morning
in Córdoba, when it leaked from a pair
of headphones a girl had left near a plate of pears,
all of us sharing plans to visit Toledo

on our way back, though all we knew of morning
and each other we learned and forgot in that simple crawl
through breakfast in a courtyard, a song
beginning its slow construction in Lani's mind, a building

of music as lovely and eternal as any building
by Gaudí, the way the memory of music can pare
away the sallow air once soaked with song,
with orange trees and sweat, how everywhere in Seville

diesel smoke hung like gray streamers above the crawl
of traffic each evening, how even morning
was a sepia fog, a breath exhaled from the last morning
dream before waking, before the daily building

back of confidence and faith revived the crawl
of hope—even Lani in her brand-new pair
of silver sandals believed that Lorca left Granada
to spare the city, not himself: once every song

was dusted over and done, once every song
hardened like a bullet in a cast of mourning,
little metal murmurs, once Lorca stopped dreaming of Málaga
and the sea and simply swallowed another fist in a building

bruised blue by evening, his face as soft as a pear
left for no one on a sill, ants crawling
up the wall in a line, certain of sugar and crawling
and a little mound of sand; once all the songs

and their memories stopped and a last pair
of moths exploded in the light of morning...
Lani finished counting the strange buildings
and began to plan. "A thousand miles to Madrid,"

she said, her finger crawling the map as she sang
the same song. "But let's forget Madrid." The buildings
fell away, a pair of cows in a field. "It's even farther to Bilbao."


*This is a one-off sestina only because I have great respect for the form and,
thus, have trashed just about every other one I've written, alas. It was part
of a larger project of poems written in the manner of Frank Gehry. I tried to
imagine how he would write a love poem, a sonnet, an elegy, a pastoral and,
finally, a sestina. I like the circularity and surprise of sestinas, so it made sense
to me to harness the form to a travel poem. I ended up really enjoying the
narrative of the poem and where it took me (both spatially and emotionally),
so I decided to bury the form so it wouldn't distract from the story. I figured
it would be more interesting to happen upon the form than to recognize it
immediately, especially given the oddly matter-of-fact story being told. It did
occur to me that the building fit the form, which is why I decided to use it.
Each poem in this series is based on a different building, and in each case I
tried to come up with the form or genre that seemed suggested by the building.*

# BROOKS HAXTON
## POSTTRAUMATIC SMALL-TALK DISORDER

When people ask me what I do,
I say,
"Whatever comes to mind,
as if you care.
I think I'll talk to someone else.
So long."

A person ought to try to get along,
which I would do,
if I knew something else
besides the same old crap to say:
"I'm glad you ask. I care
about feigned interest in my work. Mind

reading is my job. Your mind,
for instance, is a long
reel of profanities for which I care
as only sailors do:
I want to say
just those profanities myself. How else

can anyone stay sane? How else,
I mean, if we can't call to mind
endearments, or, say,
obsequies. I long
to hear your obsequies, while you do
that slow limbo in your box. Take care."

I may not care
for small talk, but what else
can anybody do,
when dimwits who don't mind
how long
the other dimwits take to say

their dim, interminable say,
insist one should care.
Fine, I care: they take too long!
Let's end all this! And something else:
death takes too long. Death I mind
enormously. I do.

But what do you say,
briefly? Have I lost my mind? Do you care?
Nobody else to anyone matters long.

# ANTHONY HECHT

## *THE BOOK OF YOLEK*

*Wir haben ein Gesetz,*
*Und nach dem Gesetz soll er sterben.*


The dowsed coals fume and hiss after your meal
Of grilled brook trout, and you saunter off for a walk
Down the fern trail, it doesn't matter where to,
Just so you're weeks and worlds away from home,
And among midsummer hills have set up camp
In the deep bronze glories of declining day.

You remember, peacefully, an earlier day
In childhood, remember a quite specific meal:
A corn roast and bonfire in summer camp.
That summer you got lost on a Nature Walk;
More than you dared admit, you thought of home;
No one else knows where the mind wanders to.

The fifth of August, 1942.
It was morning and very hot. It was the day
They came at dawn with rifles to The Home
For Jewish Children, cutting short the meal
Of bread and soup, lining them up to walk
In close formation off to a special camp.

How often you have thought about that camp,
As though in some strange way you were driven to,
And about the children, and how they were made to walk,
Yolek who had bad lungs, who wasn't a day
Over five years old, commanded to leave his meal
And shamble between armed guards to his long home.

We're approaching August again. It will drive home
The regulation torments of that camp
Yolek was sent to, his small, unfinished meal,
The electric fences, the numeral tattoo,
The quite extraordinary heat of the day
They all were forced to take that terrible walk.

Whether on a silent, solitary walk
Or among crowds, far off or safe at home,
You will remember, helplessly, that day,
And the smell of smoke, and the loudspeakers of the camp.
Wherever you are, Yolek will be there, too.
His unuttered name will interrupt your meal.

Prepare to receive him in your home some day.
Though they killed him in the camp they sent him to,
He will walk in as you're sitting down to a meal.

# BRIAN HENRY
## BAD APPLE

*[day 1]*

In this poem the cup discovered under the table,
congealed milk inside it, will emerge as a symbol
of a souring relationship, left alone until it decays
and only then doused with soap and hot water, quick fix
that hides the smell of germs but lets them live
and make her sick to the stomach a day later.

*[day 2]*

When the father thinks of his life, it's always Later,
despite the Now being there, he at the table
forgetting why, exactly, he continues to live
where he has become not a person but a symbol
of what he, until now, despised too much to fix,
and he wonders what else he will lose as he decays.

*[day 3]*

The sestina is a horrid form, it drags as it decays,
feigning movement, Now yawning into Later,
as if teleutons were enough to redeem, or even fix,
the structure, a mess of a tower—chairs on a table—
or the lack of substance despite the symbol
that sneezes itself into the poem: *to live, to live.*

*[day 4]*

Reminded by a friend that he has much to live
and be thankful for, he thinks that which decays
is already worse than dead, for it is a symbol
with no power except what it promises for later—
a burst of light that comes when one is drunk, at a table,
spine garbled by this life, too fucked up to fix.

*[day 5]*

This stanza-a-day sestina, too messed up to fix,
expects a lot of one with other ways to live,
(mow, clip, wash, shine, sweep), table or no table,
form or no form, and jerks itself off as it decays
into middling pools of amnesia, saved for later
but forgotten immediately, symbol or no symbol.

*[day 6]*

What in the end is not an idea but a symbol
wrecks the poem beyond any possible fix
despite the wish to save each step for later
and think that to write is the same as to live,
and here, it is safe to claim, the sestina decays,
sublimates like the dirt that rings the table.

*[day 7]*

That which decays does not, cannot live;
that which is a symbol will not fix
that which is held for later under the table.


*I wrote this sestina in 2002. I wanted to write a poem by writing a stanza a day. I didn't sit down to write a sestina, but on the second day, the end word of the first line happened to match up with the end word of the previous line, and the sestina just started to happen. On the third day, though, I decided to make the sestina itself the subject. The apple in the title relates to the idiom "One bad apple spoils the barrel." I thought it spoke to the construction of a poetic form like the sestina. All of my sestinas would be dedicated to Hayden Carruth, who once visited my poetry workshop in graduate school and said that any sestina not written in iambic pentameter is a fake sestina.*

# SCOTT HIGHTOWER

## *CRUISING A HUNGRY WORLD*

It is the season of meat.
Your dropped eyes would dissuade the passion
if they could. I lean in to inhale each breath
you make. You sense dark squirrels in my blood
and don't want me detecting any interest
from the banter and shifting soil

of our friendship: a flower afraid of soil;
a cage of ribs, suspicious itself of meat.
My press is driven less by fever than interest.
You try to counter what you perceive as passion,
try to forgive the garishness of my blood.
I'm not holding my breath.

Heading into my next breath,
I haven't a clue how soil
first rose up into tributaries of blood
to fill a tongue, setting in motion a dialogue between meat
and a hank of cloud. I'm not sure passion
is the residue of an excited star. That would probably interest

you. Harmonics and game strategies interest
you. You appreciate the spells a slight breath
can cast. For now, you channel your passion
the way a good farmer mounds soil
along a rivulet of water; no meat
floats red, raw, and sun-washed through the blood

of your narrow slough. Perhaps it's danger in the blood
that I revere. You veer through subjects of interest,
though none takes. I smile a nail-pinning-meat
smile. You sigh, frown, and catch your breath.
I am a persistent rivulet that breaks the soil
you've just put in place. How aggravating passion

can be when it's not your mill churning the passion.
Loosen up. I'm only indirectly out for your blood.
Actually, I'm after something else. I'm coursing the soil
of another river moving carefully with interest
along a breeze of crises. My turn for a breath.
I'm already an ear up against a door of meat.

More than passion, my circles are those of interest.
Between us, bait is not blood; though breath
too can easily soil. I'm drawn to you as river, not meat.


*I think of a sestina as a container that a poet fills up; not quite as much a
practice in obsession as a villanelle, but heading that way. I think both forms
have affinities with group folk dancing, where there is a variety of circular
configurations. While writing a villanelle always feels like a very restrictive
exercise in compacting and making quick turns, writing a sestina always feels
like an unfurling and expansive enterprise… one has to have enough material
to hit the prescribed marks while filling up that container.*

# Ernest Hilbert

## *Hel[l]ical Double Sestina:* [Metal Number One]

*for Eric "Dr. Bones" Bohnenstiel and veteran headbangers everywhere, original barbarians all*

### Overture

For hours in flames we reached for speeds of darkness—
To walls of noise forced hard and white with light—
Fulfilled a fevered trance, rank, infernal:
Such gloom! Such hymns! Such quarrels! Such undead
Majesty…But in an age of irony,
You grew serious, my demon, and died.

### 1.

You were the **chang**…before our hard day's night,
The din of every chorus sung at once,
Of hopes blackened by bad jobs, with no real love
Left, deranged and dizzy from the pit, your cross
A compass pointed at hell: Too stupid
To haul yourself from tar-black pits at last.

It's hard to feel sorry for you. You died
Like a jammed chainsaw, stern Hessian god, darkness
Your only friend, mad-drunk, right eye runny
With salt scum, tight-crotched jeans, suburban blight:
Your songs were weapons, for those we wished dead,
Tons of ammunition aimed at them all,

Brutal shock of broken noses. One last
Time may you rise, wretched, from brooding night.
Sometimes I miss you, your lowly, stupid
Discord, your chipped collar-bone. Such things once
Seemed natural, like the lonely Styx I'd cross
To get home, where there would be no love.

They told you to *grow up*, get a job and all,
Leave the tombs to those who've really died,
So you hid in fjord and swamp, a brain-dead
Convict. History is always unkind, our arks nest-
Led in dark rooms far from the shaming light.
It felt *good* in the days before irony,

To go so *fast*, yes, **yes**, so fast the Sirens' ee-
Some song could not lure our Viking ships, folderol
Beside smokehouse barbarian sweat, the light-
Ning we rode until dawn . . . and harmony died.
For years, an ache anchored my neck, then Dark Nes-
Ter turned me back on again like the undead.


2.

You changed and lost your lust to lead each night
Your lost legions to the liquor store. Once,
You knew nothing hurt so much as a love
Hurled away or held too long, but to cross
Such anger with such passion is truly stupid.
I knew that. I did, and I left you at last.

Cold beer in winter lots, last of daylight
On a humming Chevette hood, we could still raise the dead,
Every inch of us a fresh scar. We *died*
When you first hit the lights, before irony
Took it all away, the harsh glories, hot rush, all
Our lives lived for that strobing, smoky darkness.

Concrete thuds, mouthfuls of windshield, the dead
Of night bashed with black-fisted iron, E-
Vil as a botched tattoo, cold skeleton darkness
Called home, a moveable blood-feast for all,
And chains thrown in the wood-chipper; what died
Down your throat, what ruptured bulb of lost light?

You always assumed you were owed no love,
So you refused to love yourself and, at last,
Fell in love with death, so inverted your cross.
Again, I've fallen from your whiplash night
To Valhallan concussion, all hammers at once
Brought down on our enemies. Kinda stupid,

Yes, I've gone and said it, *you were stupid*,
But that never kept anyone from love.
Our East Germany of music, you were at once
Joyous and grim. Ah, *mein teufel*, where Gentians last
Bloomed, future and past are cast off to a single night.
What rivers in hell remain for us to cross?

**3.**

You attack but never advance, absorb more loss,
Obnoxious, but not really evil, drunk on the stoop, id
Above all, egoless animal, venomous night-
Crawler, cut in three yet thriving, your love
Inhuman, in three hearts and no head. Last
Call never comes. You wrecked our necks, our Once

And Backward King. You wriggle up, all affronts
Taken personally. You've slipped from your cross.
You never aged, adapted, or evolved to last,
Unwashed warrior, unleashed brute, "LEGION, *stoopid.*"
Icy volts wreak war through your crooked love.
You gnaw on grave soil, seething in the burnt-out night.

**Coda:**

I once held you, shaking . . . angry and stupid,
And, at last, was plucked from you, like dawn from night.
The black songs will rule us all once we've died.

I can't laugh or take flight, or hide from what I see.
We drank the darkness of ruthless teenage love.
So we go from death, what lives to seize us all.

*I happen to love heavy metal music. Since I am a poet and opera librettist, the outrageousness of the style continues to appeal well into adulthood. As a greasy-haired warehouse worker and dishwasher in southern New Jersey, I saw heavy metal as the only unpretentious option, not only in terms of how I listened to music, but how I chose to present myself to a hostile world. The harshness and sheer volume of the music creates a protective shell. The metalhead image was like armor donned each day. It was our way of signaling our refusal to submit, our open rebellion against everything we could think of—businesses, governments, systems of education, and discipline—against what we viewed as the obvious hypocrisies of society. Stephen Burt has remarked that the sestina "served, historically, as a complaint," its demands understood as "signs for deprivation or duress." In that regard, it is ideally suited to my aims.*

# Elizabeth Hildreth

## *In a Rut*

*for EP*

Yes, the wheel spins mud, the cloud
kicks dirt, the dialogue bubble bursts. So light
the fire from all sworn angles—inside a field
of typewriters, under a swarming sky of glass
hummingbirds. Squeeze through the bright tear
and emerge, glistening from the wall

of human jelly; reflecting against the wall
of action paintings. A child looks at a cloud
to see the shape of her own desire, to tear
that desire open and eat it in the raw light
of day. Or to crash through a crystal glass
ceiling and land broken-nosed in a blooming field

of awe. Despite reports to the contrary, field
testing one's desire against an actual wall
of operation can lead to flying shards of glass
and emergency surgery under a cloud
of heavy anesthesia. For better results, light
a cigar and declare a life born, shed a tear

of pride. Then execute an immediate tear-
down. Inspiration is a wrecking ball into the original field
of vision. Additionally, the willingness to hold a full-color light
show with ancillary slips and film loops before a hungry wall
-to-wall audience. Or, more inspired yet, a static cloud
of silence. In one experiment, babies fearlessly crawled over glass—

until they recognized human expression. At which point, glass
became terrifying and babies became tear-
splattered. Development, though beneficial, casts a cloud
of doubt and fear over that which was once as free and clear as a field
of nothingness and as warm and comforting as a roaring wall
of nonsense consumed in the heart-jumbled light

of poetry. One conclusion is that hell is light
seen too late through a shattered plate glass
window. Or, if Keats, a budding morrow over the wall
of midnight. In either case, it is okay: boredom, repetition, failure. A tear
dries faster than any other substance. Look, Eugene Field
unlikely wrote "Wynken, Blynken, and Nod" in one drafty cloud

of genius. A too-bright light on a sunken path will tear
at anyone's confidence, contentment, ego field. But there are ways, Ep.
There are walls, eyelids, their faint murmur, "If I were but a cloud…"


*I didn't consider myself to be in a rut when I was writing the poem. I try to
actively disbelieve in ruts. Then again, I emailed my friend Eric and asked
him to give me a topic and end words, so maybe I was, indeed, in a rut?
He wrote back, "Topic: ruts. End words: cloud, light, field, glass, tear, and
wall." Other than the topic and end words, I didn't have one idea in my
brain. When I first started composing on my computer, I found myself being
neurotic and deleting every line. So I lugged a giant green Remington manual
typewriter, a book of quotes, and an* American Heritage Dictionary *into
my kids' room, dumped everything on the bed, and shut the door. I started
writing at around 7:30 in the morning and worked straight through until I
finished a draft at about 4 in the afternoon. The next day I revised. Then
the next day I revised again. Then it was done, or done enough. I am such
a sentimentalist. I think it's great if anyone feels less miserable after reading
a poem. I can't claim to have had any "intent" as a writer, but the poem's
speaker is very optimistic. So, "boredom, repetition, failure," it is okay.*

# Paul Hoover

## Sestina from Sonnet 56

Love comes to us as spirit, not appetite,
But you remember when, that summer,
The true one came to your bed, new
As a glistening field.  She turned the view
From dull to full. Now fullness is rare;
You miss the light of her surprising eyes.

Everywhere you go it's her green eyes
Glancing across the room, her appetite
For sleep rustling like leaves down the rare
Hallways of winter. Her world is your summer.
The sound of her approach opens the view
Through memory, where you were brand new.

Only love can tell when love is shiny and new.
And when love takes to the street, its eyes
Dart like birds. You used to see the view
From the door of a small hotel, where appetite
Was a blessing and both of you were full. Summer
Is never the season for love to be this rare.

But the world's on fire again; everything is rare
And suddenly in danger.  Love is always new,
Even when it ages, and so it seems that summer
Might last all year. Look into her eager eyes.
Appetite needs a feeding or it's not appetite.
You want to be with her, love the only view.

Lovers are supposed to stand where the view
Is farthest. But love in the mountains is rare,
And she prefers the islands, with their appetite
For music and dancing. Buy one shoe or tear a new
Sweater, it's all the same to you. She has eyes
For the time when you'll rest together all summer.

Love that slept all winter will soon find its summer.
Love, like a poem, grows tiresome when its purview
Is only tradition: sestinas and haikus. Her eyes
Seek newer forms—free, unchained, and rare—
Just as they seek you. Is anything really new?
As in poetry, also in love: the size of the appetite.


*As soon as I came up with the concept of* Sonnet 56 *[Hoover's book of
different versions of the Shakespeare sonnet], I made a list of forms and
concepts I might follow. Sestina and villanelle went onto the list early, but the
actual composition of both came later. I'm especially proud of the ending line
of the sestina, "As in poetry, also in love: the size of the appetite." There's a
gratuitousness to poetic form. I was not convinced by John Frederick Nims, my
professor in grad school in Chicago, that there is a "natural" poetic form, such
as the heartbeat of iambic measure. Poetic form is like a riddle to be solved or
a game to be played between author and reader. We use words like "golden"
and "silvery" to describe its cadences. It's the mechanical golden bird of Yeats's
great poem, "Lapis Lazuli," designed to keep a drowsy emperor awake. The
mechanism of the sestina comes as an acknowledgment that, after all, it could
have been otherwise.*

# John Hoppenthaler

## Coconut Octopus

*O. marginatus*

Hydrostatic pressure defines the pulsing shape
of an octopus. *marginatus* dwells among sunken
coconuts, more than fifty feet deep, hiding
sometimes in their shells by drawing two halves around
its body. When faced with danger, it wraps six arms
around itself and backpedals away on a pair, camouflaged,

innocent coconut bob-bobbing along. Camouflaged,
eluding predators with admirable stealth—shape-
shifter—the suckered treads of its fluid-filled arms
rolling slowly over ocean bottom, past sunken
shipwrecks, intrusive snorklers who dive around
the coastline of Indonesia. What glorious hiding,

so utterly naked and in open sight! Such stealthy hiding
can excite, though, really, the ingenious camouflage
of *marginatus* is stereo-typed, an inherent moving around
requiring no feedback from the brain. The shape,
color, not more than an oblivious twitch of nerves, sunken
coconuts a coincidence of seascape to which it adjusts. Armed

only with primal behavior coded into the ganglia of each arm,
it could care less about the potential thrill of its hiding.
Ignorance, if not bliss. I'm looking hard at my face: sunken
blue eyes, tidal drift of hairline, the graying camouflage
of a beard. My fantasies are all about being in better shape,
anxious moments spent realizing that I've been floating around

a very long time. Every creature in the food chain is surrounded
by gourmands and midnight snackers, swollen armies
of gluttonous neighbors whose grotesque shapes
mirror the intensity of their desire. Here I am, hiding
out in the flotsam of suburbia. I'm camouflaged
as pocket lint, later as a soul who knows how low to sink,

how thrilling it is to buoy among wind-fallen coconuts.  At the
    kitchen sink,
I'm preparing octopus while a lover seems still around
to enjoy it; she's curled up on the sofa, camouflaged:
comfy bolster, shadow.  I could hold her in my arms.
*Remove ink sac, eyes and teeth. Clean well.* "Oh, hide
from me, will you?" *Place in a pot; simmer till tender.* "Oh, shapely,

shapely.  Sunken treasure; seductress." *Cut the eight arms*
*into bite-sized pieces.* Around every corner, she's hiding there.
In the coconut cream, camouflaged, roiling, assuming another shape.


*At some point in 2005, I read a newspaper article about the Indonesian*
*coconut octopus and became intrigued; a good handful of my poems have*
*begun with something I've read in a newspaper. I'd also been thinking about*
*the sestina form and considering whether or not to try and write one. It was a*
*perfect confluence. The form played the lead role in this poem's making, as I*
*feel it does whenever I choose a closed rather than open form. By its nature, a*
*sestina almost has to be wild, wacky, fluid, and quirkily synaptic—it has to be*
*to undermine the sestina's extreme artificiality. I think this poem is all of those*
*things.*

# SONYA HUBER

## *DEAR* THRASHER

*Adapted from a letter to the editor printed in* Thrasher *skateboarding magazine, April 2003*

Dear *Thrasher*, I love your skate
mag. It rocks, even though you
guys print too many shoe ads.
And what's up with the posers
doing handrails? Don't they know
real skaters do it in the street?

Well, you know even skating the street
sucks 'cause cops won't let us skate
anywhere. But kids here know
some killer secret pools and ditches. You
would shit to skate the Blood Bowl—eats posers
for lunch. Put the Blood Bowl in your ads.

I got a serious beef, though—the ads
with those skate-betty chicks standing in the street
in thongs made me think you're all Cali posers!
It makes me want to give up and screw this skate
bullshit. I mean, God, why don't you
sell your souls for cash, you know?

I don't want to ride your asses—you know
you rock my world even with the lame ads.
It's like, I need a lifeline here, you
can't imagine Rankin, Georgia—mullets, no street
courses, one shitty skate park. I skate
with four cool punks, try to steer clear of posers.

We've got a big problem in Rankin with posers.
I'm 12 and not stupid. I know
guys here think us girls can't skate—

That's crap! It's your fault. Running those ads
makes idiots here think it's street
last, clothes and babes first. It's on *you.*

Guys even rape girls in the park crapper. You
see a port-o-potty shaking with a poser
and a screaming chick inside, guys on the street
high-fiving, whatever, it's gross, and I know
this shit happens all over. So be cool and drop the ads.
It's not about tits. Get on your board and skate.

They're everywhere, you know,
Poser, thick-necked Fitch Bitches like in your ads.
I don't want 'em. I lost my cherry to the street. I'll die or skate.

*The poem was inspired by a letter to the editor in* Thrasher *magazine from a young female skater that just blew me away. With skater culture, like any subculture, there's a repetitive vocabulary of certain words, which fit the sestina form. The poem is adapted directly from her letter, which had the repetitive language plus a strong argument and amazing images, all expressed in a way that was really forceful and memorable. The subject matter directly connected with the form.*

# VICTOR D. INFANTE
## *SIX PORTRAITS IN DISINTEGRATION*

1.)
This is where we meet, in the crumbling,
navigation by skin flakes, chips of bone,
these trails of ourselves that we leave behind
as we learn what's breadth and what is breathing,
that baby teeth were our first offering,
hard truths that fell unbidden from our mouths.

2.)
My first taste of whisky was when our mouths
pulled tight—first kiss, bodies coiled, crumbling
beneath the weight of blood rush, offering
small tokens to the night of fear and bone—
set to make canticles of our breathing,
anonymous hymns to what's left behind.

3.)
Our conversation: "What is left behind?"
Inevitably on roadsides, mouths
parched—you, to the side, aloof, not breathing—
me, staring at neon and crumbling:
You, who have my eyes, wear my hair and bone.
I understand what you are offering.

4.)
Spark against spark the only offering
I have for you: What I have left behind
dissolved in the cathedral of our mouths,
what the needle of us carves in our bones:
What I once was now left to crumbling:
It's only with you that I am breathing.

5.)
Ask me what is breadth and what is breathing,
and I will stutter hymnals, offering
fragments of what will ease your crumbling
as you leave this house of mistakes behind—
When we speak, teeth remain within our mouths,
no truths fall forward, echo from our bones.

6.)
We love like neon and we love like bone,
permeate each other, as though breathing,
holding our pasts and futures in our mouths,
escalating prayers raised in offering
of what once was holy, what's left behind
and what is left when our crumbling is done.

*I actually didn't set out to write a sestina. I started with the idea of these relationships with women, some long out of mind, dissolving, and how I coped with that, how I did or didn't fight to save them. The persona's not exactly me, of course, but there's a lot of very personal emotion and exploration of masculinity in them. In the course of writing the poem, I found certain words refraining—"neon," "bone," "teeth"—and it occurred to me that what I had would hang well as a sestina. I recalled Pound's breaking the sestina into separate numbered sections, and suddenly I had a structure on which to build, one which allowed me to present each scene individually, while the repeating key words allowed each scene to echo one another—the language and the emotion connecting small heartbreaks over the course of decades.*

# KENT JOHNSON

## SESTINA: AVANTFORTE

*O your perfect, vulgate, hairy sestina.*
—David Shapiro (correspondence with the author)

It's interesting how no one has yet written a sestina about John Ashbery,
Joseph Ceravolo, Barbara Guest, James Schuyler, Frank O'Hara, and
Kenneth Koch.
After all, the New York poets wrote a bunch of sestinas, and Frank O'Hara,
of course, though he never wrote one himself, dropped the names of
poets in his poems like crazy. James Schuyler
did too. He lived at the Chelsea amongst wackos of all kinds. Once,
on the morning of this poem, when seven thousand saffron
panels billowed in the park, on a day you could take up the
tattered shadows off the grass, Barbara Guest
knocked on his door with a flat shape under her arm. Joseph Ceravolo

answered the door. What are you doing here, she said. Maybe I
should be asking *you* that question, said Joseph Ceravolo.
Well, I've got this painting, it's by Joe Brainard, I wanted to show it
to Jimmy, and it's called "Tangerines." John Ashbery
gave it to me after Frank O'Hara died, said Barbara Guest.
What do you mean Frank died, cried Joseph, I just saw Kenneth Koch
down at the San Remo, and he didn't say anything about *that!* Ha ha
hee hee, laughed James Schuyler,
arranging some jonquils in the kitchenette, you two are a stitch and a
half! And they all laughed and laughed, like a happy rain, because
the world was new, and irony was so straightforward then, in
the Kennedy era. And just then the phone rang. (It was Frank
O'Hara!)

You'll never guess what, Jimmy, said Frank. What, Mr. Frank
O'Hara?
said Jimmy, with a mock ceremoniousness. Well, don't tell Joe
Ceravolo
because I want to tell him myself, and don't tell Kenneth, either,

because you know how he takes these things, but they are here
from Holland to make a movie about me. Can you believe it? Oh
my God, Frank, squealed James Schuyler,
I *can't* believe it, that is so fantastic, and even though I am a bit
envious, I am happy, too, but please can't I tell John Ashbery,
he'll be thrilled, he loves everything Dutch, in fact he just won some
prize, and he might go there, and I'll tell him not to say a word to
Kenneth Koch...
Joseph and Barbara exchanged quizzical looks. Jimmy, what the hell
are you talking about, demanded Barbara Guest,
who was still standing there in the doorway holding her painting
like some acoustic panel waiting for sound. Oh, Barbara, do be a
good Guest
and come on in, said Jimmy, in his famous punning way, It's Frank
O'Hara,
and they're making a movie about him, and it's all in Dutch, O poor
Kenneth Koch,
he'll go mad like King George the Third, he's always wanted to be
translated into Dutch! Actually, interjected Joseph Ceravolo,
he's just been translated into Swedish, by a countess from
Minneapolis. A man shouldn't complain. . . The sun went
behind a small cloud. Barbara was absentmindedly running her
fingers across the inscription W.H. Auden had written for Jimmy
in a first edition of *Some Trees,* by John Ashbery,
it said: To my friend in Foetry and all other things, Mr. James Schuyler.

(signed) W.H. Auden. The sun came out again and gently burned the
world. James Schuyler,
she said coyly, in a Katherine Hepburn kind of way, do you think he said
Foetry on purpose, or is that just his handwriting? Barbara Guest,
said Jimmy, clearing his throat and replying in formal kind, I've tried
to figure that one out myself, it seems almost like a pun, doesn't
it, and when I asked John Ashbery
himself, he got all distant and mysterious as a girl in a Vermeer, so I
just don't know. By this time, Frank O'Hara

was beginning to wonder what had happened to Jimmy, who had
become so distracted by the conversation with Barbara he had
simply forgotten about Frank, and because he was on his lunch
hour and had to meet Leroi Jones at the Automat, Frank decided
to hang up. Joseph Ceravolo
said, Um, Jimmy, you kind of left Frank hanging, didn't you? Just
then, Kenneth Koch,

still in his twenties (or so he claimed), came bounding up the stairs,
crying out the names of northern European cities, the energy in
and around him so electric, it looked like he could take it off and
put it back on, like clothes. It's Kenneth Koch!
said Joseph. Hi Kenneth! said Barbara, it's so nice to see you! Hello?
Hello? Frank? Frank? said James Schuyler.
**From my window I dropped a nickel by mistake**, said Kenneth,
looking fixedly at the floor and nearly shouting, **so I raced
down and found there on the street, instead, a good
friend, who says to me, in Dutch, Kenneth, do you have a
minute? And I say, Yes! I am in my twenties! I have plenty
of time! And so he tells me he's been translating my
poetry, and it's going to be published! In Holland!** Jimmy
quickly hung up the receiver and a look of absolute panic came
down over his face. Joseph Ceravolo
(for this was a gift he had as a person and as a poet) radically changed
the subject with the swift and elegant authority of a guillotine:
Well, Kenneth, that is so fantastic, and even though we are a bit
envious, we are happy, too. But look at this wonderful painting
Barbara Guest
has brought to show us… Kenneth looked up. **You have
TANGERINES in it**, said Kenneth. **And hey, by the way,**
he literally yelled, as he started to do jumping jacks at a great
velocity, **What's up with Frank O'Hara?**
**Wait until he hears about Holland! Last time I saw him he
said he felt like he'd never write again! I'm writing a lot,
though! So where's he been? Huh?** Uh, said Jimmy, he's,
uh, been editing a new, um, sestina… full of, you know, cartoon
characters… by John Ashbery…

Kenneth Koch's eyes got big as pool balls. **A sestina? A sestina by the poet of *The Tennis Court Oath*, John Ashbery?**
Yes, said James Schuyler, nervously lighting a Gauloise, uh, W.H. Auden suggested he try one… I think…Just then, the phone rang again. Joseph Ceravolo, who was nearest the death-black machine, answered. Hi Joseph, the pleasant voice said. Was that Kenneth I heard shouting right before I hung up? (It was Frank O'Hara!)
Ah, hi, uh, no, no, um, there is no, ah, Olivia Oil who lives here. Sorry. Goodbye. Click. The backs of all the chairs were turned towards the sun, and then Kenneth, past his seventieth jumping jack, started to get this feeling of exaltation. **And! But!** he yelled. He yelled so loud, it was as if the conjunctions could couple, like in the form of a centaur, the living to the dead. Now wait a second, they asked for *Olivia Oil?* I mean, you've got to be fucking kidding me, said Barbara Guest.

*There is nothing more natural, seems to me, than to use names as end words in a sestina that is about the New York School of poets. As the poem itself says, most of them "dropped names in their poems like crazy." I wanted a breezy, insouciant kind of poem, and repeating the names in different patterns enabled that, like little puffs of wind pushing one line into the next. The iterated names helped to make it madcap, too, and, I hope, funny.*

*As for the quote in the epigraph: I've admired the great David Shapiro's poetry ever since I encountered it in the library of Pewaukee High School, in Wisconsin, in 1972 or '73. Years ago, after writing much poetry myself, I finally got my courage up and wrote Shapiro and told him that I didn't know if I should profusely thank him or send him a letter bomb in the mail for turning me on to poetry, back then. And so a long correspondence ensued. His quote is weird, isn't it, in a thrilling way? Thrilling in part because what he means by "hairy" is a total mystery. At least to me.*

# DONALD JUSTICE
## *HERE IN KATMANDU*

We have climbed the mountain.
There's nothing more to do.
It is terrible to come down
To the valley
Where, amidst many flowers,
One thinks of snow,

As, formerly, amidst snow,
Climbing the mountain,
One thought of flowers,
Tremulous, ruddy with dew,
In the valley.
One caught their scent coming down.

It is difficult to adjust, once down,
To the absence of snow.
Clear days, from the valley,
One looks up at the mountain.
What else is there to do?
Prayer wheels, flowers!

Let the flowers
Fade, the prayer wheels run down.
What have these to do
With us who have stood atop the snow
Atop the mountain,
Flags seen from the valley?

It might be possible to live in the valley,
To bury oneself among flowers,
If one could forget the mountain,
How, never once looking down,
Stiff, blinded with snow,
One knew what to do.

Meanwhile it is not easy here in Katmandu,
Especially when to the valley
That wind which means snow
Elsewhere, but here means flowers,
Comes down,
As soon it must, from the mountain.

# MEG KEARNEY

## *14TH STREET*

In the apartment next door, a boy plays the piano,
Chopin, mostly, though sometimes notes he's made up.
Through the woman's window climbs the noise of 14th Street:
merciless horns, squealing bus brakes, carnival-like music
from an ice cream truck belting "She'll Be Coming Round
the Mountain" over and over and over.

The phone rings; her lover coos, Can I come over?
She hesitates, weighs her desires: company, or listening to the piano,
spending the evening with her books. Can you come around
nine? she concedes. How about eight, he counters. I'll cook up
some pasta, open the red Bordeaux, put on a little music—
Eight-thirty, she sighs—Pick up some bread at Palermo's on 14th Street.

She settles on the couch with *Take Heart* by Molly Peacock. 14th Street
begins to fade like an old grief. She turns the book over;
the cover: "Hummingbird and Passion Flowers;" inside: the music
of poetry, intelligent passion of form, not so unlike the piano
sonata walking through her wall like a ghost. Up-
stairs a neighbor screams, Quiet! The ice-cream truck begins another
    round.

How many times can one listen to "She'll Be Coming Round
the Mountain"? And how *could* a woman ride six horses at once? 14th Street
is no place for country songs, or a girl from LaGrange. Up
where she's from they play a song once, and then it's over.
She closes the window, eases back on the couch. The piano
overwhelms the street noise; she can return to poems, the true music.

In "Blue and Huge," Peacock describes the ocean: "It's like music, /
a substance that can't be cut up." The woman smiles. Unlike a round
that divides a card game, the ocean doesn't end by chance. The piano
is silent. She doesn't notice, so absorbed even 14th Street
can't touch her. She uses sticky notes to mark poems she'll read over.
Just then, the door buzzer. He croons, Can I come up?

She's regretting their date. I'm not sure I'm up
to this tonight, she says as he selects a CD, puts on some music.
He pulls her toward him. Are you saying it's over
between us? he teases, knowing how to bring her around.
She presses closer, confides: I guess I have to get away from 14th Street.
Relax, he whispers. It's just you and me, and Monk on the piano.

Later, alone in bed, she wonders if her mother's still up.
It's too late to call. She can't sleep, keeps replaying that street music,
imagining a girl riding six white horses, over and over and over.

*When I wrote "14th Street," I was subletting an apartment in Manhattan
that belonged to poet Molly Peacock. Anyone who knows Molly's work
realizes she's a formal poet; what better place to try writing a sestina? I think
the walls in that place whispered poems to me, as it was a very productive
time. In writing this particular poem, I realized that sestinas can provide a
great structure to tell a story. That apartment and its location—which made it
quite noisy night and day—were the original driving forces behind the poem,
though it quickly grew beyond a poem about place.*

# WELDON KEES

## SESTINA: TRAVEL NOTES

Directed by the eyes of others,
Blind to the long, deceptive voyage,
We walked across the bridge in silence
And said "Goodnight," and paused, and walked away.
Ritual of apology and burden:
The evening ended; not a soul was harmed.

But then I thought: we all are harmed
By the indifference of others;
Being corrupt, corruptible, they burden
All who would vanish on some questioned voyage,
Tunneling through the longest way away
To maps of bitterness and silence.

We are concerned with that destructive silence
Impending in the dark, that never harms
Us till it strikes, washing the past away.
Remote from intrigues of the others,
We must chart routes that ease the voyage,
Clear passageways and lift the burden.

But where are routes? Who names the burden?
The night is gifted with a devious silence
That names no promises of voyage
Without contagion and the syllables of harm.
—I see ahead the hand of others
In frantic motion, warning me away.

To pay no heed, and walk away
Is easy; but the familiar burden
Of a later time, when certainties of others
Assume the frigid shapes of silence
And build new winters, echoing harm,
May banish every passageway for voyage.

You knew before the fear of voyage,
You saw before the hands that warned away,
You heard before the voices trained to harm
Listeners grown weak through loss and burdens.
Even in city streets at noon that silence
Waited for you, but not, you thought, for others.

Storms will break silence. Seize on harm,
Play idiot or seer to others, make the burden
Theirs, though no voyage is, no tunnel, door, nor way.

*Weldon Kees was a stylish person and a stylish writer. He wore his suits in a way that was casual and cool, not uptight and restrictive, and he matched this sestina to his strengths accordingly. Especially impressive is how he turns the forced repetitions to his rhetorical advantage. When we use the same word twice in rapid succession in normal communication, it's often because we're rewinding, editing ourselves, expressing doubt or concern about something we've just said. ("To maps of bitterness and silence. / We are concerned with that destructive silence.") This kind of unraveling via skepticism seems very Kees—it's a falling apart that is eerily under control. In other words, Kees wears the sestina and not the other way around.*—Kathleen Rooney

# LYNN KILPATRICK

## *FRANCIS BACON SESTINA*

*I've used the figures lying on beds with a hypodermic syringe as a form of
nailing the image more strongly into reality.*—Francis Bacon


except it's ridiculous, this attempt
we are always trying both to get in
and get out and what are we left
with? a hypodermic syringe
which only reminds me of his face stopping time
he ran his hands up my legs, dead,

i thought, we all end up dead
but everyone was singing *sex and sex and sex,* attempting
to forestall the tyranny of time
that's one way to remain in
reality, another is: a hypodermic syringe
use that and what's left?

what you're left
with is something more than death:
a hypodermic syringe.
she told me *they're getting married,* an attempt
(they are trying, so hard, to stay in)
there's more than one way to stop time

just as divorce is happening, there is time
to use up everything, use up what is left
i got high thinking: staying out or in
either way results in death
this is one way or another attempt
just another (hypodermic syringe)

way (this nail, this hypodermic syringe)
he was making reality, altering time
his o.d. white face almost waking, my attempt

(what remains, what is left)
i was chanting to keep him dead
his eyes singing *sex and sex and sex,* in

my skin, up my legs, and on in-
to my body, his gaze a hypodermic syringe
and onto reality with this, his dead
eyes stopping time
pretending death isn't what's left
isn't just this final attempt:

playing dead, trying to stop time
this way, nailing it in with a hypodermic syringe
using what's left, a shade of red, anything, one last attempt

*I love sestinas because of the obsessive repetition. The pattern resembles how my brain works. I like coming back to words or ideas and reworking or rethinking them. The sestina form seemed right for all this material because of the obsession/repetition. For me, the sestina is a way of thinking through problems: by the time you get back to the word again, you've travelled some mental/emotional distance and you have a new vantage point on the word/ idea/feeling/image. I think Bacon's painting does this too. It attempts to compile many different perspectives into one image. I kept Bacon's "hypodermic syringe" mainly as an experiment to see if it kept the poem nailed to reality. I was also interrogating if that was true. In life, the syringe provides an escape. But I like how the sestina forces the reader to confront it, over and over. And the poem itself is about trying to stay in/escape reality. Drugs are one way; love is one way; art, another.*

# KENNETH KOCH & JOHN ASHBERY

## CRONE RHAPSODY

"Pin the tail on the donkey," gurgled Julia Ward Howe. A larch
shaded the bathtub. From the scabiosa on the desk
The maple gladioli watched Emily Post playing May I? in the
persimmon bathtub with the fan.
"Nasturtiums can be eaten like horseshoes," murmured the
pumpkin, "but on Hallowe'en when Cécile Chaminade's
Rhapsody roars in the beeches and a bathtub chair
Holds Nazimova, a lilac palm plays mumbledy-peg with an orange
bathtub filing cabinet,
And Queen Marie of Roumania remembers the Norway maple."
Pitching pennies from the cantaloupe bathtub, I remembered the
poppy and the typewriter,
The mangrove and the larkspur bathtub. I saw a banana Carrie
Nation ducking for apples in the lamp.

Oak dominoes filled the bathtub with a jonquil. A crabapple rolled
slowly toward the Edith Wharton lamp,
Crying, "Elm shuffleboard! Let the bathtub of apricots and
periwinkles give May Robson a desk!"
"Heavy, heavy hangs over thy head," chanted the black raspberry. A
zinnia dropped from the plane tree into a rotting bathtub. Dame
Myra Hess slumped over the typewriter
And wrote, "Dear Madame de Farge: A sycamore, an aster, and a
tangerine, while playing scrub in my bathtub, noticed a fan
Of yours. Do you remember the old cottonwood tree by the auction
bridge? It's now a bathtub. The freesia is gone. And an apple
placed Queen Victoria in the filing cabinet.
Forget me not, as Laura Hope Crewes once spelt out in anagrams
while we were all eating honeydew melon. I write you this from
the bathtub and from a willow chair."

A raspberry bathtub was playing leapfrog with Sarah Allgood in the
heather. Junipers hemmed in the yellow Ukrainian chair.
In the apple tree Queen Mary of the Chrysanthemums shared a grape
rock bathtub with her insect lamp.

The cranberry juice was playing water polo with the dwarf plum tree.
Margaret Dumont approached the bathtub. A song came from
within the wisteria-covered filing cabinet—
The gooseberries were playing golf! Louisa May Alcott lifted a water
lily from the poison-oak bathtub: "Put this on the desk,
Mrs. August Belmont." In the poison sumac grove a spitting contest
was in full swing. The bathtub peeled seven mangoes, and a
petunia fan,
Known to the orchid prune as Dame May Whittie's bathtub, felt
curvaceous playing house with a eucalyptus typewriter.

The Clara Barton irises worshipped a baseball pineapple. O bathtub!
"A birch rod," wrote the typewriter
Of papaya (its bathtub keys tapped by Bess Truman sitting beneath
the cypress—or was it a grape hyacinth?), "guided the society
craps game from a red chair
To where the cherry polo faded under the holly tree." "Pear-
blossom," called Edna May Oliver to the brick bathtub, "fetch
me my fan.
It's over there on the Lydia E. Pinkham musical chairs." But peach
ash smothered the bathtub with a calendula lamp.
"Capture the flag," whispered briar rose to mandarin orange.
Standing by the bathtub, Lady Gregory thought of her spruce
desk.
"A grapefruit for your tulip," Ethel Barrymore said to the cherry
tree checkers. And the bathtub knew the embrace of the filing
cabinet.

That was the year that a calla lily bought Colette's *Ice Hockey* in the
capital of Honduras. It was the year of the bathtub Ice Age and
the flowering of the stone pear. The catalpa shivered gently in
the shade of the filing cabinet.
Then Barbara Frietchie skipped rope under the gingko tree, spitting
buttercups on the loganberry bushes. In the dim light of the
bathtub formed a typewriter.
The bathtub fell amid orange blossoms. The black walnut tree fell
amid lemon soccer balls. Marie Brizard fell under the desk.
But who won the sack race? Spirea split the bathtub. Why, here is
Susan B. Anthony holding up a raisin to the sequoia chair!

And here is the Joshua tree. Mistinguett thought about the tomato. The bathtub was nailing up the rules for seven-card stud by the light of a crocus lamp.
All of these things were confided by a pine tree to a primrose in the bathtub. Inside the pomegranate Ivy Compton-Burnett was playing hand tennis with her fan.

In her locust bathtub Maria Ouspenskaya was playing spin-the-bottle with a violet strawberry. The big fan
Who had once known Mary Roberts Rinehart, strangled by hemlock, wanted the rose whortleberry to play doctor with it in the bathtub. A tiny filing cabinet
Was reading Harriet Beecher Stowe's *One Potato Two Potato* to a blueberry in a room that contained no furniture other than a bathtub, a poplar, and a dogwood lamp.
Cowboys and Indians brought the shasta daisy to watermelon Eleanor Roosevelt. In the meantime a horse-chestnut tree had gotten into the bathtub with the typewriter.
"I saw Lily Muskmelon and Tag Football just now. They were on their way to Margaret Sanger's new place, The Baobab Tree," chorused the bathtub. "When I think that that chair
Once held Alice B. Toklas, I don't give a fig for what I catch from the live-oak tree or the cowslip!" Then the bathtub became silent as a desk.

The crabapple tree screamed. The carnation said, "I am a hundred years old!" The breadfruit fell onto the desk. In the post-office bathtub an Edith Sitwell fan
Muttered, "I want a bathtub." Forgetful of contract bridge, Alison Skipworth pulled up a chair to the yew tree and looked for *heliotrope* and *blood orange* in its filing cabinet.
The gentian finished chopping down the linden. The kumquat typewriter was attacked by Grace Coolidge. She wrote, "When I play cops and robbers I need a bathtub lamp!"

# NOELLE KOCOT

## WHY WE GO TO COUPLE'S COUNSELING

In spite of all common sense, I make my home in the rotisserie
Of your teeth. This was all prewritten on the gravity
Of a giant planet, and those slightly corrupted
Particles of light that formed the stars.
You say the Eternal. The eternal is not mine but has a Big Mission.
Despite our differences, we manage to create a hoax

Of nice weather, an unresolved moment. But the hoax
Is that I search for warmth within the cave of you, a dry rotisserie
Chicken with a mission.
I eat myself and plunge my bones into the gravity
Of crop circles filling with stars.
Our love has been corrupted,

But not corrupted
As one might deem a warped roll of film, a hoax
Of UFO pictures submerged in an ocean of fireflied stars,
But love that hangs on a rotisserie
In a Chinese restaurant, where the waiter brings us our check with a gravity
Whose mission

Is known only to us, who won't be missionary
Later that same night amid readings of Trakl's autumn and black corruption.
Gravity.
What a weighty word! And what if Newton's apple were a hoax,
Nothing more than the stuff in a pig's mouth on a rotisserie
Casting itself up into the stars

To forge a new constellation? I admit, I'm starry-
Eyed when I look at you, every moment seems a mission
Where I am the pig on the rotisserie,
Every oink I oink to you corrupted.
Surely I'm a hoax
And a half laid out in resourceful capsules, but I am in grave

Error if I believe the gravity
Of our rhetoric reaches beyond a drawing of a house with cut-out stars
Above it, some stick figures of cats and children. A hoax
It may be but my mission
Is not complete until I corrupt
All that's been said and search for warmth within my own private rotisserie,

And remember that in the last horizontal hoax of my mission's
Superfluous event, the gravity of my lion paws stretch across the ruins
    of the stars
And lie corrupted in your teeth's rotisserie.


*I discovered the sestina when I was 16. My English teacher, the late Carol
Ann Kiyak, suggested I write one. She told me how to write it, but didn't give
me any samples, and I wrote a bunch. A year and a half later, on the English
Advanced Placement exam, was Elizabeth Bishop's "Sestina," which was to
become at that moment, and remain, my first and favorite sestina.*

# LEONARD KRESS

## *MISS NEW JERSEY*

I almost dated Miss New Jersey
Once. No, this is not the punch line
To some joke. And it didn't happen
Decades after the pageant, when she'd become
Unrecognizable as such. Maybe just a year
Or two after her title, her sash still pressed

And unboxed. However, if I were pressed
I wouldn't divulge whether or not the jersey
Came off—but I admit, *it was a very good year
For small town girls*…at least that was the song line
We heard in a bar one night after we became
Friends. Good for me, too, if it happened

That her scumbag boyfriend left—which didn't happen,
Of course. She couldn't resist his full-court press,
Against spilled blood and casinos, what would become
Of him, if she left New Jersey,
Where she substitute-taught junior high music, in line
For full-time, if she stuck it out a year,

Teaching steelworkers' sons and daughters. The year
She won, she toured military bases and happened
To appear with Bob Hope, even became the punch line
Of his suggestive jokes, while he pressed
Up close. Vietnam, I thought, but it might've been Jersey's
Fort Dix. She didn't dare sing (fearing she'd become

A laughing stock) the Schubert song, *Bliss*, which became
Pageant legend. Instead, for *Mr. Hope*, it was the year's
Hit, *Tie a Yellow Ribbon*, which played well in Jersey.
Though after a single tour, it happened:
She lost her will to sing and nothing could press
Her into it. Time after time, her rehearsed line

Was "God took my voice," and with that I drew the line
On taking things further. For she was becoming
Sorrowful (a different Schubert song) and depressed.
Her inability to sing lasting almost a year.
Then she sang *Bliss* for me—I don't know how it happened—
Right before she moved away from New Jersey.


*I had recently received an email from the person who's featured in the poem—the former Miss New Jersey. I think her title came as part of the Miss USA Pageant rather than the more well-known Miss America Pageant. The email was rather general and it came as something of a surprise, since I hadn't heard from her (or heard anything about her) in over two decades. We actually met in a dance class and began going out for beers afterwards. I was living in Philadelphia at the time and she lived in South Jersey. As the poem states, we were never that close—I was never one to presume that a beauty contestant would spend much time hanging out with me, but there was this rather peculiar connection during a pretty difficult time in her life. The sestina form seemed to be the only possible way to work through the information and emotions. I think the form is the only thing that keeps the poem from getting lost in layers of irony.*

# QURAYSH ALI LANSANA

## HOMEMADE

i was made in st. stephens church
on choir pews behind an ageless pulpit.
under the almighty eye of mutha,
my cousins and i, led by aunties,
crafted stodgy hymns into poetry
with the love of God and song.

al green coloured saturday's song,
but flickering spirits painted church
sundays in deep human poetry.
our voices reached the oak pulpit,
then the small congregation, while aunties
bonnell and maudell stirred mutha

to rock and hum their gentle music. mutha
raised seven children on gospel song
and hard work. my mama, two uncles, & four aunties
talked with God in a tiny texas church
where an easy-tongued preacher stroked the pulpit,
sharing scripture as hereditary poetry.

between prayers they tilled poetry
with blood and sweat. in the garden, mutha
produced converts from her earthen pulpit:
stubborn tomatoes. melons ripe with tender song.
praising the hallowed floor of this church,
this land that knows my uncles and aunties

by name. led by my soulful aunties,
the family left calvert, texas, to inspire poetry
a little further north. they found a church
home in a place called enid, then sent for mutha.
this tired soil, this birthplace of mama's song
was now a fond remembering, a lonely pulpit.

the space between preacher and pulpit
remains sacred. one of my aunties
now resides there, naturally. her song
full of light. her love like the poetry
of my sons' laughter. i feel mutha
everywhere. i know she's always church.

kneeling at church, i consider the pulpit,
dream about mutha and cherish my aunties.
a narrow rift divides poetry and song.

# JOAN LARKIN

## JEWISH FOOD

*It's the worst—but it tastes so good.*—Gerald Stern

I came from school to warm bread
and *tsibele bulkes*: Russian rolls, onions
in wells her palm pressed in the dough, softened in sweet
butter and baked in. Little pillows, fragrant as flesh.
I'd eat a few with cold milk at two. Five-thirty, supper
was on the table, Dad home between shows and hungry

for soup with *knaidlach* and boiled chicken. I was still hungry
afterward for a heel of black bread
smeared with rendered chicken fat. *Shabbes*, supper
had to be chicken. No milk on the table. Onions,
salt, and fat were what she put in chopped liver, start of a *fleysh-
edik* meal. To end it, fruit in thin, sweet

syrup: compote—pears, prunes plumped with cooking, sweet-
ened with raisins. No one left the table hungry
or thought there was anything wrong with fattening childflesh
at three meals and between: *mon* cookies, hunks of rye bread,
batter licked from the bowl. I watched her knife cleave onions,
carrots for *tzimmes*, beets for borscht. *Pesach,* supper

was called a *Seder*—not an ordinary supper.
*Matzo* folded in a cloth napkin, goblets filled with sweet
red wine—they spilled drops for each of the plagues. Glazed onions
and brisket waited while uncles prayed. I sat there hungry,
wondering at the strangeness of a week with no bread.
In candlelight, my grandmother's warm flesh-

folds shone, the rough crepe of her peasant flesh
smoothed with Jergens lotion. She scoured sinkfuls of pots after supper
then sat and ate some of her own unleavened bread
baked with *matzo mel* and sucked sweet
tea through cubes of sugar. I sat with her, hungry
for stories of the old days, when sometimes even onions

were scarce but everyone told jokes. Onions
couldn't make you cry if you ran water while you cut their raw flesh.
She always knew you were hungry, everyone was hungry,
and she sneaked cream into your coffee, if it was a *milchik* supper,
even if you said you wanted it black. Her voice was Russian music, sweet
even when she said harsh things. I can't think of her without tasting bread—

no one made better bread. She gave me the taste for onions,
the oily flesh of carp, the cold thick sweet-
ness of sour cream on a blintz for supper. God forbid I should be hungry.


*Robert Francis wrote in* The Satirical Rogue on Poetry *that the point of
dancing while wearing 39 chains was to dance as if there were no chains. He
must have been thinking of the sestina's 39 lines—though he wrote no sestinas
himself, as far as I know. No poem can be just an exercise in imposing a form
from the outside, no matter how gracefully executed; poetry is interior. There
are many good sestinas, as this anthology makes clear, but finding one with
lyric intensity and with language that feels inevitable yet surprising is still an
unexpected gift and a source of astonishment and pleasure.*

# DAVID LEHMAN

## THE OLD CONSTELLATION

*The old constellation of wish, word, guilt, pleasure, shame.* —Judith Hall

Other people go to bed. I just sit and wish
for nothing much, just to know the word
where I hear it and not to feel the guilt
that other people associate with pleasure,
or something more primal than guilt, shame,
which is what you get for having a body.

What can be worse than not having a body?
(In my veins there is a wish.)
Money is to shit as guilt is to shame
as the sentence is to the word.
Is that understood? It's been a pleasure
to serve you, said the Commissioner of Guilt.

Some soldiers can kill without feeling guilt.
I learned I wasn't one of them. I was anybody
in a uniform, and staying alive wasn't a pleasure
but a duty. Some of the injured wished
they had died, a wish seldom put into words
without feelings of shame.

If the women we loved were unashamed,
it was because they obeyed the laws of guilt
and loved the men who wooed them with words
in praise of their yielding bodies.
I asked her, did she get her wish?
She said yes but it gave her no pleasure.

The poem's first purpose is to give pleasure
and defeat the formidable forces of shame
that would twist every healthy lusty wish
into a dark confession of guilt
and a renunciation of the body:
the word without flesh, the naked, shivering word.

I who believe in the constellations of the word
would construct a planetarium of pleasure
for my friends, where each heavenly body
can be contemplated without the shame
of a pretty librarian or the guilt
of a veteran who pulled the trigger of a wish.

The word is the result of the wish for the word.
Not every pleasure is a guilty one.
A shame it would be to forsake love's body.

## OPERATION MEMORY

We were smoking some of this knockout weed when
Operation Memory was announced. To his separate bed
Each soldier went, counting backwards from a hundred
With a needle in his arm. And there I was, in the middle
Of a recession, in the middle of a strange city, between jobs
And apartments and wives. Nobody told me the gun was loaded.

We'd been drinking since early afternoon. I was loaded.
The doctor made me recite my name, rank, and serial number when
I woke up, sweating, in my civvies. All my friends had jobs
As professional liars, and most had partners who were good in bed.
What did I have? Just this feeling of always being in the middle
Of things, and the luck of looking younger than fifty.

At dawn I returned to draft headquarters. I was eighteen
And counting backwards. The interviewer asked one loaded
Question after another, such as why I often read the middle
Of novels, ignoring their beginnings and their ends. When
Had I decided to volunteer for intelligence work? "In bed
With a broad," I answered, with locker-room bravado. The truth was, jobs

Were scarce, and working on Operation Memory was better than no job
At all. Unamused, the judge looked at his watch. It was 1970
By the time he spoke. Recommending clemency, he ordered me to go to bed
At noon and practice my disappearing act. Someone must have loaded
The harmless gun on the wall in Act I when
I was asleep. And there I was, without an alibi, in the middle

Of a journey down nameless, snow-covered streets, in the middle
Of a mystery—or a muddle. These were the jobs
That saved men's souls, or so I was told, but when
The orphans assembled for their annual reunion, ten
Years later, on the playing fields of Eton, each unloaded
A kit bag full of troubles, and smiled bravely, and went to bed.

Thanks to Operation Memory, each of us woke up in a different bed
Or coffin, with a different partner beside him, in the middle
Of a war that had never been declared. No one had time to load
His weapon or see to any of the dozen essential jobs
Preceding combat duty. And there I was, dodging bullets, merely one
In a million whose lucky number had come up. When

It happened, I was asleep in bed, and when I woke up,
It was over. I was thirty-eight, on the brink of middle age,
A succession of stupid jobs behind me, a loaded gun on my lap.

*I've long been fascinated by military code names, such as Operation Torch for the Allied invasion of North Africa in World War II. "Operation Memory" suggested a military metaphor for an autobiographical reflection. Or was memory (or its loss) a metaphor for a military experience? Perhaps both. I set out to write a poem about the war in Vietnam. (An undeclared war, Vietnam is nowhere mentioned in the poem.) "Operation Memory" is a sestina with a variable. Ordinarily, there are six repeating end words in a sestina. Here there are five fixed end words and a sequence of numbers where the sixth would go. It's a downward progression (hundred, fifty, eighteen, ten, one) plus a year (1970) and an age (thirty-eight, the age I was when I wrote the poem). I thought of Abraham trying to persuade God to spare the sinful cities: If there were fifty righteous men, would he do it? If there were twenty righteous men? Ten? I was recently asked whether the speaker commits suicide at the end of the poem ("a loaded gun on my lap"). That's one possibility; a second is that he is about to shoot somebody else; a third is that it's "a loaded gun" in metaphor only.*—Note from *The Best American Poetry 1988*

# Eric LeMay

## The Sestina of O

**O (as overseer):**

Rule one: The mouth rounds open as an O.
That shape's yours, Slave, to lavish and caress
Whatever Master thrusts in you. It'll go
Hard on your ass unless you mouth, "O yes!"
Drool, too. Unlike love, drool's a no-no.
Droolers are beat in a bib and baby's dress.

Rule two: Bare skin beats fetishistic dress.
You might perfect your mouth's fuckable O
Or show your love for Master by moaning, "Yes,"
To every slavish shame you undergo,
But leather-lock your ass from his caress
And you'll force Master to push you to "No."

Rule three: Before Master no slave says, "No."
Say it and you'll be beat, as your redress.
Master will stripe each ass-cheek's fleshy O
With welts and make you mouth your mantra (Yes)
Until your slave's mind spins in a vertigo
Of hate and love, under a whip's caress.

Rule four: Love tests the cruelest caress.
Sometimes Master's conscience whispers, "No,"
When a thrashed slave in, say, a nurse's dress
Collapses. The beating stops. The broken O
Of the slave's mouth can't spout, "Yes, Doctor, yes."
Love lets you lift your ass, to say, "Let's go."

Rule five: The ass has torments to undergo.
A vanilla lover will stroke, squeeze, caress
Your ass, French kiss your mouth, and drone out "Ooooo"
Like a dial tone, but Master makes you undress
And squat. He beats your ass until you know
You're his, a slave who, caned or strapped, cries, "Yes!"

These are the rules, Slave. You must choose: Yes
Or no? You offer your ass or else you go.
Can you take a beating as a caress?
Can you suffer for love? It's yes or no.
If yes, then bow to Master. If no, then dress,
Close your mouth, and chuck your *Story of O.*

**INITIATE:**

My mouth is Master's O. This slave's all yes.
My Master may caress my ass. I go
To him in love. No beating will make me dress.

*I took inspiration from Sir Philip Sidney, who wove a double sestina and just about every classical and European verse form there is in* The Countess of Pembroke's Arcadia *(1590). Just how far can you push form? What if, in addition to its other demands, you made it rhyme? Turns out Algernon Charles Swinburne did that in the 19th century with a poem aptly named "Sestina." He also wrote a double, rhyming sestina called "The Complaint of Lisa." Take that, Sidney. Okay, so what if you made your sestina rhyme and you included a second sestina inside of the first, so that at the caesura of each line, another set of six words played out in the sestina's 36-line pattern? You'd essentially have a double sestina compressed into a single sestina, and that might be a first. The constraints I'd hit on for my sestina struck me as severe, even sadomasochistic. If a hallmark of a good poem is that it weds form and content, why not write it about that darling of S&M subculture, the heroine of Pauline Réage's infamous* Histoire d'O? *I'm not sure I was successful, but I did have fun. And I'd like to think that, even if the poem fails, Sidney and Swinburne would have liked what it tries to do.*

# BRENDAN LORBER

## *LUCK IS THE THING WE ARE SHIT OUT OF*

*for Paul Wellstone*

I probably should've selected a higher point
There isn't a door in the world without my finger
caught in it just enough to raise regret
as an issue That and momentum over the cliff
Whatsit? Doom? Trash Masher? It forces yr hand
to take up rock science The lucky #1 rock pick

set in motion towards one's own head Pick
the size and shape Which eye the point
hits I approach my demise with missionary zeal Hand
on the keys to America's trust to finger
the hell out of The wrong face carved on the wrong cliff
Elect yet another strong stiff and regret

nothing more than stasis One man's regret
is another's successful campaign A pick
me! among the rocks of the martian landscape The cliff
between these lofty troughs & the point
of no return ie total branding of organs A left hand
from Pfizer Fist full of profit behind each subsidiary finger

So yr being a prick What do you want? The finger?
Change yr Britta Kidney every month or you'll regret
even the water you drink No hand
outs for you pal with yr marvelous pick
of the litter days & nights A return to the point
becomes inconceivable though as the cliff

dwellers develop swooping abilities & the cliff
itself extends its reach Puts a finger
on the thing that gives you a pulse The point
that propels you beyond all regret
A motive you insist is beyond choice The pick
off one by one plan until the hand

into which we've all been played the hand
is all that's left The machine on the cliff
of its own making Programmed to pick
a straw every straw A finger
in every pie There's nothing to regret
because there's nothing left at all Nothing to point

at nothing to point out No cliff to triumph over
nor perp to finger No time left to regret
No hand to receive nor give No two ideas from which to pick


*When people die, their ideas are oft interred with their bones. Wellstone was
one of the few politicians who rose to the national stage on an anti-corporate
platform. Wellstone called out the oligarchs and his fellow senators on their
dog whistle class war against the poor and middle class. A poem isn't going to
change policy, especially not a sestina, but its dedication acts as a faint beacon
that will lead someone into looking up Wellstone and finding an articulation of
their own sense of right and wrong.*

# Matt Madden

## *The Six Treasures of the Spiral: A Comics Sestina*

185

187

189

190

194

195

*Since I started working on* 99 Ways to Tell a Story: Exercises in Style *in the late 90s, I've immersed myself in the world of Oulipo (Ouvroir de Littérature Potentielle, or Workshop of Potential Literature), the literary supper club/laboratory founded by Raymond Queneau and François Le Lionnais in 1960. I found my kindred spirits when I discovered that group and its passion for constraints and formal structures and their application in literature. As it happened, around that same time, some French cartoonists had founded Oubapo (Ouvroir de Bande Dessinée Potentielle, or Workshop of Potential Comics), and after a few years' correspondence they made me a "US correspondent" to the group. When my friend Jason Little described the sestina's structure to me, I was intrigued by the possibilities of that sort of permutational repetition for comics. There are a number of ways you can adapt the concept of* repetons *to comics: you can have words repeating or images, bits of dialogue, compositional schema, keywords, or, as I did in 'Six Treasures,' whole panels.*

# Paul Mariani

## The Great Wheel

In the Tuileries we came upon the Great Wheel
rising gargantuan above the trees. Evening
was coming on. An after-dinner stroll, descending
by easy stages toward the river, a bridge of leaves
above us, broken here and there by street lights
coming on. Our time here nearly over, our return

home a shadow hovering. Paris, city of returns,
you said, for the pleasure of it, like the Great Wheel
looming there above us, all steel & light
& music, daredevil daunting, against the evening
sky with the tower in the distance winking. The leaves
still held firmly, the unthinkable descending

of what lay ahead undreamt of still, death descending
inevitably as the Great Wheel in its return,
(a descent first through summer's golden leaves
and then bare ruined branches), the Great Wheel
turning & returning. As then, with the all but evening
over us, our wives laughing by the entrance lights,

we rose above the mansard roofs, the trees, the lights,
lifting in a vertiginous ascent before descending,
as we chattered on against the coming on of evening,
our seat creaking in the rising wind, anxious to return
now to earth's solidities. Instead, the Great Wheel
merely sighed and lifted, stopping at the top, leaving

each of us alone now with our thoughts. The leaves
below, green, gray-green, gray, the dollhouse roofs, lights
like diamonds winking, aloof & distant, the Great Wheel
playing us, two middle-aged men, each descending
toward the Wheel's one appointed end, the Great Return
to earth, as the books all have it, come our evening.

For all our feigned bravado, we could feel the evening
over us, even as we stared down upon the blur of leaves,
our wives, our distant children, on all we would return
to, the way shipwrecked sailors search for lights
along a distant shore, as we began the last descent,
leaving the tents and Garden with its Great Wheel

to return, my dear dead friend, to the winking lights
along the boulevard, leaves lifting & descending,
as now the evening air took mastery, it & the Great Wheel.

*My wife Eileen and I visited Paris and Rouen and the beaches of Normandy
with our dear friends, Ed and Maureen Callahan. We were all around 50 and
had known each other by that point for almost 25 years. It was hard to escape
the looming wheel in the Tuileries when staying in the heart of Paris, and Ed
and I dared each other to get on the Great Wheel. Our wives thought we were
crazy and would have nothing to do with the idea, so Ed and I got on, and the
wheel began to ascend over the city, with all its history from Charlemagne and
the lineage of the kings and the philosophs and on through the Reign of Terror.
Then, at the top, the Wheel stopped again, and the wind picked up, and then
Ed asked me to hold his hand until we were safely down on the ground again,
and we laughed and I joked with him about that. The four of us decided that
we'd all go to the Holy Land the following year, but Ed had colon cancer. So
Eileen and I went alone, as part of a pilgrimage.*

*I knew I would write about this. The question was: what form might best
capture the sense of the early ascent and the inevitable descent we all must
experience, no matter how high we seem to ascend over the earth or the
city, even so beautiful a city as Paris, that secular City of Lights where the
Cathedral of Notre Dame still reminds me of another City of Lights. I think
I had the six terminal words early on, thanks in part to Eliot: "wheel,"
"evening," "descending," "leaves," "lights," "return."*

# Nate Marshall

## PALLBEARERS (A SESTINA)

*The ones that hold you when you can't really stand. That's crew...*
—Ang 13, "My Crew"

Dom, Kenny, Shaun, Bart, and I were close as a coffin.
Promised we would always be tight.
We made it to every middle school dance.
Weaving through crowds of awkward kids we kept moving
behind a nervous girl's hips, mesmerized by the split
of skirts and smiles at our request. We didn't know much.

In those days we never had much.
We threw our pennies like roses on a coffin
into PlayStation games to split.
Even when money was tight
we could cop a five dollar pizza, keep it moving
everybody got a slice. This was the dance

of being best friends. Teaching Bart to dance
like a black boy. Bart forgetting how much
the Polish heirloom I broke was worth. Giving Shaun advice to make
    moving
on from old girlfriends easier. Shaun helping move the coffin
of my DJ's turntables at the last show.  Helping Kenny get his jump
    shot tight.
Playing for money, only to take the winnings and split

them on bus fare. The day Shaun's pants split
in school we told him to dance
around until we found pants that weren't too tight.
We laughed but helped him avoid much
embarrassment. We covered for him like a closed coffin.
Told him watch the way he was moving.

I remember Kenny moving
to Dominic's neighborhood when his parents split.
The way he spoke about his father cold, a coffin.

We comforted him, me and Shaun showed him how to dance
through single parent life. We knew there was so much
change in our lives. But we held to each other tight.

Last summer our time was tight
and we only got together once for a few minutes before moving
on again. Shaun and Bart said since first semester they don't talk much
to Kenny. Dom hasn't been around much since he split
to work with kids in New Orleans. I've been busy learning to dance
like corporate interns do. My cubicle is quiet as a coffin.

But I remember the tight feeling in my chest, my heart split
at the sight of my grandma not moving, her body done with life's dance.
These friends love too much to split. Helped me rest, her in a coffin.

*I love the sestina for the repetition. It lends itself well to narrative because
of that, and that plays well to my instincts as a poet. Also, I really dig the
way knowledge of homophones becomes so golden in building a sestina. That
homophone use really reminds me of the inventiveness of writing raps. Sestinas
are my go-to form when I have time to kill. They are like poetry sudoku.
They are the official form of international flights, long flight delays, and
Megabus trips through the Midwest. The thing I started with in this poem
was the end words. That's a trick I learned from Mark Jarman. I wanted to
use a bunch of small, flexible words and then one that was strange or more
challenging. I think "coffin" became the word because I could think of a
variety of ways it could be used and because I often write about how death and
loss impact my life and my world. The repetition seemed to fit the storyline
naturally, because in a childhood friendship there's often a kind of repeating,
almost sitcom quality to the times you spend with those friends. There's also
a sadness to when that time in life ends that might be kind of akin to a sort
of death. I think, though, it is important that the poem ends on the image
of togetherness and support even in death. That makes the poem hopeful.
It speaks to life and the fact that life is ultimately about the relationships we
cultivate with each other.*

# HARRY MATHEWS
## *HISTOIRE*

Tina and Seth met in the midst of an overcrowded militarism.
"Like a drink?" he asked her. "They make great Alexanders over at
the Marxism-Leninism."
She agreed. They shared cocktails. They behaved cautiously, as in a
period of pre-fascism.
Afterwards he suggested dinner at a restaurant renowned for its
Maoism.
"O.K.," she said, but first she had to phone a friend about her ailing
Afghan, whose name was Racism.
Then she followed Seth across town past twilit alleys of sexism.

The waiter brought menus and announced the day's specials. He
treated them with condescending sexism,
So they had another drink. Tina started her meal with a dish of
militarism,
While Seth, who was hungrier, had a half portion of stuffed baked
racism.
Their main dishes were roast duck for Seth, and for Tina broiled
Marxism-Leninism.
Tina had pecan pie à la for dessert, Seth a compote of stewed
Maoism.
They lingered. Seth proposed a liqueur. They rejected sambuca and
agreed on fascism.

During the meal, Seth took the initiative. He inquired into Tina's
fascism,
About which she was reserved, not out of reticence but because
Seth's sexism
Had aroused in her a desire she felt she could hide—as though her
Maoism
Would willy-nilly betray her feelings for him. She was right. Even
her deliberate militarism

Couldn't keep Seth from realizing that his attraction was
    reciprocated. His own Marxism-Leninism
Became manifest, in a compulsive way that piled the Ossa of
    confusion on the Peleion of racism.

Next, what? Food finished, drinks drunk, bills paid—what racism
Might not swamp their yearning in an even greater confusion of
    fascism?
But women are wiser than words. Tina rested her hand on his thigh
    and, a-twinkle with Marxism-Leninism,
Asked him, "My place?" Clarity at once abounded under the flood-
    lights of sexism,
They rose from the table, strode out, and he with the impetuousness
    of young militarism
Hailed a cab to transport them to her lair, heaven-haven of Maoism.

In the taxi he soon kissed her. She let him unbutton her Maoism
And stroke her resilient skin, which was quivering with the shudders
    of racism.
When beneath her jeans he sensed the superior Lycra of her
    militarism,
His longing almost strangled him. Her little tongue was as potent as
    fascism
In its elusive certainty. He felt like then and there tearing off her
    sexism,
But he reminded himself: "Pleasure lies in patience, not in the greedy
    violence of Marxism-Leninism."

Once home, she took over. She created a hungering aura of
    Marxism-Leninism
As she slowly undressed him where he sat on her overstuffed art-deco
    Maoism,
Making him keep still, so that she could indulge in caresses, in
    sexism,
In the pursuit of knowing him. He groaned under the exactness of
    her racism
—Fingertip sliding up his nape, nails incising his soles, teeth nibbling
    his fascism.
At last she guided him to bed, and they lay down on a patchwork of
    Old American militarism.

Biting his lips, he plunged his militarism into the popular context of
 her Marxism-Leninism,
Easing one thumb into her fascism, with his free hand coddling the
 tip of her Maoism,
Until, gasping with appreciative racism, both together sink into the
 revealed glory of sexism.

# FLORENCE CASSEN MAYERS

## *ALL-AMERICAN SESTINA*

One nation, indivisible
two-car garage
three strikes you're out
four-minute mile
five-cent cigar
six-string guitar

six-pack Bud
one-day sale
five-year warranty
two-way street
fourscore and seven years ago
three cheers

three-star restaurant
sixty-
four-dollar question
one-night stand
two-pound lobster
five-star general

five-course meal
three sheets to the wind
two bits
six-shooter
one-armed bandit
four-poster

four-wheel drive
five-and-dime
hole in one
three-alarm fire
sweet sixteen
two-wheeler

two-tone Chevy
four rms, hi flr, w/vu
six-footer
high five
three-ring circus
one-room schoolhouse

two thumbs up, five-karat diamond
Fourth of July, three-piece suit
six feet under, one-horse town

## JULY IDYLL

My
my
guys,
July
flies
by!

I
find
I
like
my
ride:

bright
shiny
bike,
fine
tie-dye
sky,

pines,
thyme,
briar,
tiny
spiders.
Wild

briny
tides
collide,
mild
Fire
Island

nights
inspire
rhyme.
Idle,
I
comply,

write
tight
tidy
feisty
lines,
revise

twice, thrice.
  Nice try.
    High five.

# Marty McConnell

## *ONE POSSIBLE EXPLANATION OF MY UTTER AND RATHER SURPRISING LACK OF AN ADOLESCENT TOMBOY PHASE*

the girl who has a brother
is tough. twins, all
the more so. I have always
been a girl in a world
of women. of note, that I
am a woman who loves

women, but who has loved
also the woman in a man. brother,
had you been born whole, I
would have chased you all
across the cracking world,
would have buried you always

in the sand, in the yard, always
the way a girl learns to love
who has a boy in the world
whose blood matches hers, a brother
not made of dust. under all
I've ever wanted, all I

ever schemed to create, I
knew there was a boy always
waiting, waiting all
molecular and ghosted, loved
despite his nothingness. my brother,
our sisters have given boys to the world

and I have given the world
this memory of you. it is all I
can do, to say I had an almost brother
and I've never asked, but wondered always
what they would have named you. to love
is to gather all the death, all

that wants to bury us all
the time, and make of it a world
where even if there is no twin who loves
me more than their own blood, I
can live there. you were always
going to leave us, brother,

the world is temporary, brother,
like love. I wanted to hear you always,
hear us all say, say the first word, say *I.*


*I started writing this sestina in the blank back pages of another person's book*
*a year or so ago, sitting on a pier in Wisconsin watching a girl who had twin*
*brothers play with them and others, and thinking about how different my*
*childhood might have been had my mother not miscarried the boy she conceived*
*between my second and third sisters, what it might have been to grow up in*
*a household that included a brother instead of two sisters, how that might*
*have influenced my way of interacting with male-bodied people. The poem*
*was a terrible failure in all of its early forms, until, out of desperation to make*
*something of it, I started playing with putting it into various traditional forms*
*just to see what would happen. I think that, by radically re-writing it as a*
*sestina, I was able to release my expectations and aspirations for it in terms*
*of content and just focus on the form, allowing my subconscious to supply the*
*content in surprising and, quite honestly, moderately disturbing ways. It is not*
*the poem I set out to write at all, which may be the key to its success.*

# JAMES MERRILL

## TOMORROWS

The question was an academic one.
Andrey Sergeyvitch, rising sharp at two,
Would finally write that letter to his three
Sisters still in the country. Stop at four,
Drink tea, dress elegantly and, by five,
Be losing money at the Club des Six.

In Pakistan a band of outraged Sikhs
Would storm an embassy (the wrong one)
And spend the next week cooling off in five
Adjacent cells. These clearly were but two
Vital details—though nobody cared much for
The future by that time, except us three.

You, Andrée Meraviglia, not quite three,
Left Heidelberg. Year, 1936.
That same decade you, Lo Ping, came to the fore
In the Spiritual Olympics, which you won.
My old black self I crave indulgence to
Withhold from limelight, acting on a belief I've

Lived by no less, no more, than by my five
Senses. Enough that circus music (BOOM-two-three)
Coursed through my veins. I saw how Timbuctoo
Would suffer an undue rainfall, 2.6
Inches. How in all of Fairbanks, won-
der of wonders, no polkas would be danced, or for

That matter no waltzes or rumbas, although four
Librarians, each on her first French 75,
Would do a maxixe (and a snappy one).
How, when on Lucca's greenest ramparts, three-
fold emotion prompting Renzo to choose from six
Older girls the blondest, call her *tu,*

It would be these blind eyes hers looked into
Widening in brief astonishment before
Love drugged her nerves with blossoms drawn from classics
Of Arab draftsmanship—small, ink-red, five-
Petaled blossoms blooming in clusters of three.
How she would want to show them to someone!

But one by one they're fading. I am too.
These three times thirteen lines I'll write down for
Fun, some May morning between five and six.

# Sharon Mesmer

## Super Rooster Killer Assault Kit

Hey, home skillet, what is this super rooster killer assault kit crapsauce
that keeps puking up Joe Walsh kicking out the maximum nacho?
Thought you were the Imagineer? Your dandelion breeze classy smashing
with golf ball–sized Khloe Kardashian and fifteen fat gangsta fags?
I may not be as Mexican as EZ WIDE but I already called dibs on the
Twilight Shitler
Home Depot Aisle One Kitten Hittin' Technique of TV's Orville
Redenbacher.

Why a kitten? Only non-internet masturbating Orville Redenbacher,
riding a Kitler boner to nowhere, understands that fail crapsauce.
And why Home Depot? Because fuck you, that's why. And because
Governor Shitler
wants to give free healthcare to...oh, wait that was Jesus. That was
Maximum Nacho
Jethro Trollcat Jesus on "Everybody Draw Mohammad Day"
(everybody 'cept gangsta fags).
I'm pretty sure possum pee + Hennessy is now our closest thing to
classy smashed.

The story behind Jesus is that God saw us sinking into pirate-on-
possum classy smashing
and decided "Pope Francis, Gangsta Fag" would be a better name for
Orville Redenbacher,
Gangsta Fag.
Big Wong don't take no crapsauce.
And at this point in modern society, with Joe Walsh kicking out the
maximum nacho,
the only thing lamer than a Home Depot Aisle One Kitten Hittin' Shitler

is Wang Chung running on glossolalia. But do you really give a
   landlord's shitler?
Nope. 'Cause you are possum pee + Hennessy 24/7 classy smashed
for Easter Week, down with el youtube sexo booty sourcings of
   Turbo Al and Max Macho,
featuring the mandingo sweatpants of Orville Redenbacher
having crab-on-its-back sex at the social security party—that's some
   crapsauce,
emo dude. How does diaper keep AIDS off emo panda gangsta fag?

When emo panda gangsta fag looks like My Chemical Gangsta Fag
douche-twerking it to "Hey Kids, It's Kitten Hittin' Time" by Shitler.
Sorry: golf ball–sized Khloe Kardashian already called forever dibs on
   crapsauce—
her Lucky Neckbone Sweatpants and 24/7 Easter Week classy smashing
are vying with Super Rooster Killer Orville Skywalker and his lover
   Taco Redenbacher
for the title of Last Year's Most Un-Mas Macho Maximum Nacho.

Boy, home skillet, you sure do love Joe Walsh kicking out the
   maximum nacho
with golf ball–sized Khloe Kardashian and her fifteen fat gangsta fags.
The *Home Depot Aisle One Twilight Kitten Hittin' Technique* of TV's
   Orville Redenbacher
is no way as Mexican as EZ WIDE but it already called forever dibs on
   your double-shitler
24/7 possum pee + Hennessy classy smashed-inspired
"Super Rooster Killer Assault Kit" unrhymed iambic pentameter crapsauce.

Newsflash, Stu: Wang Chung glossolalia ain't no maximum nacho…
   not even with crapsauce.
Not even with Orville Redenbacher, gangsta fag with benefits, classy
   smashed
and kickin' out the jams at the *Home Depot Aisle One Kitten Hittin'
   Party with Shitler.*

Not even.

*Since this is a flarf poem, I put each word or phrase through Google and composed from the results. Pretty much right away (which surprised me), a kind of voice/narrative started to emerge, so I just kept to that "feeling." I thought at first it was a fool's game (and who's to say it wasn't, ultimately?) because I was expecting random chance to provide content for something so traditionally prescribed. But then I began to see the poem actually taking on a volition, and I was entertained by the idea that something so determined could also contain such caroming weirdness. And it seemed to take on extra weirdnesses as I went along, and so I just trusted that I'd end up at some super weirdness point-of-no-return...thus the extra two words at the end.*

# ANIS MOJGANI

## THEY RAISED VIOLINS

Before I was born I was a string.
My sister was a cello. My brother a sleeping bird.
My father's memories are of eggshells.
My mother's are of tablecloths and petals.
The water was warm. The days like bones,
long and white. Our eyes soft mice. Our mouths cranberries.

Before I was born Mother grew cranberries.
Father spoke English and carried pockets filled with violin strings.
The first time they say *I love you,* the clouds are playing bones
above them. Mother's eyes are warm. Father's heart is a new bird
learning to stand. Mother places her hand in Father's hair. It becomes petals.
My father. A crab. Smiling, his tired shoulders free of their shell.

Replacing claw for wing, Father spends the evening pasting stars out
     of eggshells.
Staring into her eyes, he swears he can see in their cracks the cranberries
she used to grow. Emptied of fruit, her hands now are full with petals.
Father smiles, teeth white as string,
Mother looks to where they are tied. *Look. The birds,*
he says, pointing at the sky. *The feathers have left their bones.*

The clouds finish their game. They start throwing the bones
at the earth. The rain falls. It sounds like shoes on eggshells.
Gathering on the roof is the nakedness of the featherless flock.
They begin to eat the roof, taking bites like it is cranberry,
the ceiling starts leaking, water washes inside in strings,
the feathers of the birds float on the floor like petals.

Feathers like petals. Father's hair falls like petals. Mother's memories
     are of petals.
Father collects them and starts sticking them onto Mother's bones
then pulls out the bones and leaves only the feathers. He takes a string

from the unraveling of his pants leg and ties it around her elbows and
     her eggshells,
making a child's telephone. *Cranberry? Are you there Cranberry?*
he says to her. Mother's eyes are hazel birds,

turning into green ones. Father is pink birds.
They are flamingos. They talk apple. They speak petal.
Their life together is a crayon of color unnamed. A pebble. A cranberry.
A prayer. They stretch their youth between each other's bones
and pour their memories into morse code tapped out onto the shells
     of eggs:
a viola. A summer. A September. A little one. A string,

tied around a bushel of berries until the juice squeezed itself into a
     flock of birds.
My father tied his violin strings under their wings. My mother took
     the petals
of his hair, fed them to us. Our bones hold tightly—as thin, as safe as
     eggshells.


*I can't remember what spiraled me to try writing sestinas. It was probably
ten years or so after learning about them. I just wanted to play with what I
thought seemed like the logical way of approaching, instead wanting to explore,
something fantastical that would allow me to play with its constrictions.
Though maybe that is the logical and popular way writers approach it, I don't
know. After all, I've only written a handful. I can't remember what prompted
the lines. I think it was somewhat connected with my wanting to create an
image-based fairy tale about my parents. I had a line or two that had come out
in some earlier writing. I think it may have been a variation of the first line,
like "I was born small as a violin string," "my sister was a cello." And that
line was where I returned when I thought to take the sestina for a whirl.*

# Rick Moody

## *Radio Sestina*

The nave of the jazz dives blows a merry old air.
Not the free jazz. Or not at the end of the set.
The ballads. Though he thinks he can't, he can;
Though he thinks he won't, he might.
By the by, don't trust a cat who's given to lie,
As that cat hard sells. This player he goes back to the well,
And even if, as an alto man, he seen better days, well,
He can still pluck gossamer clusters from the air.
Can still scale the modal and be-bop heights. Lie
In the arms of mathematicians, you know, set
Theorists, e.g. Look, keep the beams on bright, don't stare. Might
Of militarists, unnecessary here. A can
Of elbow grease, that's all, for the nave of jazz, he's can-
Do, man. Dips the pen of his craft into the inkwell.
It's swell. Least, until the day when his eyesight gives out. Then: might-
Have-been. Could-have-done. Etc. He starts to sound like an air
Raid siren, or a rhino bellowing from his lair. Hey, it's art. There's a set-
To, at the jazz dive. Going disco. The promoter used to lie
Back and slyly collect meager profits. Now, jazz, a "pack of lies,"
Dude says. "In all candor, fella does what he thinks he can,"
And then this dude, he cranks the television set,
Inks a deal, while watching the patrons bus-stopping in the well
Of his club, like it's a streetwalkers' fair, *en plein air.*
Girls looking like if they don't yet, they might.
Good for business, dog. No jazz bands, now, even if the players are mighty
Prophets. Flugelhornists, they lie
Low. Same with the vibes guys. Violists. They air
Dry their laundry, eat mac and cheese, save where they can,
It's like a living hell, musician's life, like radio, whose impoverishment is well
Documented. Man has a brain, man has his radio set
At defiance, set at naught. Set
At the left of the dial. All you who might
Rush pell-mell into the contemporary. Know well
Where you fly, this region where the tuba players of lullabies lie

In state. Here the house music vampires do their can-can,
Delouse love slaves out in the cabana. Yes, where'er
You fly, hell. Through the static, a voice, "Might just as well
Prolong this set of lies, since I'm already on air,"
Mister D.J. exclaims, "And don't wanna get my ass canceled."

*"Radio Sestina" was just a desperate effort to write a sestina on command.
True, it has a lot of music in it, and it also has some radio in it. At the time,
I was making occasional pieces for radio (for a show on WNYC called "The
Next Big Thing," whose demise I often lament), and I was therefore thinking
about radio, and about the relationship of radio to music, in the larger sense.
Music in language and in sound.*

*I work with found text poetry and collage poetry and process-oriented poetry a
bit. That is, I like "experimental" poetry a great deal. But I don't necessarily
rear up and write in one of the old forms very often (except maybe tanka and/
or haiku). I probably write one or two poems a year really, which is not so bad,
as I have been publishing almost 25 years now. So that means 25 poems.*

# CARLEY MOORE

## MECHANICS

"Don't you see!" I cry in the dream, "It's my alarm clock!"
At 4:38 the red numbers turn into appointments.
Having a small back does exempt one from history,
but it does not allow for excessive stopping both curbside and roadside.
What's enormous in the middle
and not about to get away?

I'm inside and very nearly away,
but already I know the hands of that clock—
begrudging, dusty and always in the middle
of two numbers or two living rooms or two appointments.
This was supposed to be the tree-lined roadside
of someone else's history.

He said, "I am history's
tallest order!" and left on a bike I'd already given away.
The house and barbeque are all roadside
like ships on the hem of a wave. The clock
bobs for its own appointment...
middling, middling.

I'm sorry about the middle finger and the middle
manager who insist on only one history.
I try and try to keep my appointments—
to walk purposefully into the Away,
but even the undertow has a clock
of its own; an excuse for never appearing roadside.

Did he leave the already-spoken-for bike roadside
or in the yellow middle
of a field without a time clock?
He thought, "Mechanize! Become the history
you deserve before you go away!
Run headfirst to all of your appointments!"

I am the underwater version of my earliest appointment
and the lake you see while asking for roadside
assistance. I always say I want to get away
but instead organize a trip to the middle
of a past ocean vacation. This must be history
just without clocks.

He wasn't the roadside historian kept in
the middle by appointments and clocks.
We both thought of ourselves as walking away.

*"Mechanics" is my attempt to reconcile small histories—personal stories,
memoirs, the daily details of life like insomnia, clock-watching, and break-
ups—with the capital-H history that gets told in textbooks and by historians.
It's probably an homage to people like Joe Brainard and Eileen Myles who
consistently use the personal to get at something larger and more cosmic/
historical, albeit in a subtle, lyrical way. I am also trying to think about the
ways in which our lives are ordered by time, clocks, and mechanization, and
yet often, we, I, the speaker, find ourselves in the swells of chaos, out in the
ocean, or in the middle of a field of sunflowers. Ultimately, I'm trying to say
that even those chaotic, natural spaces have their own histories and clocks, and
a way of teaching us about history and time.*

# LENARD D. MOORE

## *A QUIET RHYTHM OF SLEEP*

March midnight creeps upstairs
while my wife and daughter sleep
on the new brass bed that darkness blankets
as a hard wind rattles the panes
and thunder booms like artillery rounds
blasting the vast night.

I sit downstairs writing about night
while slight snoring scatters upstairs
as the TV talks of exploding rounds
like those that shattered my father's sleep
in a building with shivering panes
on a green cot without blankets.

In the jungle no one needed blankets.
Terror must have gnawed bones at night
like rigid wind splinters panes
and infinite chill climbs stairs.
No matter how hard I try I can't find sleep
while late night TV resonates rounds.

I imagine how my father ducked rounds
beneath a sky like heavy blankets
that smothered soldiers in sleep
and snuffed out lifelong dreams of night.
I pray to the Man Upstairs
to rid that charred land of constant pains.

With pen I tap sturdy brilliant panes
in this house of memory where rounds
are falling like rain; here it is safe upstairs:
my woman and child rest beneath blankets,
their chests lift and fall with night
in a quiet rhythm of sleep.

I wish my father might fathom such sleep
without the rattling of cracking panes
in the dubious, dwindling night,
without patrolling like a guard making rounds
but wear his nights beneath blankets
as peace settles like dust motes upstairs.

My wife and daughter sleep without dreaming panes
and rounds shaking away the inkblack night.
I imagine my father walking upstairs, blinking at blankets.


*I wrote "A Quiet Rhythm of Sleep" on May 21, 1999. In fact, I finished
writing the first draft at 3:45am. I believe the poem went through about
four revisions. It took a few hours for me to write the first draft. I think the
simplicity and straightforwardness came natural to me. I would dedicate my
sestina to the memory of my daughter, Maiisha L. Moore (1982–2004).*

# Jeffrey Morgan

## When Unreal Girlfriends Die: The Manti Te'o Sestina

Sadness pulls its drawstrings tight and a tragedy
that never happened becomes loss we
can't answer for by carving a rectangle in the ground.
This kind of duplicity is so much more than two.
A tabernacle of coaches, a clowder of teammates;
we are poor indeed when only life measures death.

We do not know what to do with imaginary death.
We do not know what to do with our hands after tragedy.
We reach to slap the butt of a teammate,
only to learn the play has been called back. Who are we
when we are not ourselves, of more than two
minds and unable to make sense of manicured ground?

We have seen a man throw another man to this ground.
We have looked at this prostrate man and expected death,
only to have him wave from the stretcher, to
disappear into tunnels underneath us. We are tragedy,
but we are also love. We are confused. We
are everything including the strange hatred of teammates.

Trust is a sacred bond to break, ask any teammate
not to touch the microphone in his face. What are the grounds
for fake reconciliation? A fake love says no we
were never, and no we will not be in death.
We wear the threadbare uniform of this tragedy,
each rip cleaving the ridiculous thing more in two.

Whatever this is, it is not this, too.
It is not a man running so hard into a teammate
that for an instant they switch bodies, switch tragedies.
It is not a pile of men searching for a ball on the ground,
a stadium full of eyes symbolizing death.
All the whistles blowing: There is no I in we.

What is a man with an undead girlfriend to do? We
are listening to the answers, listening to
our voices fumble in the false valley of the shadow of death.
What does it mean, the dog pile of reporters, teammates,
coaches, all of us who visit and revisit the ground
of our latest failure, that we are grateful for each tragedy?

Only this: It is hard to exhume tragedy,
and bad luck to touch the yard lines on the ground
once fake death has put its helmet on a teammate.

*I can't effectively summarize the real-life events of then–Notre Dame football
player Manti T'eo's girlfriend death hoax conspiracy. Nobody can. However,
if anyone out there has no idea what I'm talking about, I urge you to look into
it. It's like amateur night at a Greek tragedy. It's like David Lynch suddenly
got very interested in Notre Dame football. I don't know what it's like. The
whole thing had all the elements of a ripping yarn, except that there were just
too many moving pieces and unknowable motivations. The best part was how
frustrated reporters got covering the whole strange affair. They kept repeating
the facts they knew, but the thing simply would not cohere. In other words, it
was a real-life sestina.*

# Tomás Q. Morín

## Canso of the Dancing Bears

They call this place Bulgaria. We still say earth
rising and falling. No matter, we descend
carefully, the three of us, the face of the risen
ground (Musala Peak, if you will), until we get
clear of the fern rot, the fume and hiss of lead
and sulfur mines. Late afternoon, we pass the closed

eyes of a rose farm where night has begun to close
on the empty stomachs of children. The earth
purples one last time and the sun completes its descent.
By morning we reach the caravan, not yet risen
from its slumber. In Greece, where they tend to get
philosophical, even at a circus, the ringmaster leads

the show with our introduction, *The only good bear*—they lead
us quickly in—*is a dancing bear! Keep your eyes closed
and your ears covered if you can't stand to see the earth
shaking bears!* So we dance, or at least we give the sense
of an oafish novice lifting his feet, rising
to the music of a mandolin. How does a bear get

to dance you ask? It starts with a heated needle, we get
a knee to the neck, and then we see a hand leading
us by our pierced muzzles to a pile of ashen coals
where we are taught how mankind once left the earth
when he rose on two feet. Tired of carrying the scent
of our mothers, we rub against the children, then rise

and leave the cow-trodden roads of the country, the ryes
and oats, the beet-laden fields to find work in the ghettos
of Sofia and Varna, where we can earn as much as 100 lev
for a wedding, 150 for a birth. In New Delhi, an uncle closed
out his life making 4000 rupees a month. Unearthly
amounts of money can be made if only our descendants

can learn not to hate the children of man. Unruly dissent
will be our undoing if we can not learn how to rise
to the eager crowds, how to make the beautiful get
hysterical with laughter and joy. Don't be misled,
we don't envy man his position, money, or clothes,
nor do we even wish to rid him from the earth.

An unpeopled earth would only beget catastrophe. Chaos
would descend upon us all; the sun would close its eye,
and who would then rise and lead us to the music of our dying?

*The poem was inspired by a banner on the side of my internet browser meant
to draw attention to an organization championing the rights of dancing bears.
I couldn't resist clicking on it. Once I had, I was faced with all the horrible
details of how bears are made "to dance." I then researched the use of dancing
bears in all the countries where they were used, so that I could get a good idea
of how different cultures interacted and appreciated this type of sideshow.
Once I had spent some time educating myself about this terrible practice, I
chose my pattern for repeating the end words. Rather than use the typical
sestina pattern, I decided to model mine after Edmund Spenser's "Ye wastefull
Woodes, beare witnesse of my woe" from* The Shepheardes Calender.

# PAUL MULDOON

## THE LAST TIME I SAW CHRIS

In Amagansett, for crying out loud, setting the arm of his French helpmeet
toward a funky-as-it-gets exhibit in the Crazy Monkey,
a crosscut saw
in the window not quite making up for this not quite being Long
    Island Sound,
the gobs of tar
on his and his buddy's pants

suggesting they might have been willing participants
in some recent keelhauling. Blown, too, the opportunity to meet
and greet an incipient Jack Tar
or wannabe grease monkey
in an outhouse wired, for the love of Mike, for sound.
When he turned away from me I could have sworn I saw

a woman on a seesaw
from the seventies, still flying a flag for the seventies. That's what was
    with the hot pants.
The politest way of putting it would be to say she and I'd been trying
    to sound
each other out, thought it seemed unlikely ever the twain would meet.
She was just back from Benin. No monkey
business without an overcoat, for crying out loud. No losing the ship
    for a ha'p'orth of tar.

Not ship, I was treading water. *Sheep.* A sheep being the avatar
of no god we know of, always the best kind. For she was musing on
    an ancient saw
having to do with a monkey
and paying p(e)an(u)ts
to the guide, for the love of Mike, who'd led her hunting trip. A
    hartebeest meet
summoned by a hartebeest bugle, a sound

that had barely the strength to resound
through the bush. Boots and saddles. The clench of Wright's coal tar
as she suddenly deemed it meet
to turn the other cheek, for crying out loud, looking back at me as if
    she saw that I foresaw
the needle tracks just above the line of her pants
when her arms would set from years of firing up, as if I foresaw the monkey

on her back ("*les ans, mon ange, les ans manqués*"),
as if I might look forward from an era in which we were all still
    relatively sound
in wind and limb to an era of night sweats, gasps, and pants,
for the love of Mike, now threatening to tar
all of us, straight or gay, with the same brush, the god who oversaw
our not knowing of him yearning now to mete

out retribution as the hartebeest pants for cooling streams, *taratantara,*
    *taratantara,*
our breathing indistinguishable now from the sound of a saw
through the breast of a monkey, for crying out loud, through
    monkey- or other bush-meat.


*Having written a bunch of sestinas, I tend to avoid them, partly because I
don't like to repeat myself. Having said that, I remain open to the possibility
that a poem may announce itself as a contender for that form. It seems to
be one of the most splendidly paradoxical of ways of working things out.
Everything is at once nailed down and up in the air. I'm pretty sure I wrote
this one along with a group of students. We'd agreed on the six end words, and
everyone in the class used them. One of the beautiful serendipities is that the
word "monkey" was one of those end words, but I'd no idea that the gallery
was waiting for me. "For the love of Mike" is an Irishism, I'd say, but one
that has some currency in the U.S. It's used as the title of a Frank Capra film
starring Claudette Colbert. A lost film, it seems.*

# Amanda Nadelberg

## My New Pet Word Is Mozzarella

My new pet word is mozzarella
and I like how it sounds. You
mozzarella me when you park the
car. When you open the mail with
your teeth. Teeth are not tools my
friend's mom says and she's a

dental hygienist. I could go for a
walk around the lake if the weather is mozzarella
tomorrow. If not we could drive my
car to the beach and sit inside and talk about your
problems. That could be fun. My friend with
the dental hygienist for a mom lives in the

nicest place in Chicago. Tall ceilings and the
bathtub has a marble bench for soap and there's a
back door with a wooden stairs all nice with
porches, the kind that Tom, my old mozzarella,
used to have in St. Louis. Please, leave your
shoes on. I need to vacuum soon anyway. My

carpet gets so dirty because it's white. I take my
shoes off but it still looks dirty so I vacuum the
floors often. My sister said she loved your
gift. She says they've always wanted a
mechanical icebreaker. Emptying the mozzarella
is everyone's least favorite thing to do. With

the work day being so much longer now, and with
the past few years and the rise in hatred of Israel my
sister has an even harder time with mozzarella.
She says that when they go to hear the
Philharmonic the whole audience is crying such a
shame in jeans on linen seats. As an Israeli your

uniform is a pair of jeans. Before they got expensive, before your
uncle invented pairs for $250 so that we might sit with
more expensive asses, Israelis were born in a
pair of blue jeans and a loose shirt. Tonight my
favorite station is playing the Israel Philharmonic Orchestra and the
sound, their sound makes everything sad, like the Mozzarella

has made all things in Israel sound sad like a piece
of unfortunate history. The Mozzarella is, to use one
of your phrases, my idea of Donald Duck without his tail.


*I've always enjoyed writing sestinas with end words that are seemingly
"less expensive" (i.e., prepositions and articles are keys to the kingdom).
The sestina's form drives the content most of all. It's fine to have a nugget
expectation of direction, but after a while, what I always forget I love about
them is how you are bullied by these words into a narrative and sometimes it
becomes a surprise, the direction taken. It would be fun to a write a sestina
without a narrative.*

# MARILYN NELSON
## *TWO MASTERS*

*c. 1750*

For the first few years of living with my master
I was pretty much involved with household business—
fetching things, carding wool. Thus I went on,
submissive and obedient, following orders
every day with faithfulness and honesty,
earning my master's complete confidence.

As I grew taller and stronger, his confidence
in me set harder tasks for me to master,
as if he would measure the depth of my faithfulness.
Of course, I had no say in this business,
my business being to do as I was ordered,
to be the beast pulling Master's family on.

One morning, Master had given me a task and gone
away for the day. Swaggering with confidence,
his peach-cheeked son gave me a contrary order.
I told him I'd promised to complete a job for my master.
I had no right to refuse his enterprise,
he yelled, in his eyes no spark of charity.

He snatched a pitchfork. I weighed *fight* against *faith*
for one moment, then snatched the other one.
We faced off like devils going about their business,
he big with arrogance, claiming authority,
I defending my promise to my master,
and Master's confidence that I would fulfill his orders.

I held off three men my upstart master ordered
to tie me up. At last he gave up hope
and ran to his mother. As soon as he left I mastered
my temper and volunteered to put on
the hair-rope bond and be carried to him, confident
that he knew hurting me hurt Master's business.

He had me suspended on a gallows made for the business
of butchering cattle, and loudly gave orders
for twig whips to be cut. But he lost courage
and did no more. And the leopard-skin shield of faith
protected me while, by my wrists, I hung on
the gallows for refusing to serve two masters.

No man can be faithful to two masters.
All of life's business is centered in trust.
Even in an insane world, there must be some order.

# ETHAN PAQUIN
## ORATIO MODERNA

o the times you poured a dour muscatel,
god, bastard—you are the wrong god seated
for this, our new wilderness. there is trash
that appears friendlier than thou. some neon
accusations—"Hoagies" and "Live Strippers"
and "Oil-in-a-Minute"—what is this skyline,

what is the _____. here in this miniature skyline
there are shades of smoky musk. do tell
all the minions of the flesh—strippers,
pornographers, painters—to be seated
and await the sermon. they will as neon
tubes be jolted to awakening. no more trashy

thoughts. yes, you, my dear god, trash-
remover in the sky, lord of sky and circle and line
and my best teacher, beam revelatory neon-
bright awareness. all theology is so much musculature,
flex'd on the weak or wicked, supposedly. sit,
will you? listen—like water—that which strips

away the _____ to a bareness. strippers
got it right: remove the rhinestones, that trash
(makeup, bras, ad inf.). all the johns seated
in the front row wear hats resembling the skyline
of Buffalo. they are, yes, intoxicated by muscatel
and various human whiffs. look at all the neon

reminding us of how real it is, that goddamned neon—
ungodly invention, luring us in. all the strippers
got us hooked on their new breast versions. muscatel
never tasted so good, realer than psalmery. trashed,
one can saunter through a really tiny kitten's skyline
when hammered—gin, varied theocracies, etc. seated

at the podium, one can say "bitch-ass trick"; seated
at the podium, one can boom a voice distinct as neon
and farther and wider than any damned skyline
known to nobody but those in touch—strippers,
minions of "hellish agency," professors, Eurotrash,
all knowledgeable on their coke and shiny muscatel;

seated 'neath a neon skyline, bleach'd strippers
and sluts and hardy priests, all cheap, all get trashed
on cheap and heady and varied, all heady, muscatels.

# RICHARD PEABODY

## SPAGHETTI WESTERN SESTINA

I worry about the bags of dollars
left by "Blondie," the Man with No Name
after all of the bad guys have taken a bullet,
worry about the bags after it's clear Tuco won't die
in the graveyard where the big gundown has transformed the West
with gold coins and spilled blood and highly operatic desert.

I want to live in that place, that's really Spain—Europe's only desert.
And somehow I want Tuco to collect all of those dollars
from the bags he split open with a shovel in the imaginary west.
Because without a horse I can't imagine how he's going to carry
    them, name
or no name. And I wonder how Lee Van Cleef can just die.
And oh my God—are those flies crawling on his face? One bullet

and he drops. I expected him to be more diabolical than that. One bullet.
And "Angel Eyes" drops like a solitary crow circling the endless desert.
And I wonder what it's like to be Eli Wallach, a nice Jewish guy who
    doesn't die
in this movie, but who also starred in *The Magnificent Seven* for many
    more dollars.
An actor's an actor no matter what, no matter how big their name.
But c'mon—would you ever guess he'd play in two of the best Westerns

ever made? No way. The only West Eli knew was West
Brooklyn. Am I right? I'll bet he wouldn't let flies crawl on his face
    or take just one bullet.
I've seen every Spaghetti Western by now. The ones with name
stars and the ones with actors like Edd Byrnes or Alex Cord, shot in
    the same desert
towns in Almeria, Spain. I love the Sergio Leone Dollars
Trilogy, and his classic *Once Upon a Time in the West*. The way Henry
    Fonda dies

is fabulous. I'm sure he was tickled that he got to gnaw scenery and die
on screen. Not something he did often. And is it just me or does the
    Old West
make more sense with Leone at the helm? Bandits shooting up the
    place for dollars.
Bullets flying everywhere. Family, kids, bystanders taking a bullet.
I heard they had to shoot new footage for TV versions of these desert
shoot 'em ups. Harry Dean Stanton's intro about the Man with No Name

assures the American audience that he's not really a bounty killer sans name
but a U.S. government–trained agent. Censors should just do the
    right thing and die.
Thank God the Italians shot all of these movies in the 60s, in the desert.
*Django, My Name Is Trinity, Sabata, Death Rides a Horse.* The Old West
just isn't the same without Ennio Morricone's soundtrack complete
    with bullets,
harmonicas, and soaring choruses. But back to the bags of dollars.

Sure, Clint left all those dollars. The Man with No Name was fair in
    his way.
The Good? An ominous question mark. Better than a bullet or dying
    under the big sky.
The Ugly gets off easy—wandering mythic Western deserts with a
    fistful of dollars.


*I started a James Bond–themed sestina, and that got stuck in the literary mud.
The Spaghettis flashed as a motion picture alternative in that I'll bet nobody
has written a sestina about those movies, and then I was out of the mud and
cruising. Sergio Leone relied on repetition, and the form actually seemed to fit
Ennio Morricone's operatic soundtracks. I think it dovetailed together right
from the start.*

# Kiki Petrosino

## CRUSADERS

The note you dropped became a bird.
It sleeps in my chest.
Wings abjure in dreaming white.
How fast it dreams.
How slur.
A silence in the canebrake.

When we came to the canebrake
I tore my yellow coat. You spoke to a bird.
Tall slur
of sunlight on the water's chest.
In dreams
you take my coat into your white

shell mouth. I race among the hard white
stalks of cane, breaking
my feet sharply against their gloss. I dream
a bird
lands on the wooden desk in my chest
to slur

its bones with ink. You slur
above me like white
linen rolling outward from a tea-chest.
Come.  We can sleep in the canebrake.
I know a bird
who drops down. Dreams

are falling from its beak. And some dreams
even slur,
so that the bird
may stay and speak to both of us, more white
for our time in the canebrake
sleeping chest

to chest.

How the bird trebles in our dreams
of what can break.
Inclining hard into the slur
of small exits. White
houses fold. Each roof a bird

moving in the slur
that cane-stalks make as turning white
we fill with birds—


*I wrote this sestina over several sessions in an Iowa City coffee shop. Every time I made a significant edit, I saved the draft as a new document, just to see how many I could burn through. After about a dozen saves, though, I stopped tracking my adjustments. It was too difficult to bring the sestina to completion if I thought consciously about each individual strand. Taken together, the end words became their own thing; they demanded to be treated as a unit. It was like they'd agreed to live together and not be separated. Thus, in my memory, writing this sestina felt like playing the harp. And I don't even play the harp.*

# CARL PHILLIPS

## BIRDLAND

For attention upon arrival, arrive naked,
save for a single rhinestoned pair of field-
glasses. Affect a perfectly natural interest
in ornithology, i.e., profess to know
the male when you see him, or that in any cast
of starlings, no two are the same; let the eye,

with no prompting—like any bird's eye—
attend to the ankle, whether banded or naked,
in flight, and fly with it. As for the casting
of the hard trick, drawing birds from the field
to within some more observable range, know
this too is easily mastered: play to the interest

in any sudden appearance of food, stir interest
by not stirring—remember this, their eyes
are most liable to settle on what they know
or believe to be safe clearing: a pool, the naked
body stumbled upon in some field,
not turning for the wind, one bloodless finger cast

as signal flag, softly waving, broadcasting
it's safe to go down, come closer. A cool disinterest
is, above all, essential, in the particular field
you've entered. Fear, too keen a light in the eye,
and you'll have lost all the edge your body's naked-
ness gave you—any bird worth half a tail-shake will know

what you've pretended all this time not to know,
or really don't, anymore, already having all but cast
to either side what clear vision remains, eyes nakedly
parading the room, in each a dangerous uninterest
in what the other one sees, a failure of the eyes
to telescope, hence a marked inability to field

whatever meets them head-on. In this case, a field
of birds you begin to sense you already know
from somewhere, to do with that space the mind's eye
now slowly pulls forward, a room, windows of overcast
sky, and in the room the only point of real interest,
what the two bodies, sheetless, bone-naked,

closed-eyed, and busy shifting the casterless
bed elsewhere, miss: the sound a naked interest
will make—birds alighting in a field they know.


*I probably started writing this from watching birds lift from and settle into a
field, something I love to watch. But I soon realized I was somehow writing
about a particular flock, some idea in my head of gay men in a club, though I
had yet to go to a club and had yet to understand my being gay. I like how the
original birds got transformed in that way.*

# Ezra Pound

## Sestina: Altaforte

Loquitur: En *Bertrans de Born.*
*Dante Alighieri put this man in hell for that he was a stirrer-up of strife.*
*Eccovi!*
*Judge ye!*
*Have I dug him up again?*
*The scene is at his castle, Altaforte. "Papiols" is his jongleur.*
*"The Leopard," the* device *of Richard Cœur de Lion.*

### I

Damn it all! all this our South stinks peace.
You whoreson dog, Papiols, come! Let's to music!
I have no life save when the swords clash.
But ah! when I see the standards gold, vair, purple, opposing
And the broad fields beneath them turn crimson,
Then howl I my heart nigh mad with rejoicing.

### II

In hot summer have I great rejoicing
When the tempests kill the earth's foul peace,
And the lightnings from black heav'n flash crimson,
And the fierce thunders roar me their music
And the winds shriek through the clouds mad, opposing,
And through all the riven skies God's swords clash.

### III

Hell grant soon we hear again the swords clash!
And the shrill neighs of destriers in battle rejoicing,
Spiked breast to spiked breast opposing!
Better one hour's stour than a year's peace
With fat boards, bawds, wind and frail music!
Bah! there's no wine like the blood's crimson!

IV

And I love to see the sun rise blood-crimson.
And I watch his spears through the dark clash
And it fills all my heart with rejoicing
And pries wide my mouth with fast music
When I see him so scorn and defy peace,
His lone might 'gainst all darkness opposing.


V

The man who fears war and squats opposing
My words for stour, hath no blood of crimson
But is fit only to rot in womanish peace
Far from where worth's won and the swords clash
For the death of such sluts I go rejoicing;
Yea, I fill all the air with my music.


VI

Papiols, Papiols, to the music!
There's no sound like to swords swords opposing,
No cry like the battle's rejoicing
When our elbows and swords drip the crimson
And our charges 'gainst "The Leopard's" rush clash.
May God damn for ever all who cry "Peace"!


VII

And let the music of the swords make them crimson!
Hell grant soon we hear again the swords clash!
Hell blot black for always the thought "Peace"!

# MICHAEL QUATTRONE
## *TICKER*

......In other developments,
the autopsies on the dead may be
complete as early as Thursday morning.
The autopsies on the living remain
pending.  They will be performed
with a full orchestra and spectacular

lightshow... Meteorologists expect a cooler
weekend... Housing developments
are on the rise. Creation outperformed
destruction in the markets this May. Be
that as it may, most experts remain
skeptical... Thousands are mourning

comedian Siggy Smolka, who died this morning
of natural causes. "Spectacular!"
raved the *Times,* when he performed
*Carcinogentlemen!,* about the development
of the southern tobacco lobby. Dismay be-
fell the Hollywood crowd... "We remain

optimistic," said actor Johnny Tremain,
"about the war" ... Yesterday morning
the President spoke to Congress: "Maybe
you should know, I have speti—, texta—, uh ... *spectacular*
cancer." He ordered the development
of an innovative procedure, to be performed

by multiple, titanium, super-formed
robots.  He will be in DC for the surgery, Maine
for a six-week recovery... A development-
ally disabled teenager was executed this morning
in Texas. Cheering crowds deemed it a "spectaclear
[sic] demonstration of justice." This may be

the start of a new era," commented Governor May B.
McClantock. "It's just super!" … For med-
ical personnel who wish to inspect a "Q-lar-
va," said to cause wide-spread diarrhea, blocks remain
firmly in place… Insurance companies are mourning
the loss of billions due to recent developments

toward an AIDS vaccine. Further such developments may be
discouraged in the morning by government officials, who remain
convinced the cure has underperformed, is "less than spectacular" …

*During its composition, I discovered that (for me, anyway) the sestina is an
inherently humorous form and should be treated as such. Something about its
rigidity—I still need a teleuton cheat sheet on hand when attempting one—
invites irreverence and encourages deviation and surprise. I guess that means
that a sestina is especially delightful to me insofar as it fails to be a sestina.
The loose form of a news ticker helped me skip around from subject to subject
without too much transition, but also ended up giving the poem its political,
and therefore cynical, flavor. The silliness of reframing teleutons by their
phonetic syllables probably helped me address some dark subject matter more
easily than I otherwise could have done. It made me think of Bill Hicks, a
great hero of mine.*

# NED RUST

## *PROPHETIC SESTINA*

The last
shall be
first and
the first
shall be
the last

But, for the not quite first or last—
because not completely first or last—
it is not clear where they shall be,
They could be second to first now, or be
someplace else in the middle (that is not the first
and not the last). And

you can't combine—for example first and
a last
together shall not be
the last.
Nor shall they be first.
But what shall they be?

And, come to think on it, by what measure shall last be
first? And
shall it be
the last
even when the last
is similar to the first?

Because to be first
is to be
far from the last
(or people won't see the difference and
and the impression won't last)
and that'd be

a shame, to be
the first
And then last—
but not really be—
due to anonymity and,
to begin with, looking much like the last.

Which prompts the thought that maybe the reason that the first
Shall supplant the last is because it's all a matter of perspective and
we instead should say, Whatever shall be, shall be.


*I don't recall the inspiration-nugget itself, but I remember wondering how
short I could make one. (I at least aspire to have a thing against verbosity.) I
also recollect where I penned most of it. It was whatever year the Book Expo
America was last in Washington, D.C. [2006], and I was working in
publishing and was supposed to be escorting a bestselling author from one place
to another after he finished an interview. So I was sitting in some downstairs
hallway and there was one chair. And I sat down and started scribbling on
the back of the folder that held the author's itinerary. As luck would have it,
he didn't ask for the folder when he was done with the interview. Writing a
sestina is like managing a crossword, only it leaves you with something some
people don't mind looking at. I've never been able to get anybody to spend
much time reading my completed crosswords.*

# Carly Sachs

## Indecent Docent: Sex-Deprived Tina

Let's begin here with the use of color.
I find the painting to be overtly sexual, I think
it was intentional, I mean the artist
must have realized how erotic paint
can be, the opposite of undressing you
know, what I'd give to be ten years younger

because everyone wants to fuck someone younger
or someone whose skin is a different color
than yours. Don't tell me that you
don't have these fantasies. The problem is that I think
too much. I mean, what if I could paint
like that, you know, I'd be a fucking artist

and I've always wanted to fuck an artist
or perhaps a sculptor, but I'm not getting any younger.
What artist would want to paint
me naked? Who wants to see that? Only a color-
blind artist maybe, would get me, I think
you know, the whole essence of me, you

know. Now I know what you're
all thinking. I couldn't get an artist
to fuck me. Well, you know what I think.
Fuck you! I was hot-to-trot when I was younger,
you know, like if my sex were a color,
it would be like Jackson fucking Pollock with paint

all over the place. This one time I bought these body paints,
but it wasn't the same, you
know. Like it was too forced, so we tried watercolor
but then we felt more like kids than artists,
you know. It was better when we were younger,
less inhibition, less shit to think

about. That's why I come here, to stop thinking
about myself. I think about the way paint
changes everything. The way it hides things, it makes me younger,
I think. To come here, sort of like Dorian Grey, you
know, he had that artist
paint him, but you saw his true colors

shining through, eventually, because the color of thoughts
is that thing that artists like to paint
so you can see yourself younger, you know.


*I had been working on a series of poems about art, and immediately this Tina
character popped up. I had been visiting museums and watching the docents
give tours—mostly older women, or prim and proper younger women, and I
imagined what it would be like if the tour went awry. I imagined going on a
tour with someone who had their own personal agenda or just had a really bad
or off day, and they were trying to do their job but couldn't quite pull it off. I
think using humor and writing in the voice of someone else helped me to break
into the form instead of letting the form control or break me. Maybe Tina is
the most enlightened version of ourselves. I think we all have that wildness
and freedom in us, and I don't know about anyone else, but there's an appeal
in being completely uncensored. It's ironic that the form created that space for
me—it's one of the reasons I love this poem and will continue to play with
form.*

# MICHAEL SCHIAVO

## *"BE CAREFUL, CORTELYOU, HOW YOU TELL HER"*

It seemed to fall from the sky like an anvil or piano,
The weather extraordinarily pleasant for Buffalo
In autumn, in wartime. We had several rented instruments
To choose from, each a democratic machine, a garment
To each who played. The catch was the kazoo, made of tin,
Though all were slightly out of tune. Even the mannequin

Who stood in the window couldn't maintain he was an assassin
For long. The music was such that every piano
And piccolo, every last one, stank of an ideal even the tin
Gods could agree on. But that was later, in Idaho,
In the spring. We were still upstate, picking peppermint,
Waiting for a note so we could tune our instruments

Before the summer warped them. "Instruments
Such as these must be preserved!" declared the mannequin,
Much to our surprise. Unlike his profession to be so ebullient.
Still, one can't hate a man who plays ragtime piano
With such panache. I hadn't heard such passion since Mexico,
The bullfighters with flowers in their hair, banging tin

Cans as they entered the ring. And after the tin
Came the paper, then the silver and gold, such instruments
Making winter pass quickly (so it seemed) in Jericho.
"Stand firm, or sit down, but don't befriend assassins,
Even if you know their names. A man can play piano
To an empty room and earn a better night's retirement."

The point was lost long ago. Overrun by perfidious rodent,
Both cellar and attic are in bad need of cleaning, and Tin
Pan Alley has gone the way of kudzu; the piano
Needs a coat of wax and a good stripping. "New instruments
Come in various disrepairs and love the mannequins
Best when they're shipped straight from El Dorado

This evening to you." And then, of course, there is Rochambeau,
Who, having defeated the British at Yorktown, went
On to have a middle school named after him. The assassins
In the audience know what I mean. They are made of tin,
And do not rust so easily, except in rain. Each instrument
Is ours, and we share in its playing as we share this piano...

Forget the piano, friend—we will always have Tupelo.
We will always have an instrument called a president,
Something made of tin that can't help but be a mannequin.

*The poem's title is from a quote made by President McKinley to George
Cortelyou after he was shot. Cortelyou was McKinley's personal secretary
(and later, under Teddy Roosevelt, the first Secretary of Commerce and
Labor), as a stand-in for the poet who, after being tasked with giving the
report, must describe a corrupt democracy to a populace unready or unwilling to
see into the roots of the corruption. More absurdly, this voice seems to suggest
that Art (Expression) is the way to correct it. (The "her" of the original quote
refers to McKinley's wife, Ida.) It was written mainly around mid-November
2003, deep into the Iraq War, before Hussein had been captured but well after
"Mission Accomplished." There's an indictment of a particular president, but
more broadly it echoes what Emerson writes in "Compensation" about the
nature of that position: "The farmer imagines power and place are fine things.
But the President has paid dearly for his White House. It has commonly cost
him all his peace and the best of his manly attributes. To preserve for a short
time so conspicuous an appearance before the world, he is content to eat dust
before the real masters who stand erect behind the throne."*

# LAWRENCE SCHIMEL

## *ENDLESS SESTINA*

Sunlight helps to hold delirium
at bay. Seated, warm, I desire
nothing more than my dreams
can provide: escape from death,
from sliding into despair
contemplating my destiny.

I do not like to call it destiny
for I took delight
in the flesh—mine, theirs. While I now despair
my end, I do not—cannot—regret my desire;
who knew it would lead so nimbly to death?
Sun on my face, I sit near the window and dream:

before me on an endless field stands Morpheus,
himself, and I wonder if I am facing my destiny,
a vision of how I will look just before Death
comes to claim me. I must be delirious;
gaunt and drained as he looks, I still desire
him. A frustrated libido is an easier despair

than one's own death. Despair
is such a constant companion, even my dreams
are full of her. The angst of wanting—of needing to be desired—
is every boy's unavoidable destiny.
I beg him, "I can show you such delight..."
But Morpheus has other things on his mind than *le petit mort.*

He is a banshee, foretelling my death
with a keening wail of despair.
I shiver at the sound, cold, and know delirium
and night sweats wrack my body, invading even my daydreams.
I know what I cannot avoid; therefore, call it destiny.
Who am I trying to fool with this desire

for time, the chance to be desired
again, if only once more before I die?
Before I die! How cruel Fate!
I am so far sunk into despair
I can't even get laid in my own dreams!
This abstinence is only delirium.

Morpheus, help me fight my destiny!
Let me be desired! I won't give way to despair!
I'll rage against the dying of delight!


*I love the narrative power of the sestina, how the story seems to automatically
unfold, once you establish the six end words. This sestina was written when
Neil Gaiman and Ed Kramer were compiling an anthology of other writers
writing in the Sandman universe of Neil's comics. Neil had just sent me a
rhyming pantoum he'd written, "The Old Warlock's Reverie," and I also
greatly admired his "Luther's Villanelle." So I set myself to task writing a
formal poem that would be suitable for the collection. And the idea of drawing
from the* Endless *for the end words just came to me and I ran with it. In the
mythology of the Sandman universe, Destruction voluntarily abandoned his
responsibilities, so I felt justified in not including him. At the same time, the
youngest of the Endless, Delirium, was originally known as Delight, so in
that same end word "slot" I alternate between using Delirium and Delight
in each successive stanza. So in many ways, there are in fact seven Endless
included in the poem... although in only six end word slots, using the form to
parallel the events in the comic (with Delight becoming Delirium).*

# JASON SCHNEIDERMAN

## THE BUFFY SESTINA

*(first episode of the new season, before the opening credits)*

Buffy is upstairs sharpening her large collection of stakes
when her mother comes upstairs and says, "Would it be bad,
just this once, not to go out staking vampires again tonight?"
After all—she had just defeated an apocalyptic force! Time
for a break? Buffy never has time for a break. Angel gone,
her stakes sharp, she kisses her mom and hops out the window

into the back yard. Buffy is familiar with this small window
at the beginning of every season (school year), when her stakes
are enough to fight her battles, and whatever the big coming
evil will be— it hasn't started to build yet. What big bad
will it be this season? She pulls her coat against the night
and there's Willow! Her best friend! She certainly has time

for Willow! They walk, explicate the summer, say, "Time
to go back to school." Suddenly, a vampire seizes this window
of relaxed defenses, and grabs off-guard Willow. Oh this night-
ly threat! Willow screams and resists. Buffy turns, her stake
at the ready. "Meet my friend, Mr. Pointy!" she says. Bad
blood-sucker, he lets Willow go. He wants to fight. He goes

at Buffy with everything, and Buffy (blue coat, boots) comes
back at him hard. The fight is oddly even. For a long time
(forty seconds say), he gets in good blows. He hurts her bad,
she looks finished. She isn't getting back up again. A doe
leaps into the cemetery. All are distracted. Willow makes a stake
from a broken bench piece and the vampire tries to run into the night.

But Xander arrives, blocks the exit with his own stake. This night
is going terribly now (for the Vampire)! The vampire goes
around to a crypt and tries to run inside, but it takes time
to pry open the gates. Too much time; Xander almost stakes
the vamp, but he stops to quip, and the effort goes bad.
The Vampire throws him hard into the boarded up window

253

of the crypt. Willow runs over, pulls a board from the window
for a new stake. Buffy's back up. Oh, what a luxury this night
is! Forever to fight just one, lone vampire. Xander's bad-
inage soundtracks the fight. Willow lunges and misses, coming
close, but too far left. Buffy kicks the vampire in face, stake
brandished. He goes down, and she's on top of him this time.

Buffy stakes the vampire. He's dust. Whew! Wait. Bad. Crypts
don't have windows. The night is heavy and dark. That took a long time!
What's coming begins to come. Let's un-board that window.

*My husband and I were watching seasons of Buffy as they came out on*
*DVD, and we'd watch almost an entire season in a weekend. I got very used*
*to the rhythm of the seasons... the arc that never included summer, and it felt a*
*bit sestina-like—to cycle through the same events, but with endless variation.*
*I wanted to capture the pleasure of the repetition, to enjoy the formal play of*
*the season's arc, and the sestina seemed like the best container.*

# Esther Schor

## Sestina: Tegucigalpa

*for James Merrill*

Mother I sent you sixteen postcards from Tegucigalpa
which I remember only vaguely. Running to meet the mail
in the time of heavy rains
I pulled my poncho over my head and with it a gust of chili
which had escaped the pot. The Señora used crystal
always, even for breakfast; after lunch we slept.

Sometimes I planned my comings and goings while I slept
for it was quiet and easy to sleep in Tegucigalpa,
easy to dream; though often there would come the clean rattle of crystal
from the kitchen where Maria washed, cooked, took in the mail
when the bell rang. My dreams were as full as her Indian eyes; her
    hair reeked of chili;
she made faces and a point of warning me about the rains,

threatening me with a pale wooden spoon. (Where there are rains
there is mud.) For years Maria had slept
at the Señora's and she told me one blue evening she was chilly
at night, lonely without her husband and child holed up in northern
    Tegucigalpa;
might as well have been New York. No mail
from them ever. Last Christmas they brought her crystal

radio which she plays low, tentatively. Enough of her. I sent you a
    postcard of the crystal
faces of Five Lakes, which we visited during the hot rains
of July. There we bargained with the Indians. Remember I wrote that male
Indians dressed more brightly than female Indians, like peacocks; we
    ate, stayed the night, slept
in a seedy hotel near Antigua, then returned to Tegucigalpa
just in time for a full lunch. More frijoles, more chili.

I wrote you a card about that chili,
how it was hot like taking an iodine bath, how I nearly broke the crystal
water goblet the first time. The Señora babbled about my baptism. In
    Tegucigalpa
they never ask if you'd prefer this or that, they don't stay in when it rains;
I began to feel within me a second, gentler heartbeat; I spoke
    sentences; I ate and slept.
Now I can thank you for writing; I mean, I appreciate your mail

which came at the right times. You should have seen me nurse my mail,
your tissue-paper leaves that flew to me like infants, small and
    precious; once I sent you chili
powder in an aerogramme. Now I want to ask how far I went, how
    many hours I slept.
I think I wrote you that I smashed my watch crystal,
put the old Omega in a drawer. After some time I learned to live by
    the regularity of rains,
learned what one needs to know in Tegucigalpa.

So the odor of chili is washed away with the rains,
I have stopped receiving mail. Time is etched in the patterns of crystal
in Tegucigalpa, where for months and months I slept.

# Ravi Shankar

## *How Duggan Knew*

"If it's too damn silly to be said, it's sung,"

was Olson's standard excuse for not going to musicals.
He was a grizzly bear's man, spit chaw, knew how to use
a chainsaw, wore flannel, crushed beer cans between his hands,
preferred to piss outside, even in a sleet storm.
How he came to marry the daintiest girl in town, no one knew

except for Old Admiral Duggan, who wouldn't hand
a handicapped toddler an umbrella in a rainstorm.
Duggan had purchased all the land in the subdivision for a song
after the Korean War, then made more than the IRS knew
selling it to the man responsible for the longest-running musical
in Superiorpace Opera House history. Well it's not correct use

to say "responsible," I suppose, since far as Duggan knew
the man didn't write one chord in a song,
had never shown the ability to write anything in his own hand
save checks. Let's say he *financed* the longest-running musical
in Superiorpace Opera House history, which, incidentally, was "Use
It or Lost It: A Tale of Extravagance," in the tradition of Sturm

und Drang 18th-century German playwriting, save for the use
of meta-theatrical dramaturgy whereby the actors knew
they were acting, and sometimes badly, and purple-veined storm
clouds and pseudo-sun were projected onto a video screen, the final song
crooned by the heroine-slash-villain while she held the hand
of the cowboy she'd been trying to kill, accompanied by musical

flourishes that included an amplified kazoo, electronic storm
remixes, dueling banjos, and, from the Afro-Cuban tradition, hand-
held cabasas. Anyway, Old Duggan wasn't musical,
but green's green, however it sounds. He kept one plot of land to use,
a secluded parcel that, when all was said and done, he knew
he'd die in, building a sprawling ranch in the style of a Song

dynasty imperial palace, with carved doors, latticed windows, musical
archways that let in afternoon light, and, for his own personal use,
an indoor pond stocked with fresh trout. No one even knew
Duggan was still alive, until Olson, who as a teenager used to storm
around the neighborhood looking for porch ornaments to break, one song-
less summer morning, convinced one of the Juarez twins to give him a hand

job. Though she had sung second tenor in the choir, she could use
her form for less musical purposes, and deep in the woods, mid-storm
and -gyration, Duggan, hand in his robe, saw. That's how he knew.


*My parents live in Manassas, Virginia, which is known for the Battles of Bull
Run and Lorena Bobbitt. They bought one of the first houses built in this
development, which now is totally suburban, but back in the day was a kind
of incursion into rural farmland. Growing up there, I palled around with some
neighborhood kids, and we discovered that a Korean War veteran who had
gone out of his gourd still lived around there, down a dirt road, where he lived
alone, raised goats, played opera at punk rock volumes, and chased any kids
out of his yard with a shotgun. He seemed really demented to us at the time, so
we would often sneak up to peek in his windows or tease his goats. One of my
friends, Dave Evans, swore to us that one day he looked in the window and
saw old Admiral Duggan in his bathrobe with a stack of Penthouses and a jar
of vaseline and, well, the rest is my sestina...*

# Peter Jay Shippy

## *The Lyricist and His Rock Star*

I'm eating moussaka at the Greek's
when you step in for smokes with that cat
who comports as your superego.
On the jukebox an a cappella
version of "Only You" makes me woozy—
or is it the stale ouzo? Less and less

my waitress whispers, but more and more
I toss poison darts at that geek
who stares at me from my spoon—boozy
and hung by horny toes, like a fruit bat.
Why sad? Wasn't our love a priori?
Like a socialist on Super Tuesday,

I was forgone—like a superfecta
ticket at Suffolk Downs, worth less and less
furlong by furlong. Your A&R
team took one look at me and cried, "Eek!"
I'm the type who Scrabbles Q with qat.
I'm the stripe who fills songs with doozy

idioms where beggars are choosy
and love is hallowed as a superbug.
I look away and recall Angkor Wat,
where the video for "More & More"
was filmed. I sat under a sacred teak
rewriting beats while you went à deux

with that creep sitcom actor, that A-list
hack who speaks like he fucks—like an Uzi—
rat-a-ta-ta. He called me *word freak*
when I verbalized in polysemous polysyllables and *supercomputer*
when I did tips in my head—less and less
as I ate, by then, mostly solo—the rat's

gnat
or edo-mala to his à la mode.
You text messed the end to our amore *and more
powwow to you and all that are newsy!*
Don't bah for me, I have my superglue
and weekly enemas with Irish leeks.

Now I write, more or less, for an oozy
Osaka band that sounds like gats à gogo—
a supergroup. Wait 'til you hear our squeak.


*Is there anyone who actually composes a sestina? Seriously—I'm curious, so
I can find them and cuff them! Not me. It's like wrestling Hokusai's great
wave: if the poem wakes up alive, it's a thousand miles from where it began.
That's probably why so many critics—the Justices—don't trust the form.
They don't trust abandon.*

# Rachel Shukert

## Subterranean Gnomesick Blues; or, The Gnome Who Whet My Fleshy Tent

In lands where the waters are clear
And the forests virginal, where the heavens
Are full only of birds and stars—
Before writing a poem about it, I find it helpful to masturbate.
I believe this is also true of camping,
For there is no privacy once you pitch the tent.

Indeed, I had pitched a bonny tent
And my next task soon was clear;
Hastily I had gone off camping
And beard of Zeus! My sainted heavens!
I had completely forgotten to masturbate!
So thus I lay, and, twitched 'neath the stars,

Beneath my eyelids, I saw a host of stars
Of pornographic nature—But ho! A rustling in my tent!
Oh go away! Can't you see I'm trying to masturbate!
And in the corner, 'twas all too clear
As I raised my fist to curse the heavens—
A gnome stood setting up his gear for camping.

"Sorry to disturb you while you're...*camping,*"
Said he dryly, his gray eyes twinkling stars.
"It seems I am drawn here by the heavens
Here to make my home inside this tent,
For to the nose of a gnome there is nothing more clear
Than the scent of a woman as she masturbates."

He dropped his tiny drawers to masturbate
And, as he did, I forgot all about camping.
Confused I was, but in sooth, one thing was clear—
This gnome's cock could threaten all the stars
Of my earlier fantasy; and what good's a tent
If not to screw a gnome preordained by the heavens?

And so smiled the heavens!
And no longer had I need to masturbate!
And so his red-coned hat tore through my tent!
And so blew up his pouch of things for camping!
For small Gnostic/Gnomic/Paracelsusian lovers come to us like stars
And we must take away our fingers to make their entry clear.

No longer can I masturbate unless I think of camping—
What cursed stars, what blasphemous heavens
On a clear night sent a priapic gnome into my tent.


*I love repetition, for emphasis, or for comedy; I'm obsessed with that ephemeral moment when you repeat something just enough times that what was stupid, or pointless, or just boring suddenly becomes hilarious. And then, when you repeat it enough times that it stops being hilarious and then becomes stupid and pointless and boring again, which of course, it always was. So that was something I thought a lot about—what is something odd enough that the absurdity of the repetition will lift it to another realm?*

# Patricia Smith

## Looking to See How the Eyes Inhabit Dark, Wondering about Light

*In December 1999, Stevie Wonder sought to undergo an operation to partially restore his sight. He made the round of talk shows, trumpeting the possibilities, before the story dropped off the radar. Doctors had declared that he was not a good candidate for the procedure.*

*Look.* When he assumes he is alone, he absently claws the air for light.
See how he pulls the sun toward himself. Even as he conjures,
    wonders,
eyes spit their cruel blanks, drench him in mud. His mama is the
    dark;
dark is his daddy. A shiver in his lids becomes his next church, his
    eyes
wonder at the black bottomless flash, the siphoning of narrative. He
    can see
light as it exists in memory—lush, fleeting, then maddening. *Made ya
    look.*

Darkness strives to be his comfort. But he is obsessed by the need to
    look,
eyes flat, roiling, his head adjusting *as if*. He tilts toward each tongue
    of light,
wonders at its evil sweet, squints, strains. Dark whispers, *if you must see,
see the gifts I have given*—the unflinching knowledge of self, the wild
    wonder
light has birthed in you, how it blooms without answer. He touches
    his eye.
*Look.* He lifts the lid, pokes the dead orb with a finger, cries out again
    to dark.

Seasons change only on his skin. Chill and steam nudge the edges of
    dark.
Wondering what year, what June, what clock it is, his useless eyes
    look,

light upon layered shadow, scan the unraveled empty. He curses
those eyes,
eyes that simply loll and water and grow impossibly wide, clawing for
light.
Look how completely he has learned the language of the hand, stark
wonder
darkening weary palms as he presses them flat against against,
wanting to see.

Eyes, they say, can be sexed, propped wide, flooded with daybreak.
He'll see
lightning, dim dance, maybe a minute of day. Doctors tout the
shattered dark,
look beneath trembling lids for doors, promise his child's face. And
he wonders—
wonder being the only response he trusts—as hope is unleashed. It
hurts to look.
Dark, desperately clutching, woos him, redefines beauty as the
absence of light.
See his torso ripple, how he fights with his own fingers, how he
weeps for eyes.

Wonder how long it will take before those who whisper the promise
of eyes
look hard at the one-soul religion they've crafted, scan their data and
finally see
dark as it owns him—numb to their screeching miracles,
overpowering the light?
Light is overrated, they decide. Best not to shock the system, rip
holes in the dark,
see up close the cacophonous stanzas sight scribbles over time. It
hurts to look.
Eyes overwork, tangle lessons best learned by touch. It's much safer
to wonder.

Light a match, wave it back and forth, watch him follow the waltzing
heat. Wonder,
darkly, what hollow blessings he has left to cling to. He follows music
with his eyes,

sees the notes rollick black upon black. He snakes his balding head,
   pretends to look,
looking like a man who has never watched another man move. Now
   it's easy to see—
eyes would ruin him. Shadow puppets have answered every question.
   The dark,
wonderful, forgiving, takes his hand and leads him, like a lover, away
   from the light.

*Light simply makes us wonder and crave the dark.*
*I've seen how desperately you look for me.*


*I have about a million little tiny wire-rimmed notebooks. I carry one with me always, to jot down ideas, discoveries, uncanny description, little news items, recollections, oddities, snippets of conversation, anything that might eventually lead to a poem, a short story or an essay. Once I fill a notebook, I throw it into a little cardboard box. When one box is filled, I start to fill another box. That memory of Stevie making the rounds of the talk shows was buried in one of those notebooks for years. It wasn't until after I'd officially studied the sestina that I realized it was the form that story had been asking for. Once I had the six words, I had the engine that drove the poem forward. I just took advantage of the fact that the lines of the sestina don't have a set length, which allowed me to get much more "story" into the space. I'm always flirting with essay or short story, consciously blurring the lines between prose and poem. Most of my work is heavily narrative, so I'm frequently daring borders. I love a long, textured line.*

# JAY SNODGRASS

## *JUDAS PRIEST*


A hologram of antlers pierces my bankbook.
The clear blue invites me to confess.
On the street women twist subtle fingers.
They break my skull, switch holsters
for a clearer shot at my head.
When I think of you I'm filled with opposition.

In outer space, up-start contestants position
airy thoughts thick as the cream in the book
of my brain, digital recordings in my head
seeping through my eyes they confess
of their own brutal concentration, holster
the rain through the path stones like fingers

tickling the wind chimes, tap demon finger
notes on the march. The popular position
is animal feet, her legs up in holsters.
I step up the pace with my stretching the book
until the funeral flowers delineate, confess
to the popular media who peeks over your head

leaving nothing picked-over to get ahead
of the channels making her choices, slick fingers
to order this, inimical smacked skin, confess
to the flowers, debarred flowers resisting positions
of submission, petals raised high like the book
says as chain link fences, posts in their holsters

her modern casements, empty pistol holsters
like barriers and breezes holding up her head
so your shadow-blitz won't go to her head
the twisted valley of joints, falling finger
adjusts as birds on electric wires to the on position
of film screens touch their valley lips to confess.

What makes me a holy man is I confess
to putting the gun back alone in its holster.
But to Fashion I'm just a face in the right position
to be baton-worthy beaten, crack my wide head
into a smile, so much an apparition of fingers
pulling open just the right red pages of a book.

The fingers, I'm afraid, positioned between strangers.
My fear is the book of enraged billboards, holstered.
My head is the color of gas station attendants' uniforms.

# SPARROW

## *COWBOYS*

Cowboys often read the newspaper
As they lie beneath Polaris (a star);
They most enjoy reading gossip columns,
Especially about tennis pros
And rich blonde widowed millionairesses
Who live in Panama Beach, Florida.

Cowboys imagine that in Florida,
Under a bulging sky, a newspaper
Covers the face of a millionairess
As **Rod Stewart,** the renowned blond pop star,
Struts by, with a margarita a pro
Bartender mixed (an Irish guy named Colum).

In the cowboy-imagined scene, a column
(White) supports **Paris Hilton,** Florida
Vacationer, drinking with a golf pro
Named Eduardo. The next day's newspaper
Will report them necking beneath the stars
Outside the mansion of a millionairess

In Palm Beach, where many millionairesses
Find their names—in bold—in **Liz Smith**'s column,
Linked with **Ben Affleck,** the megastar,
Sojourning briefly in Florida
Before his next movie (the newspapers
Reveal): a cop/suspense flick called *The Pro,*

Costarring **Sandra Bullock,** and pro-
Duced by **Ron Hanler,** whose millionairess
Wife, **Meg Ryan,** is in the newspaper—
Actually, in **Rex Reed**'s column—
Because her new film, shot in Florida
(Tampa), is a hit. And now Meg's star

Will rise again. Her fans rejoice. "Real stars,"
Observes the Cowboy, who is a pro-
Fessional horseman, "can be in Florida,
Maine, anywhere—with millionairesses,
Roughnecks, cops—they spread magic." A column
Of campfire smoke lifts over the newspaper:

Photos of rock stars, millionairesses,
Pro wrestlers; **Dave Barry**'s humor column
(From Florida). The Cowboy burns his paper.

# HEIDI LYNN STAPLES

## EMBRYONIC SESTINA

I don't know what we were expecting
when we took off our clothes, lay down together,
got up, lit a candle, put on some music,
got down, put it in, did the ol' in-n-out, the kiss
kiss, the go ahead, the it's about time don't you think?
We are in our thirties. And ready. Pretty much. Maybe.

Each of us lives that gropeful life of the scribe;
so, when I knocked on his door, he was expecting
his ordinary miracle—black ink
on a blank page, a story begun. Rather,
"What do you see?" "One line." "Look again." His
eyes asquint, he held in the light the stick...

"Two lines. I see two lines." Our eyes click-
ed, seemingly in slow-motion, in disbe-
lief. Soon, we were in bed again. Tho' this
time not talking, barely touching, expecting
nothing more than the tender sight of the other
smiling, staying sweet like that till the brink

of dawn, the new day's light lit in blues and pinks.
Lovely. Until I started in with the feeling sick,
everything about body a bother,
no matter that I'd read, heard, knew sick to be
true, this was not what I was expecting—
ick-blech-retch wretched as the later Isis,

fears of hepatitis, toxoplasmosis,
listeriosis. "No soft cheeses." "No adult drinks."
"Oh! No you can't bike/roller-skate/ski. You're expecting!"
"Now hold your arm still—You'll feel a little prick."
"Oh no, you'll never quite get rid of the flabby."
"Rest now. Soon, you'll never get a breather!"

Then, inside, a feeling like a change in the weather.
Swims like the breeze in the trees and the light amiss,
a rippling water—what's that? That's the baby.
Kickingly soft as an eye-lash kiss. In the blink
of a quiet, quietly quick the quick-
ening. One cell unfolded unto expecting

a mother, a father, O what are you expecting
of this tribe, this globe, once a microbe, old magic
link with all that ever was and will be? This is…

# MARK STRAND

## CHEKHOV: A SESTINA

Why him? He woke up and felt anxious. He was out of sorts,
out of character. If only it would go away. Ivashin loved Nadya
Vishnyevskaya and was afraid of his love. When the butler told him
the old lady had just gone out, but that the young lady was at home,
he fumbled in his fur coat and dresscoat pocket, found his card,
and said: "Right." But it was not right. Driving from his house in
the morning to pay a visit, he thought he was compelled to it by
the conventions of society which weighed heavily upon him. But
now it was clear that he went to pay calls only because somewhere
far away in the depths of his soul, as under a veil, there lay hidden a
hope that he would see Nadya, his secret love. And he suddenly felt
pitiful, sad, and not a little anxious. In his soul, it seemed to him, it
was snowing, and everything was fading away. He was afraid to love
Nadya, because he thought he was too old for her, his appearance
unattractive, and did not believe that a young woman like her could
love a man for his mind or spiritual character. Everything was dim,
sharing, he felt, the same blank character. Still, there would rise at
times in him something like hope, a glimpse of happiness, of things
turning out all right. Then, just as quickly, it would pass away.
And he would wonder what had come over him. Why should he, a
retired councillor of state, educated, liberal-minded, a well-traveled
man; why should he, in other words, be so anxious? Were there
not other women with whom he could fall in love? Surely, it was
always possible to fall in love. It was possible, moreover, to fall in
love without acting out of character. There was absolutely no need
for him to be anxious. To be in love, to have a young pretty wife and
children of his own, was not a crime or a deception, but his right.
Clearly, there was something wrong with him. He wished he were
far away … But suddenly he hears from somewhere in the house the
young officer's spurs jingle and then die away. That instant marked
the death of his timid love. And in its vanishing, he felt the seeds
of a different sort of melancholy take root within him. Whatever
happened now, whatever desolation might be his, it would build
character. Yes, he thought, so it is only right. Yes, all is finished, and

I'm glad, very glad, yes, and I'm not let down, no, nor am I in any way anxious. No, certainly not anxious. What he had to do now was to get away. But how could he make it look right? How could he have thought he was in love? How out of character! How very unlike him!

# CHRIS STROFFOLINO

## *IN MEMORY OF MY ROCK BAND: SESTINA*

Your "trickle down" band sounds sterile! So at the next rehearsal
You have to break out into a groove, even though your guitarist
Has moved to Boston, though he hasn't exactly quit the band.
Perhaps you should be "groping for a new sound" while waiting
To see if any labels will bite on your classic last. You can't rest
On laurels in the disktrays, walkmans & iPods of your many friends

In low places. You don't want to brag or think of your friends
As misguided, flatterers, nor of all the parties as but rehearsal
Rooms for the "big chance" on which you quixotically rest
Your hopes to bypass the local scene confines like your guitarist
Did by giving up his "unrealistic needs" he got sick of waiting
To see fulfilled in opting for a family instead of a band

But the woman he moved to be with is also in a band.
Can it last if he chose her over his bands and friends
And in the process made himself vulnerable, by waiting
When she's out schmoozing at shows or at her own rehearsals
While he spends nights alone trying to forget he's a guitarist?
You try to give him advice, but your envy gets in the way. Let it rest

Or "Let It Be" as Paul said in his jealousy toward Yoko. The rest
Sided with John, and even played with The Plastic Ono Band,
But you're afraid you'll sound like Wings, and, damn, you miss your guitarist!
He was someone to perform with as well as one of your best friends.
Without him you feel empty as the post-*Tim* Replacements at rehearsals
And performances. The drummer and bassist are getting tired of waiting

For you to book another gig, and you're sick of waiting
For them to lock in to the pocket. But you can't rest
So you bring a new batch of songs to teach them at rehearsals
And they like them, but you feel less a member of a band
Than a "singer songwriter" playing songs for friends
Who happen to be a rhythm section, and damn you need a guitarist

(Or a better drummer who can keep up with a smart woman bass-guitarist!)
To make up for your inability to play more than chords while waiting
For the instrumental bridge in which to solo, or some new friends
Who happen to run a cheap analog recording studio to help the rest
Of the musicians realize you can excel through overdubs as a studio band
And thus get on the radio for which your live gigs have been but a rehearsal...

Airwaves or bust! Sterile! Maybe you and your girlfriend could be a band!
With her, rehearsals are not waiting rooms, nor a mere excuse to
    hang out with friends
Or shop for a new drinking buddy who just happens to be a mean guitarist.

*Starting with a "formal problem" and taking relatively randomly chosen words
that balance more "general" or "universal" words (friends, rest, and waiting)
with more specific words ("rehearsal," "guitarist," "band") seemed like a good
recipe for creation of this sestina, especially since the word "rest" is commonly
used in at least two different ways. I had no idea when I began it what I
was going to say, but I knew that it would focus on the social relationships
of bands: how many bands, whether good or not, whether famous or not,
become dysfunctional families. Once the form is established in a sestina, the
task is to see if those end words can actually create some kind of narrative. If
it manages to "say something" that can reach the prose intelligence, I always
consider that "gravy." Some "rock critic" talk emerges alongside the confession
(Replacements, Beatles), but I was just primarily happy that I sustained the
form, with some humor and "music," regardless of what I was saying!*

# Jade Sylvan

## Facebook Sestina

Par-human, hairless palms once reached to build
a fire to supply a warming light
for weary gatherings of kin and friends.
They huddled round the burning glow to share
fresh meat, new information, and the like,
or maybe to forget they were alone.

As usual, it took one man alone
whose feet caught in a need. He paused to build
a novelty that radiated like
theodicy imbued with sacred light
and drew lone hunters in to rest and share.
A chosen few were honored as his friends.

They gathered, gaunt and staggering, now friends,
from hauling heavy secrets all alone
with open mouths and fingers, parched to share
their blueprints just to see what they could build
together, and the weight became so light
soon no one could recall what it was like.

We've all been interwoven. I mean, like,
intertwined and twisted with our friends.
Like how a basket looks so frail and light
and each one of its reeds would tear alone,
but when they bear each other they can build
a vessel strong enough to hold its share.

Hold on to questions too sedate to share,
like, "Are we what we are or what we like?"
There will be time for that, but first we build.
Your friends like you and you like all your friends,
which should incite the spark to move alone.
We've lots to do before we lose the light.

Perhaps these structures strike you oddly light.
Perhaps you've mortared more than your fair share
and pulled the curtains, certain you're alone,
to ask the floorboards if you even like
those rough experiments you call your friends,
the visage of proclivities they build.

Then, all alone, you stare into the light
and build to bridge the hollows we all share,
eyes burning flint like memories of friends.


*I was at a human evolution exhibit in the Natural History Museum in
D.C. a couple years ago, and they had one of those "Evolution of Humans"
timelines. You know the type: long line with little illustrations of Cro-
Magnons with evolutionary turning-points marked at things like "Developing
Language" and "Burying the Dead." This one had marked "Gathering
at the Hearth" as one of these turning-points. I've always been interested in
evolution, and I've seen a ton of these timelines, but I'd never seen "Gathering
at the Hearth" listed alongside "Fashioning Tools" as a major event in human
evolution. I realized that this was the earliest form of networking, and that the
reason the scientists suddenly considered networking to be an intrinsic part of
being human was probably things like Facebook. The sestina form fit perfectly.
I decided to use half Facebook words ("like," "friends," "share") and half
non-Facebook words ("light," "alone," "build") as the repeated words. Then
it was just a puzzle.*

# DAVID TRINIDAD
## *DETECTIVE NOTES*

Mrs. White with the Candlestick in the Hall
Prof. Plum with the Lead Pipe in the Lounge
Col. Mustard with the Rope in the Dining Room
Mrs. Peacock with the Wrench in the Kitchen
Mr. Green with the Revolver in the Conservatory
Miss Scarlett with the Knife in the Study

Prof. Plum with the Knife in the Study
Col. Mustard with the Candlestick in the Hall
Mrs. Peacock with the Lead Pipe in the Library
Mr. Green with the Rope in the Lounge
Miss Scarlett with the Wrench in the Kitchen
Mrs. White with the Revolver in the Ball Room

Col. Mustard with the Revolver in the Billiard Room
Mrs. Peacock with the Knife in the Study
Mr. Green with the Candlestick in the Kitchen
Miss Scarlett with the Lead Pipe in the Hall
Mrs. White with the Rope in the Lounge
Prof. Plum with the Wrench in the Library

Mrs. Peacock with the Wrench in the Conservatory
Mr. Green with the Revolver in the Dining Room
Miss Scarlett with the Knife in the Lounge
Mrs. White with the Candlestick in the Study
Prof. Plum with the Lead Pipe in the Hall
Col. Mustard with the Rope in the Kitchen

Mr. Green with the Rope in the Kitchen
Miss Scarlett with the Wrench in the Library
Mrs. White with the Revolver in the Hall
Prof. Plum with the Knife in the Billiard Room
Col. Mustard with the Candlestick in the Study
Mrs. Peacock with the Lead Pipe in the Lounge

Miss Scarlett with the Lead Pipe in the Lounge
Mrs. White with the Rope in the Kitchen
Prof. Plum with the Wrench in the Study
Col. Mustard with the Revolver in the Conservatory
Mrs. Peacock with the Knife in the Ball Room
Mr. Green with the Candlestick in the Hall

Mrs. White with the Candlestick in the Lounge
Prof. Plum with the Rope in the Kitchen
Col. Mustard with the Revolver in the Study


*I think of "Detective Notes" as a kind of anti-sestina. I chose the form because the six end words matched the six suspects in the Clue game. I thought it would be fun to mull over the various combinations of suspects, murder weapons, and rooms in the context of a sestina—the poor detective overcome with choices—and that that would point out the ridiculousness of the form. It turned out to be excruciatingly difficult to write. You have to surrender to the form, the rules of the game, and trust that you will be led to a satisfying conclusion, that the poem will hold together. There's no way of knowing, when you're in the middle of writing the thing, if it will all work out. The poet Tim Dlugos, talking about the sestina, called this "driving in the dark."*

# PLAYING WITH DOLLS

Every weekend morning, I'd sneak downstairs to play
with my sisters' Barbie dolls. They had all
of them: Barbie, Ken, Allan, Midge, Skipper and
Skooter. They even had the little freckled boy,
Ricky ("Skipper's Friend"), and Francie, "Barbie's
'MOD'ern cousin." Quietly, I'd set the dolls

in front of their wardrobe cases, take the dolls'
clothes off miniature plastic hangers, and play
until my father woke up. There were several Barbies—
blonde ponytail, black bubble, brunette flip—all
with the same pointed tits, which (odd for a boy)
didn't interest me as much as the dresses and

accessories. I'd finger each glove and hat and
necklace and high heel, then put them on the dolls.
Then I'd invent elaborate stories. A "creative" boy,
I could entertain myself for hours. I liked to play
secretly like that, though I often got caught. All
my father's tirades ("Boys don't play with Barbies!

It isn't *normal!*") faded as I slipped Barbie's
perfect figure into her stunning ice blue and
sea green satin and tulle formal gown. All
her outfits had names like "Fab Fashion," "Doll's
Dream" and "Golden Evening"; Ken's were called "Play
Ball!," "Tennis Pro," "Campus Hero" and "Fountain Boy,"

which came with two tiny sodas and spoons. Model boy
that he was, Ken hunted, fished, hit home runs. Barbie's
world revolved around garden parties, dances, play
and movie dates. A girl with bracelets and scarves and
sunglasses and fur stoles. . . . "Boys don't play with dolls!"
My parents were arguing in the living room. "All

boys do." As always, my mother defended me. "All
*sissies!*" snarled my father. "He's a creative boy,"
my mother responded. I stuffed all the dresses and dolls
and shoes back into the black cases that said "Barbie's
Wonderful World" in swirling pink letters and
clasped them shut. My sisters, awake now, wanted to play

with me. "I can't play," I said, "Dad's upset." All
day, he stayed upset. Finally, my mother came upstairs and said: "You're a boy,
David. Forget about Barbies. Stop playing with dolls."


*When I wrote "Playing with Dolls" in the early 90s, I was experimenting
with combining subjects from popular culture with traditional poetic forms.
Barbie seemed the perfect choice for the sestina. There was something
fetishistic about the repetition of the end words—like fondling the doll's
accessories. I always felt I had cheated by using "and" as one of the six words.
Years later, I heard Suzanne Buffam teach the poem, and she talked about the
way "and" functioned with the other end words: "boys and Barbies," "boys
and dolls." How that added, almost tauntingly, to the sense that it was wrong
for the boy to be interested in dolls. I felt quite smart listening to her justify my
use of a conjunction as an end word.*

# QUINCY TROUPE

## SESTINA FOR 39 SILENT ANGELS

there was no screaming to announce hale-bopp comet's second tail,
no screaming when those 39 people left their bodies—
their containers—behind, covered their faces with purple
silk shrouds, folded triangles, lay down smiling & fell into the steep sleep
marshall applewhite had prescribed for them deep inside that death
mansion in rancho santa fe, they knew themselves as angels,

sleuths at creating web sites, cruising the internet, space angels
flying on wings of ancient dreams upward to hale-bopp comet's tail,
(& the only way to get there through the invisible doorway of death)
launched through skies of their minds, they willed their bodies
on earth, as people of jonestown did, to be recycled through sleep,
bodies board-stiff & bloated, looking for peace, skin purple,

going black as the clothes they wore, covered 39 faces with purple
symbols the color of lenten holy week when jesus rose up to join angels,
39 travelers wore black nike shoes, weaved through 39 catacombs of sleep,
dreamed themselves up like 39 shooting stars to hale-bopp comet's tail
of silver ice, where they would transform their bodies—
18 buzz-haired castrated males, 21 females surfing death's

internet—to pass through heaven's-gate's needle eye—& death
not even a stopover here for these souls to rest dressed in black & purple,
quarters for phone calls, 5 dollar bills for whatever urges their bodies
needed—before flying through space 39 dreams, they would be truly angels
rendezvousing with the mothership hidden inside hale-bopp comet's tail,
live with extraterrestrials there in a sleeve of silver ice after sleep

cut them loose to flow through steep mystery above as sleep
like rocket fuel fell away over stages, left them asphyxiated in death
after phenobarbital, apple sauce, & vodka, they knew the silver ice tail
as the sign they were waiting for to cover themselves with shrouds of purple,
leave behind computer screens—skies—they flew purely as angels
now toward a higher source than conflicting urges of their bodies—

a tangle of web sites, conquered & controlled, their bodies—
surrendering the improvisation of living, they swam in sleep,
drifting slowly as motorless boats on the sea—were homeless angels,
took 39 pot pies & cheese cakes for their journey, they kissed death
hard with dry mouths, 39 people down from 1000, pursed lips of purple
open in wonder, they flew up to enter hale-bopp comet's tail

of silver ice particles, gaseous bodies grinning there like death
skulls flashing inside sleep, inside where eye am dreaming now of purple,
faith flashing bright as new angels inside hale-bopp comet's third tail

# Lewis Turco

## The Vision

It came upon me while I was on the crapper
of my father's parsonage, my eyes
boring into the porcelain of the tiles
before me on the wall. The tiles were white.
They spread across the vacancy of time
that seeped into my mind and filled that blank

jug of puberty with a vast Mont Blanc
of sorrow and ennui. On that crapper
I saw that I would have to fill up time
with something more than the nothing that met my eyes,
the emptiness that seeped out of those white
ranges of porcelain whose trackless tiles

led finally to death. I feared those tiles
worse than I feared my death, that ultimate blank-
ness waiting for me on the snowy white
crest of age. I saw life was a crapper
that had to be filled with something. If I closed my eyes
perhaps I could dream myself to a better time

than this one snowing before me. There was no time
to dream. What could I do? I could fill tiles
with words. I could write. I filled my eyes
with reading every day; I could fill blank
sheets with my own words. I rose off that crapper
thinking I might pave my way with white

sheaves laden with stories, poems—I could write
my way to death by filling my living tome
with endless lines of type till I came-a-cropper
at last and alas! perhaps, on the devil's tines,
if I kept my gaze steady and didn't blink,
and if I did not try to romanticize

my life with gods and demons, with the sighs
of wishful thinking, with the little white
lies of religion that covered up the blank
of existence with the stuff that fills a crapper.
I pulled myself out of the abyss of tiles
ready to take on life and move in time.

I'd use my eyes to read. Perhaps in time
I'd use those words to write, to fill up tiles
with something more than blankness on that crapper.


*Everything in "The Vision" is true and accurate, as I remember it. What you read as your eyes walk through it is what happened. It was a true, if weird, vision, and what I decided to do with my life after I experienced it is what I have done.*

# Laura Van Prooyen

## *Lenten Sestina*

A carpenter vows to give up
the buzz of his saws and promises forty days
of rotating blades in silence. Without
sound he meditates on the way
he splinters the board, and himself; the scent
of wood, a surprising delicacy that stirs

his thoughts to the woman who once stirred
in his bed. Surely, he thinks, she has given up
chocolate and is driven mad by its scent.
He recently stopped counting the days
since he'd seen her, but the way
she twisted hair around her finger leaves him without

defense. He knows why he must be without
her, but in this noiseless vacuum his head stirs
down the spiraling staircase to the way
her back arched when she lifted up
but not quite off—hours seemed to melt into days.
When she had to go, he would not shower her scent

off his skin. This love, this woman, had sent
prudence off packing; he was left simply without
judgment. He breaks with a cigarette, smokes in a daze,
wonders at how the wing of such a lovely bird stirs
the air, forever changing what has been known up
to this point. Self-inflicted penance of silence—a way

to make amends with himself and try to discover the way
back to something divine. The fresh and earthy scent
of wood, he hopes, will conjure up
some vision of Christ. For years he has been without
much heavenly conviction, so he waits for something to stir
his spirit. The answer, he concedes, must be in these forty days.

His saws have been ordered quiet for less than a day,
but already his morning work has offered way
to small solace. He did not consider, however, that stirring
his coffee would clink the spoon or the scent
of rich cream would leave him without
remorse, make him lift his eyes up,

but stir his spirit further from the cross and send
him longing for past days, asking no forgiveness for the way
he lived without conscience and loved until his strength was used up.


*I used the sestina form for "Lenten Sestina" for the way it accommodated
the cyclical nature of (perhaps my own) faith and doubt. At the time I was
composing this poem, a neighbor was building a shed. His saws were so blasted
loud, I couldn't think. I willed them silent. I imagined how great it would be
to have that power, to render particular sounds silent. So the carpenter in the
poem rotates through memory and desire, belief in and the urge to denounce his
god.*

# Martha Modena Vertreace-Doody

## *Señora Mamacita*

*a sprung sestina*

### i/

Pregnant, Luisa mobiles crocheted lanterns in paper
nets above the empty crib. Nine months
into her waiting, she carries the child who already knows
her voice until moist twilight. Her womb
decides it will be so, unlike two others, babies
entering months too soon,
leaping from blackness to utter black,
world to world.
She pillows my head
as if to cradle me, make me the girl she bears,
drown me in her sea-salt blood
under the embroidered yoke of her dress
where I lie dreaming that my mother
is a mermaid,

### ii/

that my mother
has spelled my name
on her heart's valves, aorta, its paper-
thin walls, as I breathe my moist breath
believing all oceans fill with her blood.
Time was, my mother pressed news clippings in her books,
old photos whose triangular edges she knew
would stand out among four-leafed clovers
which burned their shadows in my head.
Clovers like a ghostly garden, or memory
of a garden I crawled in as a baby.
On her knees in her modern kitchen, grinding corn
on her *metate,* the flat pestle her black
grandmother had used, her mother as well,

### iii/

Luisa corrects my *gringa* Spanish, teaching me black
magic names for grief: *mamá* and *murió* and *muerte*.
I imagine I am her bones, the mother
of her flesh tight across my face and hands.
She tells me to name the baby,
her belly sieving my whisper like wind
through a field of clematis whose papery
leaves beg for words, but *do not write it down*
she tells me, touching my head
with her lips, *do not let paper own her name*
*before she does.* A question of blood.
A storm is coming, the bruise of sky wrapping the trees.
Evening rides hollow feathers of knowing
fish hawks whose wings split the washed air

### iv/

without a sound. On the last night of spring, knowing
what I know, I will wash a linen handkerchief
then drape it over a rosebush. When it dries, the black
moon of morning writes the name of the husband I do not want
in the folds, the print of a bloodless
sacrifice to the god of love. My aunt names me
"John's niece," as if my dark mother
haunts the bare walls of my house, as if "Martha" is half
the story; "John," the other half, head
of the light-skinned family my aunt keeps from me like money
I have not earned, John's sister's black baby.
My aunt brands my hands with his mark,
a wordless wound copied on blank paper,
proof of having survived, his genes intact,

## v/

his brown eyes brooding through mine; like mine, his paper
lenses scratched by the truth of voices behind closed doors.
Time is amber, the matter of all life. Luisa knows
hydrogen/ nitrogen/ oxygen/ carbon; believes talismans keep her fat.
I trust my uncle's homegrown Appalachian jack stories: a baby
springs up, made of mountain ash to fend off witches, warning
against killing things in sevens—pine cones, black
beetles, pigeons in the chokecherry. Standing at the foot
of my bed, my mother came to wake me, kiss my forehead,
say good-bye, good-bye, good-bye, holding onto the moment
until I could see her. My blood
could feel her clip the tops of mango trees, cull purple fruit,
the sweet roundness of a mother's
breasts, over vines weaving hand-print leaves

## vi/

into the gate trellis where my mother
had let me pick grapes, figs, mulberries—anything grown wild.
With her wooden clothespins shaped like women, I hung paper
dolls from the tendrils. In the downtown park,
Picasso's woman shoulders a jug as if her own blood
sloshed inside, all one bronze movement—
from head, torso, cavity of navel to cleft—knowing
how to walk without crushing the jagged teeth of dandelions,
as if everything—everything rests near her head;
as if Earth's center spins backwards inside its skin.
She leaves footprints in the air for Luisa's baby
to follow if she wanders too far. On a grocery bag,
Luisa draws Red Horn, her father's god, with a child's black
crayon, calls the sketch a torch whose flame

## Envoy/

only unborn babies touch without burning. And so?
And so Luisa points to a peacock screeching omens,
its thousand blue-black eyes sequin
the Floridian heat. Half-blind, I hear
a wasp buzz against the paper door he seeks
in the dragonfly's wings
without knowing he seeks.
Feeder bands of silent lightning
mark the western edge of the hurricane while the child's head
crests at her opening. Chestnut mares stand
hoofdeep in flood runoff, watching a new mother
born of pure moonlight, Jupiter spinning, brilliant above the dark
as I help Luisa, be for her the mother she does not have,
my hands run red with her *mestiza* blood.

*At a writers' workshop in Dublin, Ireland, one of the writers had a sestina.*
*At that time, I had never heard of a sestina. The movement of the poem*
*fascinated me. After I came back, I tried to write one for myself. The form*
*seems to control the movement. The process was similar to learning to speak*
*another language! Somewhere, I ran into the idea of writing a sprung sestina.*
*"Señora Mamacita" is the only one I've written. I found myself arguing*
*with the repetitions. Later, I started writing the traditional sestina, which has*
*become my favorite poetic form. The sestina seems to demand a certain amount*
*of willingness to let the poem steer itself. I find that as I write a sestina, the*
*poem seems to take a different turn than I had expected.*

# ANNE WALDMAN

## HOW THE SESTINA (YAWN) WORKS

I opened this poem with a yawn
thinking how tired I am of revolution
the way it's presented on television
isn't exactly poetry
You could use some more methedrine
if you ask me personally

People should be treated personally
there's another yawn
here's some more methedrine
Thanks! Now about this revolution
What do you think? What is poetry?
Is it like television?

Now I get up to turn off the television
Whew! It was getting to me personally
I think it is like poetry
Yawn    it's 4 AM yawn    yawn
This new record is one big revolution
if you were listening you'd understand methedrine

isn't the greatest drug no not methedrine
it's no fun for watching television
You want to jump up have a revolution
about something that affects you personally
When you're busy and involved you never yawn
it's more like feeling, like energy, like poetry

I really like to write poetry
it's more fun than grass, acid, THC, methedrine
If I can't write I start to yawn
and it's time to sit back, watch television
see what's happening to me personally:
war, strike, starvation, revolution

This is a sample of my own revolution
taking the easy way out of poetry
I want it to hit you all personally
like a shot of extra-strong methedrine
so you'll become your own television
Become your own yawn!

O giant yawn, violent revolution
silent television, beautiful poetry
most deadly methedrine
                    I choose all of you for my poem personally

# MILLER WILLIAMS

## THE SHRINKING LONESOME SESTINA

Somewhere in everyone's head something points toward home,
a dashboard's floating compass, turning all the time
to keep from turning. It doesn't matter how we come
to be wherever we are, someplace where nothing goes
the way it went once, where nothing holds fast
to where it belongs, or what you've risen or fallen to.

What the bubble always points to,
whether we notice it or not, is home.
It may be true that if you move fast
everything fades away, that given time
and noise enough, every memory goes
into the blackness, and if new ones come—

small, mole-like memories that come
to live in the furry dark—they, too,
curl up and die. But Carol goes
to high school now. John works at home
what days he can to spend some time
with Sue and the kids. He drives too fast.

Ellen won't eat her breakfast.
Your sister was going to come
but didn't have the time.
Some mornings at one or two
or three I want you home
a lot, but then it goes.

It all goes.
Hold on fast
to thoughts of home
when they come.
They're going to
less with time.

Time
goes
too
fast.
Come
home.

Forgive me that. One time it wasn't fast.
A myth goes that when the quick years come
then you will, too. Me, I'll still be home.

# JONAH WINTER

## SESTINA: BOB

According to her housemate, she is out with Bob
tonight, and when she's out with Bob
you never know *when* she'll get in. Bob
is an English professor. Bob
used to be in a motorcycle gang, or something, or maybe Bob
rides a motorcycle now. How radical of you, Bob—

I wish I could ride a motorcycle, Bob,
and also talk about Chaucer intelligently. Bob
is very tall, bearded, reserved. I saw Bob
at a poetry reading last week—he had such a Bob-
like poise—so quintessentially Bob!
The leather jacket, the granny glasses, the beard—Bob!

and you were with my ex-girlfriend, Bob!
And you're a professor, and I'm nobody, Bob,
nobody, just a flower-deliverer, Bob,
and a skinny one at that, Bob—
and you are a large person, and I am small, Bob,
and I hate my legs, Bob,

but why am I talking to you as if you were here, Bob?
I'll try to be more objective. Bob
is probably a nice guy. Or that's what one hears. Bob
is not, however, the most passionate person named Bob
you'll ever meet. Quiet, polite, succinct, Bob
opens doors for people, is reticent in grocery stores. Bob

does not talk about himself excessively to girlfriends. Bob
does not have a drinking problem. Bob
does not worry about his body, even though he's a little heavy. Bob
has never been in therapy. Bob,
also, though, does not have tenure—ha ha ha—*and* Bob
cannot cook as well as I can. Bob

never even heard of paella, and if he had, Bob
would not have changed his facial expression at all. Bob
is just so boring, and what I can't understand, Bob—
yes I'm talking to you again, is why you, Bob,
could be more desirable than me. Granted, Bob,
you're more stable, you're older, more mature *maybe* but Bob…

(Months later, on the Bob-front: My former girlfriend finally
      married Bob.
Of Bob, she says, "No one has taken me higher or lower than Bob."
Me? On a dark and stormy sea of Bob-thoughts, desperately, I bob.)


*I had been writing mainly incomprehensible graduate school garbage. I can't
remember how I came up with the idea for writing a sestina with only one
end-word. It just "came to me"…! I had been recently dumped by a woman
who was then dating a man named Bob. It was a painful, chaotic, and even
vaguely tragic time in my life—for a variety of reasons; being replaced by
a man named Bob was just the icing. Anyhow, I started viewing comedic
writing as a way of getting through these really dark periods. My goal, at
that point (and at many future points), was to crack myself up. When your
life has turned into a nightmare…, laugh! Also, I think the idea of mocking
a ridiculous poetic form really appealed to me—and continues to appeal to
me. As we know, with the sestina form, there is just so much comic potential.
But… that's not a very funny sentence, is it?*

# Sestina: A Cowboy's Diary

May 14: Another miserable night. Rain
fell. Wind blew. Was on my horse the whole night.
Cattle left us. Not one beefe
to be seen. May 15: Hunt beeves
is the word. May 16: 195 beeves
recovered 14 miles from camp. Beeves

well near starved. May 18th: Indians came & tried to take our beeves.
Would not let them. May 19th: Scarfed jerky in rain.
May 22: Wind & rain & lightning: 200 beeves
got away. Was on my horse the whole night.
May 23rd: had to cross a river with beeves.
Was attacked by a beefe.

May 24th: Was attacked by another beefe!
May 27th: Dad-blamed beeves!
Stampede last night. Lost 2 men. Beeves
ungovernable. Rain
heavy at times. Can't recall a more miserable night.
May 30th: Beeves

ran, in the a.m. In the p.m., attended lecture on beeves
at local university. Very interesting. Found out that a beefe
will not defend his self against a beefe. That night,
hunt whores was the word. Found beeves
instead—100 of them. Another stampede in the rain.
Next morning we found more beeves.

June 1st: I thought I saw some beeves
but was mistaken. Went into town for counseling. Beeves
occupied my thoughts. When I close my eyes, I see rain
and that same strange image again and again: a beefe
with the body of a man is yodeling to the other beeves
who somehow turn into ladies of the night.

June 2nd: This cognitive approach seems to be working. Last night, only had one bad dream about beeves.
Therapist says: Lay off the beeves.
Gave me a great book called "Men Who Love Beeves
Too Much." Very insightful. It makes a good point about how a beefe don't care about me, and yet I give and give. June 3rd: Rain.

June 4th: More rain. June 5th: Hard night.
June 9th: Found one stray beefe. Then lost 3 beeves.
June 10th: Found beeves. June 12th: Lost beeves...


*Before I became a children's book author, I worked as a children's book editor at Knopf. And let me tell you, I saw some real stinkers from the unsolicited manuscript pile—which often inspired my adult poems! Let's face it, bad writing is just funny. This sestina was actually inspired by a real cowboy's diary from a young adult book about cowboys. That's where them thar "beeves" came from, I tell you whut.*

# Louis Zukofsky

## *Mantis*

Mantis! praying mantis! since your wings' leaves
And your terrified eyes, pins, bright, black and poor
Beg—"Look, take it up" (thoughts' torsion)! "save it!"
I who can't bear to look, cannot touch,—You—
You can—but no one sees you steadying lost
In the cars' drafts on the lit subway stone.

Praying mantis, what wind-up brought you, stone
On which you sometimes prop, prey among leaves
(Is it love's food your raised stomach prays?), lost
Here, stone holds only seats on which the poor
Ride, who rising from the news may trample you—
The shops' crowds a jam with no flies in it.

Even the newsboy who now sees knows it
No use, papers make money, makes stone, stone,
Banks, "it is harmless, " he says moving on—You?
Where will he put *you?* There are no safe leaves
To put you back in here, here's news! too poor
Like all the separate poor to save the lost.

Don't light on my chest, mantis! do—you're lost,
Let the poor laugh at my fright, then see it:
My shame and theirs, you whom old Europe's poor
Call spectre, strawberry, by turns; a stone—
You point—they say—you lead lost children—leaves
Close in the paths men leave, saved, safe with you.

Killed by thorns (once men), who now will save you
Mantis? what male love bring a fly, be lost
Within your mouth, prophetess, harmless to leaves
And hands, faked flower,—the myth is: dead, bones, it
Was assembled, apes wing in wind: On stone,
Mantis, you will die, touch, beg, of the poor.

Android, loving beggar, dive to the poor
As your love would even without head to you,
Graze like machined wheels, green, from off this stone
And preying on each terrified chest, lost
Say, I am old as the globe, the moon, it
Is my old shoe, yours, be free as the leaves.

Fly, mantis, on the poor, arise like leaves
The armies of the poor, strength: stone on stone
And build the new world in your eyes, Save it!

# ACKNOWLEDGMENTS

This book is very much a collective effort, and there are many people to acknowledge and thank. Thank you to my student assistants at The College of Saint Rose: Brenda Hanaburgh, Alex Tunney, Alexandra Korcz, and Jessica Furiani, all of whom helped with copying, researching, and interviewing the poets included here; to James Cummins and David Lehman, who encouraged and advised on this project at crucial periods; Frederick T. Courtright for immeasurable assistance in navigating the world of permissions; Cristin O'Keefe Aptowicz for relentless work as a confidence-building life coach; John Warner at *McSweeney's*, for taking me on as a sestina editor and in many ways starting me off on this sestina-editing journey; my colleagues in the English Department at The College of Saint Rose; Marj Hahne, for super-duper-proofing and emotional rescues; Keaton Maddox, for taking this baby past the finish line; Derrick Brown and everyone at Write Bloody for the courage to take this wacky project on; everyone who helped this project along, including, but not limited to, Sandra Beasley, Kathleen Rooney, Ernest Hilbert, Marilyn Nelson, Kevin Larimer, Jonah Winter, Michael Costello; and finally to my wife, Maisie Weissman, who supported this project in more ways than she knows. As Freddie Mercury sings, "I thank you all."

# CONTRIBUTOR NOTES

**Sherman Alexie** is the author of, most recently, *War Dances* (Grove Press), and *Face* (Hanging Loose Press). He is the winner of the 2010 PEN/Faulkner Award, 2007 National Book Award for Young People's Literature, 2001 PEN/Malamud Award for Excellence in the Short Story, and a Special Citation for the 1994 PEN/Hemingway Award for Best First Fiction. *Smoke Signals*, the film he wrote and co-produced, won the Audience Award and Filmmakers Trophy at the 1998 Sundance Film Festival. He lives with his family in Seattle.

**Shane Allison**'s editing career began with the best-selling gay erotic anthology *Hot Cops: Gay Erotic Stories* (Cleis Press), which was one of his proudest moments. Since the birth of his first anthology, he has gone on to publish over a dozen gay erotica anthologies such as *Straight Guys: Gay Erotic Fantasies, Cruising: Gay Erotic Stories, Middle Men: Gay Erotic Threesomes, Frat Boys: Gay Erotic Stories, Brief Encounters: 69 Hot Gay Shorts, College Boys: Gay Erotic Stories, Hardworking Men: Gay Erotic Fiction, Hot Cops: Gay Erotic Fiction, Backdraft: Fireman Erotica*, and *Afternoon Pleasures: Erotica for Gay Couples*. Allison's work has appeared in five editions of *Best Gay Erotica* and *Best Black Gay Erotica*. He is the author of *Slut Machine* (Queer Mojo) and the poem/memoir *I Remember* (Future Tense Books). Allison is at work on a novel and currently resides in Tallahassee, Florida.

**Steve Almond** is an American short story writer and essayist. He is the author of ten books, among them *Candyfreak: A Journey through the Chocolate Underbelly of America* (Mariner Books), *Rock and Roll Will Save Your Life* (Random House), and *God Bless America: Stories* (Lookout Books), as well as three books he has published himself.

**Scott Edward Anderson** has been a Concordia Fellow at the Millay Colony for the Arts, and received both the Nebraska Review Award and the Aldrich Emerging Poets Award. His work has appeared in the *Alaska Quarterly Review, Anon, Blueline, The Cortland Review, Cross Connect, Earth's Daughters, Isotope, La Petite Zine, Many Mountains Moving, Nebraska Review, Poetica, River Oak Review, Slant* and *Terrain*. He was a founding editor of *Ducky Magazine* and writes at TheGreenSkeptic.com and seapoetry. wordpress.com.

**Alan Ansen** (1922–2006) was the author of two books of poetry, *The Old Religion* (1959) and *Disorderly Houses: A Book of Poems* (1961). Born in Long Island, New York and educated at Harvard, Ansen was a widely-read scholar who knew many languages. Ansen worked as W. H. Auden's secretary and research assistant in 1948-9 and was the main author of the chronological tables in Auden's *The Portable Greek Reader* and *Poets of the English Language*.

**Cristin O'Keefe Aptowicz** is the author of six books of poetry, most recently *The Year of No Mistakes* (Write Bloody Publishing), as well as *Dear Future Boyfriend, Hot Teen Slut, Working Class Represent, Oh, Terrible Youth* and *Everything is Everything*. She is also the author of two books of nonfiction: *Words In Your Face: A Guided Tour Through Twenty Years of the New York City Poetry Slam* and *Curiosity: Thomas Dent Mütter and* *the Dawn of Modern Medicine*, forthcoming from Gotham Books/Penguin. Aptowicz's most recent awards include the ArtsEdge Writer-In-Residency at the University of Pennsylvania, a National Endowment for the Arts Fellowship in Poetry, and an Amy Clampitt Residency.

**John Ashbery** is the author of more than twenty books of poetry, most recently *Quick Question: New Poems* (Ecco). He has won nearly every major American award for poetry, including the Pulitzer Prize, the National Book Award, the Bollingen Prize, the Ruth Lilly Poetry Prize, the Griffin International Award, the MacArthur "Genius" Grant, and a National Humanities Medal presented by President Obama at the White House in 2012. Ashbery's first book, *Some Trees* (1956), won the Yale Younger Poets Prize, judged by W.H. Auden. Other books include *The Tennis Court Oath* (1962), *The Double Dream of Spring* (1970), *Self-Portrait in a Convex Mirror* (1975) and *Houseboat Days* (1977). Ashbery has also published *Other Traditions: The Charles Eliot Norton Lectures* (2000); *Reported Sightings* (1989), a book of art criticism; and a novel, *A Nest of Ninnies* (1969), with James Schuyler.

**W.H. Auden** (1907-1973) was the author of many works including books of poetry, collections of non-fiction writing, plays, and librettos. Auden is widely considered the (or one of the) greatest and most influential poets of the twentieth century. His work spans a wide range of forms and is noted for its incorporation of popular culture, current events and vernacular. He was a frequent collaborator with novelist and memoirist Christopher Isherwood. Auden received the Pulitzer Prize for Poetry in 1948, and was a Chancellor of the Academy of American Poets from 1954 until his death.

**Sandra Beasley** is the author of *I Was the Jukebox*, winner of the Barnard Women Poets Prize, and *Theories of Falling*, winner of the New Issues Poetry Prize. Honors for her work include the Lenoir-Rhyne University Writer in Residence position, the University of Mississippi Summer Poet in Residence position, a DCCAH Artist Fellowship, the Friends of Literature Prize from the Poetry Foundation, and the Maureen Egen Exchange Award from Poets & Writers. Her most recent book is *Don't Kill the Birthday Girl: Tales from an Allergic Life*, a memoir and cultural history of food allergy. She lives in Washington, D.C.

**Jeanne Marie Beaumont** is author of *Burning of the Three Fires* (BOA Editions, 2010), *Curious Conduct* (BOA, 2004), and *Placebo Effects*, a National Poetry Series winner (Norton, 1997). She coedited *The Poets' Grimm: 20th Century Poems from Grimm Fairy Tales*, and teaches at the 92nd St. Y and in the Stonecoast low-residency MFA program.

**Aaron Belz** lives in Hillsborough, North Carolina, and teaches at Durham Technical Community College. He has published two books of poetry, *The Bird Hoverer* (BlazeVOX, 2007) and *Lovely Raspberry* (Persea, 2010), and has a third forthcoming, *Glitter Bomb* (Persea, 2014). For more information, please visit belz.net.

**Tara Betts** is the author of *Arc and Hue*, a Ph.D. candidate at Binghamton University, and a Cave Canem fellow. Betts's work has appeared in *Essence, Bum Rush the Page*, Saul Williams's *CHORUS: A Literary Mixtape, VILLANELLES*, both *Spoken Word*

*Revolution* anthologies, and *A Face to Meet the Faces: An Anthology of Contemporary Persona Poetry.* She is co-editor, with Afaa M. Weaver, of *Bop, Strut, and Dance.*

**Elizabeth Bishop** (1911-1979) was an American poet and short story writer. Her work was noted for its wit and precision. She was the Poet Laureate of the United States from 1949 to 1950, received the Pulitzer Prize for Poetry in 1956 for her collection *Poems: North & South/A Cold Spring,* and was the winner of the National Book Award in 1970 for the collection *Complete Poems.* She was awarded two Guggenheim fellowships as well as an Academy of American Poets fellowship.

**Star Black**'s most recent book of poems, *Velleity's Shade,* was released by Saturnalia Books in 2010. She is the author of three books of sonnets, *Waterworn, Balefire,* and *Ghostwood;* a collection of double-sestinas, *Double Time;* and a book of free verse, *October for Idas.* Her collages have been exhibited at Poets House and The Center for Book Arts. Black currently works as a Visiting Assistant Professor at Stony Brook University and as a photographer based in New York.

**Paula Bohince** is the author of two poetry collections, both from Sarabande: *The Children* (2012) and *Incident at the Edge of Bayonet Woods* (2008).

**Jenny Boully** is the author of five books, most recently *of the mismatched teacups, of the single-serving spoon: a book of failures* (Coconut Books). Her other books include *not merely because of the unknown that was stalking toward them* (Tarpaulin Sky Press), *The Books of Beginnings and Endings* (Sarabande Books), *[one love affair]\** (Tarpaulin Sky Press), and *The Body: An Essay* (Essay Press). Her chapbook of prose, *Moveable Types,* was released by Noemi Press. Boully's work has been anthologized in *The Best American Poetry, The Next American Essay, Great American Prose Poems: From Poe to the Present,* and other places. She teaches at Columbia College Chicago.

**Geoff Bouvier**'s first book, *Living Room,* was selected by Heather McHugh as the 2005 APR/Honickman Prize winner and was published by Copper Canyon Press. His second book, *Glass Harmonica,* appeared in 2011 from Quale Press. In 2009, he served as the poet-in-residence at the University of California-Berkeley. For five years, he wrote long-form magazine journalism with *The San Diego Reader,* publishing over 50 cover stories. Bouvier's poems have appeared in such journals as *American Poetry Review, Boston Review, Denver Quarterly, Jubilat, New American Writing,* and *VOLT.* He holds an MFA from Bard College and is currently a Ph.D. student at Florida State University.

**Catherine Bowman**'s most recent poetry collection is *The Plath Cabinet* (Four Way Books, 2009). Her poems have appeared in literary journals and magazines including *TriQuarterly, River Styx, Conjunctions, Kenyon Review, Ploughshares, The Los Angeles Times, Crazy Horse, The New Yorker,* and *The Paris Review,* and in six editions of *The Best American Poetry.* Her honors include fellowships from Yaddo and the New York Foundation for the Arts. Bowman is Director of the Creative Writing Program at Indiana University, and also teaches at the Fine Arts Work Center in Provincetown. She lives in Bloomington, Indiana.

**Derrick C. Brown** is one of America's most beloved and well-travelled performing page poets. He is a former paratrooper for the 82nd Airborne and is the president of one of what *Forbes* and *Filter Magazine* call "one of the best independent presses in the country," Write Bloody Publishing. He is author of four books of poetry. *The New York Times* calls his work "a rekindling of faith in the weird, hilarious, shocking, beautiful power of words."

**Stephen Burt** is Professor of English at Harvard. His latest book of poetry is *Belmont* (Graywolf, 2013); earlier books of poetry and criticism include *Close Calls with Nonsense: Reading New Poetry, Parallel Play,* and *Randall Jarrell and His Age.*

**Casey Camp** is an artist, writer, and all-around fine gentleman. He loves to work at the intersection of poetry and visual art, typically within the bounds of sequential narrative art. Some people would just call this "comics." When not crafting art, he can typically be found getting his fix in any matter of competition that he can find nearby. No contest is too big or too small. He lives near Atlanta, Georgia with his wonderful wife, Emily, and daughter, Lennon.

**Jenna Cardinale** is the author of *Journals*, a chapbook from Coconut. Her poems have appeared in some really great places, including *Horse Less Review, Barn Owl Review,* and *A Sul de Nenhum Norte,* a magazine of writing translated into Portuguese. She lives in New York with a pit bull named Maybe.

**Patricia Carlin**'s books include *Quantum Jitters* and *Original Green* (poems), and *Shakespeare's Mortal Men* (prose). She has published widely in journals and anthologies, including *Boulevard, Verse, BOMB, Pleiades, POOL, American Letters & Commentary,* and *The Literary Review*; she has received fellowships from The MacDowell Colony and VCCA. She teaches literature and poetry writing at The New School and co-edits the poetry journal *Barrow Street.*

**Shanna Compton**'s books include *Brink* (Bloof, 2013), *For Girls & Others* (Bloof, 2008), *Down Spooky* (Winnow, 2005), *Gamers* (Soft Skull, 2004), and several chapbooks. A book-length speculative poem called *The Seam* is forthcoming in 2014. Her work has been included in *The Best American Poetry* series and other anthologies, and recent poems have appeared in *Verse Daily, Poetry Daily, Court Green, The Awl,* and the Academy of American Poets Poem-A-Day feature.

**Jeffery Conway** is the author of *The Album That Changed My Life* (Cold Calm Press, 2006) and two collaborations with David Trinidad and Lynn Crosbie, *Phoebe 2002: An Essay in Verse* (Turtle Point Press, 2003) and *Chain Chain Chain* (Ignition Press, 2000). His work is included in *Saints of Hysteria: A Half Century of Collaborative American Poetry* (Soft Skull Press, 2007) and forthcoming in *Rabbit Ears: TV Poems* (Poets Wear Prada, 2013). He is currently at work on "Descent of the Dolls," a Dante-esque collaborative epic about the 1967 film *Valley of the Dolls,* with poets Gillian McCain and David Trinidad. Poems from his newest manuscript, *Showgirls: The Movie in Sestinas* appear in *Court Green, Vanitas, Clementine, Columbia Poetry Review,* and *Marco Polo.*

**Alfred Corn**'s tenth book of poems, titled *Tables*, appeared in January with Press53. He has also published a novel, titled *Part of His Story*; two collections of essays; and *The Poem's Heartbeat*, a study of prosody. Fellowships for his poetry include the Guggenheim, the NEA, an Award in Literature from the Academy of Arts and Letters, and one from the Academy of American Poets. He has taught at Yale, Columbia, and the University of California, Los Angeles. He spends half of every year in the U.K., and Pentameters Theatre in London staged his play *Lowell's Bedlam* in the spring of 2011. In 2012, he was a Visiting Fellow of Clare Hall, University of Cambridge, preparing a translation of Rilke's *Duino Elegies*, a residency that led to his being named a Life Fellow.

**Michael Costello** was born in Buffalo in 1976 and was educated at SUNY Fredonia before receiving an MFA in Creative Writing from The New School. Since then he has published in numerous print and online journals, including *The Del Sol Review, MiPo, eye-rhyme, The Columbia Poetry Review, La Petite Zine, Tarpaulin Sky*, and *Essays & Fictions*; he was also included in *The Best American Poetry 2004*. Currently, Michael lives and works in Cambridge, MA.

**Laura Cronk**'s first book of poems, *Having Been an Accomplice*, won the 2011 Lexi Rudnitsky First Book Prize from Persea Books. Her work has appeared in the *Best American Poetry* Series. She coordinates the Riggio Honors Program: Writing & Democracy at The New School, and is the poetry editor for *The Inquisitive Eater*. For many years she curated the Monday Night Poetry Series at KGB Bar.

**James Cummins**'s most recent book of poems is *Still Some Cake* (Carnegie Mellon, 2012). His first book, *The Whole Truth*, a sequence of sestinas about the Perry Mason characters, was reissued in 2003 in the Classic Contemporary Series at Carnegie Mellon University Press. Other books include *Then & Now* (Swallow/Ohio University Press, 2004) and *Jim & Dave Defeat the Masked Man*, co-authored with David Lehman and collecting all the sestinas written by the two poets (Soft Skull Press, 2006). His awards include a National Endowment for the Arts Fellowship, an Ingram Merrill grant, and fellowships from the Ohio Arts Council; in addition, his poems have been reprinted in five editions of *The Best American Poetry, The Oxford Book of American Poetry*, and *180 More*. Cummins is curator of the Elliston Poetry Collection at the University of Cincinnati, where he is also a Professor of English.

**Peter Davis**'s books of poetry are *Hitler's Mustache, Poetry! Poetry! Poetry!* and *TINA*. He writes, draws, makes music and teaches in Muncie, Indiana. His website is http://www.artisnecessary.com.

**Sharon Dolin** is the author of five books of poetry, most recently *Whirlwind* (University of Pittsburgh Press, 2012) and *Burn and Dodge* (University of Pittsburgh Press, 2008), winner of the AWP Donald Hall Prize in Poetry. She was a featured poet at the 2012 Dodge Poetry Festival. Her other honors include the Pushcart Prize, a Fulbright fellowship, and artist residencies at Yaddo, MacDowell, Fundación Valparaiso in Spain, and the VCCA Moulin à Nef in France. She teaches at the Unterberg Poetry Center of the 92nd Street Y and directs The Center for Book Arts Annual Letterpress Poetry Chapbook Competition.

**Denise Duhamel** is professor of English at Florida International University, and the author of numerous poetry collections, including *Blowout, Ka-Ching, Two and Two,* and *Queen for a Day: Selected and New Poems* (all from University of Pittsburgh Press). The recipient of numerous awards, including an NEA fellowship, she has been anthologized widely and served as guest editor for *The Best American Poetry 2013.*

**Drew Gardner** was raised among the crumbling industrial husks, pine forests, and sprawling suburbs of central New Jersey. His books include *Sugar Pill* (Krupskaya) *Petroleum Hat* (Roof) and *Chomp Away* (Combo). His CD of conducted music and poetry, *Flarf Orchestra,* was put out by Edge. He lives in New York City.

Former Chairman of the National Endowment for the Arts **Dana Gioia** has published four full-length collections of poetry, as well as eight chapbooks. His poetry collection, *Interrogations at Noon,* won the 2002 American Book Award. Gioia's 1991 volume, *Can Poetry Matter?,* was a finalist for the National Book Critics Circle award. His poems, translations, essays, and reviews have appeared in *The New Yorker, The Atlantic, The Washington Post Book World, Slate,* and *The Hudson Review.* He has won numerous awards, including the 2010 Laetare Medal from Notre Dame. He divides his time between Los Angeles and Sonoma County, California.

**Sarah Green** lives in Athens, Ohio, where she is a third-year doctoral candidate in Creative Writing at Ohio University. Her work has appeared in *Best New Poets 2012,* the 2009 Pushcart Prize Anthology, *Mid-American Review, FIELD, Gettysburg Review, H-ngm-n, Forklift Ohio, Inter/rupture, Leveler, Cortland Review, Redivider,* and elsewhere. A singer-songwriter with the Americana duo Heartacre, Sarah is also an enthusiastic 826 volunteer. Her lesson on teaching sonnets to fifth graders can be found in the 826 National curriculum book *Don't Forget to Write.*

**Beth Gylys,** currently a Professor at Georgia State University, has published two award-winning collections of poetry, *Spot in the Dark* (Ohio State 2004) and *Bodies that Hum* (1999 Silverfish Review Press), and two chapbooks: *Matchbook* (La Vita Poetica Press, 2007) and *Balloon Heart,* which won the Wind Press chapbook award (Wind Press, 1998). Her work has appeared in many journals and anthologies.

**Marilyn Hacker** is the author of twelve books of poems, including *Names* (Norton, 2010), *Essays on Departure* (Carcanet, 2006) and *Desesperanto* (Norton, 2003), an essay collection, *Unauthorized Voices* (Michigan, 2010), and thirteen collections of translations from the French. Her awards include the National Book Award, the Lenore Marshall Prize, two Lambda Literary Awards, the PEN Voelcker Award, and the international Argana Prize for Poetry from the Beit as-Sh'ir/ House of Poetry in Morocco. She lives in Paris.

**Donald Hall** has published numerous books of poetry, most recently *The Back Chamber* (Houghton Mifflin, 2013), *White Apples and the Taste of Stone: Selected Poems 1946–2006* (Houghton Mifflin, 2006), *The Painted Bed* (2002), and *Without: Poems* (1998), which was published on the third anniversary of his wife and fellow poet Jane Kenyon's death from leukemia. Other collections include *The One Day* (1988), which won the National Book Critics Circle Award, the Los Angeles Times Book Prize, and a Pulitzer Prize nomination; *The Happy Man* (1986), which won the Lenore Marshall

Poetry Prize; and *Exiles and Marriages* (1955), which was the Academy of American Poets' Lamont Poetry Selection for 1956. His honors include two Guggenheim fellowships, the Poetry Society of America's Robert Frost Silver medal, a Lifetime Achievement award from the New Hampshire Writers and Publisher Project, and the Ruth Lilly Prize for poetry. In 2006, Hall was appointed the Library of Congress's fourteenth Poet Laureate Consultant in Poetry. He lives in Danbury, New Hampshire.

**James Harms** is the author of eight books of poetry including, most recently, *Comet Scar* (Carnegie Mellon University Press, 2012) and *What to Borrow, What to Steal* (Marick Press, 2012). He chairs the Department of English at West Virginia University, where he also teaches in the MFA Program.

**Brooks Haxton** is the author most recently of *They Lift Their Wings to Cry* (Knopf, 2008) and *Uproar: Antiphones to Psalms* (Knopf, 2006). Other collections include *The Sun at Night* (Knopf, 2001), *Nakedness, Death, and the Number Zero* (Knopf, 2001), and translations of Victor Hugo, Heraclitus, and selected poems from the ancient Greek. He has received numerous awards, including fellowships from the National Endowment for the Arts and the Guggenheim Foundation. Haxton teaches at Syracuse University's Program in Creative Writing and at the Warren Wilson MFA Program for Writers. He lives with his family in Syracuse.

**Anthony Hecht** (1923–2004) was an American poet, literary critic, and translator. Hecht was one of the inventors of the double dactyl. He won the Pulitzer Prize for Poetry for his second collection of poetry, *The Hard Hours* (1968), which dealt with his experiences as a soldier in World War II. Including the Pulitzer Prize, Hecht won many awards and fellowships from The Academy of American Poets, the Ford Foundation, the Guggenheim Foundation and the Rockefeller Foundation. He was a Chancellor Emeritus of The Academy of American Poets. He taught over fifteen years at the University of Rochester and also taught at Yale, Harvard, and Bard.

**Brian Henry** has published nine books of poetry, most recently *Brother No One* (Salt Publishing, 2013). He has translated Tomaž Šalamun's *Woods and Chalices* (Harcourt, 2008) and Aleš Šteger's *The Book of Things* (BOA Editions, 2010), which won the 2011 Best Translated Book Award.

**Scott Hightower** is the author of five books of poetry, most recently *Self-evident* (Barrow Street Press, 2012). *Part of the Bargain* (Copper Canyon Press, 2005) was winner of the Hayden Carruth Award for New and Emerging Poets. Other collections include *Natural Trouble* (2003) and *Tin Can Tourist* (2001). Hightower's translations of Spanish-Puerto Rican poet Aurora de Albornoz have garnered him a Willis Barnstone Translation Prize. He lives and works in New York, and sojourns in Spain.

**Ernest Hilbert** is the author of two collections of poetry, *Sixty Sonnets* (2009) and *All of You on the Good Earth* (2013), as well as a spoken word album recorded with rock band and orchestra, *Elegies & Laments,* available from Pub Can Records. He hosts the popular blog E-Verse (www.everseradio.com) and works as an antiquarian book dealer in Philadelphia, where he lives with his wife, an archaeologist.

**Elizabeth Hildreth**'s poems, translations, and essays have been published in *Hayden's Ferry Review, Bookslut, McSweeney's, Parthenon West, Michigan Quarterly Review*, and *Forklift, Ohio*, among other journals. She recently published *Coses Petites* (Little Things), a translation of a collaborative collection of poems by Catalan poets Anna Aguilar-Amat and Francesc Parcerisas. She is a member of Poems While You Wait, a group of poets who sit in public spaces with manual typewriters and compose poems for passers-by about any topic they request.

**Paul Hoover** has recently published the poetry collections *Desolation: Souvenir* (2012); *Sonnet 56* (2009), consisting of 56 formal versions of Shakespeare's sonnet of that number; *Edge and Fold* (2006); and *Poems in Spanish* (2005). The Mexican poet María Baranda has translated his recent work into Spanish and published it in a bilingual edition, *En el idioma y en la tierra* (Conaculta, 2012). With Maxine Chernoff, he edited and translated *Selected Poems of Friedrich Hölderlin* (2008), winner of the PEN-USA Translation Award. With Nguyen Do, he edited and translated the anthology, *Black Dog, Black Night: Contemporary Vietnamese Poetry* (2008) and *Beyond the Court Gate: Selected Poems of Nguyen Trai* (2010). Professor of Creative Writing at San Francisco State University, he edited *Postmodern American Poetry: A Norton Anthology* (1994), a second edition of which appeared in 2013. With Maxine Chernoff, he edits the annual literary magazine *New American Writing*.

**John Hoppenthaler**'s books of poetry are *Lives of Water* (2003) and *Anticipate the Coming Reservoir* (2008), both with Carnegie Mellon University Press. With Kazim Ali, he has co-edited a volume of essays on the poetry of Jean Valentine, *This-World Company*. For the cultural journal *Connotation Press: An Online Artifact*, he edits "A Poetry Congeries." He is an Associate Professor of Creative Writing and Literature at East Carolina University.

**Sonya Huber** is the author of two books of creative nonfiction, *Cover Me: A Health Insurance Memoir* (2010) and *Opa Nobody* (2008). She has also written a textbook, *The Backwards Research Guide for Writers: Using Your Life for Reflection, Connection, and Inspiration* (2011). Her work has been published in literary journals and magazines including *Creative Nonfiction, Fourth Genre, Crab Orchard Review, Hotel Amerika, The Chronicle of Higher Education*, and the *Washington Post Magazine*. She teaches in the Department of English at Fairfield University and in the Fairfield Low-Residency MFA Program.

**Victor D. Infante** is a poet, editor, and journalist living in Worcester. He edits the online literary journal, *Radius: Poetry From the Center to the Edge* and is the author of *City of Insomnia* (Write Bloody). His poems and stories have been published in *The Collagist, Pearl, Chiron Review, Word Riot*, and *The Nervous Breakdown*, and anthologies such as *Poetry Slam: The Competitive Art of Performance Poetry, Spoken Word Revolution Redux* and *Aim For the Head: An Anthology of Zombie Poetry*. He is a co-editor of the recent *Best Indie Lit New England* anthology. There are rumors linking him to a shadowy sect of Discordian nuclear physicists, Manichean philosophers, and clowns, but really, what are the odds that's true?

**Kent Johnson** has authored, edited, or translated nearly thirty collections in some relation to poetry. *A Question Mark above the Sun: Documents on the Mystery Surrounding a Famous Poem "by" Frank O'Hara* (Punch Press, 2011), named a "Book of the Year" by the Times Literary Supplement, was published in an expanded edition by Starcherone/Dzanc Books in 2012. His translation and annotation of César Vallejo's only known interview is forthcoming as a chapbook from Ugly Duckling Presse. He lives in Freeport, Illinois.

**Donald Justice** (1925–2004) was an American poet and teacher. Born in Florida, he went on to earn an M.A. from University of North Carolina and a Ph.D. from University of Iowa. Throughout his career, Justice released thirteen books of poetry. His first, *The Summer Anniversaries*, won the Lamont Poetry Prize in 1961. His *Selected Poems* won the Pulitzer Prize for Poetry in 1980. His honors also include grants from the Guggenheim Foundation and the National Endowment for the Arts. He taught creative writing at several institutions including Syracuse University, The University of California at Irvine, and Princeton University.

**Meg Kearney**'s most recent collection of poems, *Home By Now* (Four Way Books, 2009), was winner of the 2010 PEN New England LL Winship Award. Its title poem is included in Garrison Keillor's *Good Poems: American Places* anthology (Viking Penguin, 2011). *The Secret of Me*, her novel in verse for teens, was released in 2005 by Persea Books. A sequel, *The Girl in the Mirror*, came in 2013. Kearney's poetry has been featured on Poetry Daily and Garrison Keillor's "A Writer's Almanac," and has been published in such publications as *Poetry, Agni*, and *Ploughshares*. She is Founding Director of the Solstice Low-Residency MFA in Creative Writing Program at Pine Manor College in Chestnut Hill, MA. A former Associate Director of the National Book Foundation (sponsor of the National Book Awards), she is the recipient of fellowships from New Hampshire Council on the Arts, Virginia Center for the Creative Arts, New York Foundation for the Arts, and the Academy of American Poets Award. A native New Yorker, Meg currently resides in New Hampshire with her three-legged black Lab, Trooper.

**Weldon Kees** (1914–1955) was a Nebraska-born poet, novelist, and short story writer. His first collection of poems, *The Last Man*, was published in 1943. His second collection, *The Fall of Magicians*, first appeared in 1947. Kees was also a painter who had one-man shows at galleries including the Peridot Gallery. He also played jazz piano, which he learned after moving to San Francisco. Kees disappeared mysteriously in 1955, his car found abandoned on the Golden Gate Bridge. He is considered an important mid-twentieth century poet of the same generation as John Berryman, Elizabeth Bishop, and Robert Lowell.

**Lynn Kilpatrick**'s first collection of short stories, *In The House*, was published by FC2. Her fiction has recently appeared in *Alfred Hitchcock Mystery Magazine* and *Hotel Amerika*. Her essays have been published in *Ninth Letter, Creative Nonfiction*, and *Brevity*. She earned her Ph.D. in Fiction from the University of Utah and an M.A. in Poetry from Western Washington University. She teaches at Salt Lake Community College.

**Kenneth Koch** (1925–2002) was a poet, prose writer, and playwright. He was a noted member of the New York School of poetry. Koch also wrote and spoke about poetry education, including the books *Lies and Dreams: Teaching Children To Write Poetry* (1970) and *Making Your Own Days: The Pleasures of Reading and Writing Poetry* (1998). He won Bollingen Prizes for both *One Train* (1994) and *On The Great Atlantic Rainway: Selected Poems* 1950-1988 (1994) and was inducted into the American Academy of Arts and Letters in 1996.

**Noelle Kocot** is the author of six books of poetry, most recently *Soul in Space* (Wave Books, 2013). Her other books are *4* (Four Way Books, 2001), *The Raving Fortune* (Four Way, 2004), *Poem for the End of Time and Other Poems* (Wave, 2006), *Sunny Wednesday* (Wave, 2009) and *The Bigger World* (Wave, 2011). Kocot has also translated some of the poems of Tristan Corbière from the French, which appear in *Poet by Default* (Wave, 2011). Her work has been included in three editions of *Best American Poetry* and *The Norton Anthology of Postmodern American Poetry*, among other anthologies. She has received awards from The National Endowment for the Arts, The Fund for Poetry, The Academy of American Poets and the Lannan Literary Foundation, among others. Kocot lives in the wilds of New Jersey and teaches writing in New York City.

**Leonard Kress**'s recent poetry collections include *The Orpheus Complex, Living in the Candy Store, Braids & Other Sestinas,* and forthcoming *Surplus.* He has also translated the 19th century Polish Romantic epic, *Pan Tadeusz* by Adam Mickiewicz. He teaches philosophy, religion, and creative writing at Owens College in Ohio.

**Quraysh Ali Lansana** is author of five poetry books, most recently *mystic turf* (Willow Books, 2012). Other collections include *They Shall Run: Harriet Tubman Poems* (Third World Press, 2004) and a children's book titled *The Big World* (Addison-Wesley, 1998). He is the editor of eight anthologies, including *Dream of A Word: The Tia Chucha Press Poetry Anthology* (Tia Chucha Press, 2006). Lansana is Associate Professor of English/Creative Writing at Chicago State University, where he served as Director of the Gwendolyn Brooks Center for Black Literature and Creative Writing from 2002-2011. *Our Difficult Sunlight: A Guide to Poetry, Literacy & Social Justice in Classroom & Community* (Teachers & Writers Collaborative, 2001, with Georgia A. Popoff) was a 2012 NAACP Image Award nominee.

**Joan Larkin**'s poetry includes *My Body: New and Selected Poems* (Hanging Loose Press, 2007) and *Legs Tipped with Small Claws* (Argos Books, 2012). *Blue Hanuman* is forthcoming from Hanging Loose. Her previous books include *Housework, A Long Sound, Cold River,* and Sor Juana's *Love Poems* (translated with Jaime Manrique). Larkin is currently Conkling Writer in Residence at Smith College and is a member of the faculty of Drew University's MFA Program in Poetry and Poetry in Translation. She has taught at Brooklyn College and Sarah Lawrence College, among many other places. Her honors include the Poetry Society of America's Shelley Memorial Award, the Audre Lorde Award, the Lambda Award, and fellowships from the National Endowment for the Arts and the Academy of American Poets.

**David Lehman**'s books of poetry include *Yeshiva Boys* (Scribner, 2009), *When a Woman Loves a Man* (Scribner, 2005), *The Daily Mirror* (Scribner, 2000), *Valentine Place,* and *Operation Memory.* He and James Cummins collaborated on a book of sestinas, *Jim* *and Dave Defeat the Masked Man.* Lehman is the editor of *The Oxford Book of American Poetry* and series editor of *The Best American Poetry.* He won ASCAP's Deems Taylor Award for his nonfiction book *A Fine Romance: Jewish Songwriters, American Songs* (Schocken, 2009); he also wrote and designed the traveling exhibition based on the book, which visited 55 libraries in 27 states in 2011 and 2012. Among Lehman's other books are a study in detective novels (*The Perfect Murder*), a group portrait of the New York School of poets (*The Last Avant-Garde*), and an account of the scandal sparked by the revelation that a Yale University eminence had written anti-Semitic and pro-Nazi articles for a leading newspaper in his native Belgium (*Signs of the Times: Deconstruction and the Fall of Paul de Man*). He teaches in the graduate writing program at the New School in New York City.

**Eric LeMay** lives in Athens, Ohio. More of his work is available at ericlemay.org.

**Brendan Lorber** is a poet, essayist, editor, and cheerful misanthropologist. He's the author of the forthcoming *Ruin & Desire: Radical 21st Century Poetics & the Secret Path of Ecstasy Within Despair*—a rigorous cautionary tale and wild-eyed how-to guide on wrecking everything. He is also the editor of *Lungfull!*, an annual poetry anthology in which appear contributors' rough drafts along with the final versions so you can see the creative process as it happens. He's written several poetry chapbooks, most recently *Unfixed Elegy and Other Poems.* With the Lungfull! Team, he curates the Zinc Reading Series in New York City. The recipient of numerous grants from the New York State Council on the Arts, he produces *The Acculorber Weekend Weather Report*, which is not about the weather.

**Matt Madden** is a cartoonist who also teaches at the School of Visual Arts and in workshops around the world. His work includes *99 Ways to Tell a Story: Exercises in Style* (Penguin), a collection of his comics adaptation of Raymond Queneau's *Exercises in Style*; a translation from the French of Aristophane's *The Zabome Sisters* (First Second); and *Drawing Words & Writing Pictures* and *Mastering Comics*, (First Second), a pair of comics textbooks written in collaboration with his wife, Jessica Abel. The couple are also series editors for *The Best American Comics* from Houghton-Mifflin Harcourt. He is currently on an extended residency in Angoulême, France with his wife and their two children. You'll find recent news at http://www.mattmadden.com.

**Paul Mariani** is the University Professor of English at Boston College. He is the author of five biographies: *William Carlos Williams: A New World Naked* (a National Book Award finalist); *Dream Song: The Life of John Berryman; Lost Puritan: A Life of Robert Lowell; The Broken Tower: A Life of Hart Crane*; and *Gerard Manley Hopkins: A Life.* Mariani has published seven volumes of poetry, most recently *Epitaphs for the Journey: New, Selected & Revised Poems, Deaths & Transfigurations,* and *The Great Wheel.* The author of the spiritual memoir *Thirty Days: On Retreat with the Exercises of St. Ignatius,* Mariani's awards include a Guggenheim Fellowship, National Endowment for the Arts and National Endowment for the Humanities Fellowships, as well as the John Ciardi Award for Lifetime Achievement in Poetry. He is currently completing a biography of Wallace Stevens for Simon & Schuster and is working on a memoir of growing up on the mean streets of New York in the 1940s.

**Nate Marshall** is from the South Side of Chicago. He is an MFA candidate in Creative Writing at the University of Michigan, was the star of the award-winning full-length documentary *Louder Than A Bomb,* and has been featured on HBO's *Brave New Voices.* His work has appeared in *Vinyl Poetry, Learn Then Burn,* and *The Spoken Word Revolution: Redux,* on Chicago Public Radio and in many other publications. He is also an Assistant Poetry Editor for *Muzzle.* A semi-finalist for the 2013 "Discovery"/ Boston Review Poetry Contest, Marshall has been a teaching artist with organizations such as Young Chicago Authors, InsideOut Detroit, and Southern Word. He is the founder of the Lost Count Scholarship Fund that promotes youth violence prevention in Chicago. Marshall has performed poetry at venues and universities across the US, Canada, and South Africa. He is also a rapper.

**Harry Mathews** is an author of numerous works of poetry and five novels, including the critically acclaimed *Cigarettes, The Conversions,* and *Tlooth.* He is the winner of an NEA Grant in fiction writing and the 1991 National Academy and Institute of Arts and Letters Fiction Writing Award.

**Florence Cassen Mayers** has written 73 Sestinas. 2 are here. 19 have appeared individually, in journals, quarterlies, and anthologies. She is author/designer of 13 children's books, all published. Her collection of sestinas is in search of 1 publisher.

**Marty McConnell** is the author of *wine for a shotgun* (EM Press, 2012), the director of *Vox Ferus,* and a co-founder of the louderARTS Project. Her work has recently appeared in *A Face to Meet the Faces: An Anthology of Contemporary Persona Poetry, City of the Big Shoulders: An Anthology of Chicago Poetry, Indiana Review, Crab Orchard, Gulf Coast,* and *Southern Humanities Review.* She is also the 2012 National Underground Poetry (NUPIC) Champion, and appeared twice on HBO's *Def Poetry Jam.* She lives in Chicago.

**James Merrill** (1926-1995) was a poet, novelist, essayist, and playwright most known for his Pulitzer Prize–winning poetry collection, *The Divine Comedies* (1977). Other awards include two National Book Awards for the collection *Nights and Days* (1966) and *Mirabell: Books of Number* (1978), and the National Book Critics Circle Award for the epic poem *The Changing Light at Sandover* (1982).

**Sharon Mesmer**'s recent poetry collections are *The Virgin Formica* (Hanging Loose) and *Annoying Diabetic Bitch* (Combo Books). Other collections include *Vertigo Seeks Affinities* (Belladonna), *Half Angel, Half Lunch* (Hard Press) and *Crossing Second Avenue* (ABJ Press, Tokyo). Four poems appear in the newly-released *Postmodern American Poetry: A Norton Anthology* (Second Edition). Fiction collections are *In Ordinary Time* and *The Empty Quarter* (Hanging Loose) and *Ma Vie à Yonago* (Hachette, in French translation). An excerpt of her story "Revenge" appears in *I'll Drown My Book: Conceptual Writing By Women* (Les Figues). A two-time NYFA fellow and Fulbright Specialist, she teaches at NYU, the New School, the Poetry Project, and online for the Chicago School of Poetics.

**Anis Mojgani** is a two-time National Poetry Slam Champion and winner of the International World Cup Poetry Slam. A TEDx Speaker and former resident of the Oregon Literary Arts Writers-In-The-Schools program, Mojgani has performed for audiences as varied as the House of Blues and the United Nations. His work has appeared on HBO, NPR, and in such journals as *Rattle*, *Paper Darts*, *Union Station*, and *Used Furniture Review*. Anis is the author of three poetry collections, all published by Write Bloody: *Over the Anvil We Stretch*, *The Feather Room*, and *Songs From Under The River*. Originally from New Orleans, he currently lives in Texas with his wife and their dog, Trudy.

**Rick Moody** is a New York–born novelist and short story writer. His works include the novels *Garden State* (1992), *Purple America* (1996) and *The Diviners* (2005). His first novel, *The Ice Storm* (1994), was made into a feature film, and his memoir *The Black Veil* (2002) won the PEN/Martha Albrand Award for the Art of the Memoir. He has received a Guggenheim Fellowship and his work has appeared in *The New Yorker*, *Esquire*, *Harper's*, and *The New York Times*.

**Carley Moore**'s poetry and essays have been published or are forthcoming in *American Poetry Review*, *Aufgabe*, *Drunken Boat*, *Fence*, and *Swink*. She teaches writing in the Liberal Studies Program at New York University and is a Book Review Editor for the website *Writing in Public*. Her debut young adult novel, *The Stalker Chronicles*, was published by Farrar, Straus, and Giroux in 2012. She blogs at www.carleymoorewrites.com.

**Lenard D. Moore**, a North Carolina native, is the Founder and Executive Director of the Carolina African American Writers' Collective and Co-founder of the Washington Street Writers Group. Moore's poems, essays, and reviews have appeared in such places as *Agni*, *Callaloo*, *African American Review*, and *Crab Orchard Review*. His work has appeared in anthologies such as *The Haiku Anthology* (Norton, 1999) and *The Garden Thrives: Twentieth Century African American Poetry* (HarperCollins, 1996). He is the author of the collections *The Open Eye*, *Forever Home* and, most recently, *A Temple Looming* (WordTech Editions, 2008). He has also been featured on several radio and television programs, including the TBS Documentary *Spirit of the Ark* and Voice of America. A Cave Canem Fellow and former President of the Haiku Society of America, Moore teaches Advanced Fiction Writing and African American Literature at Mount Olive College.

**Jeffrey Morgan** is the author of *Crying Shame*. His poems have appeared in places like *Barrow Street*, *Bat City Review*, *Bellevue Literary Review*, *Painted Bride Quarterly*, *Pleiades*, *Third Coast*, and *West Branch*, among others. His favorite sestina is John Ashbery's "Farm Implements and Rutabagas in a Landscape."

**Tomás Q. Morín** is the winner of the 2012 APR/Honickman First Book Prize for his collection *A Larger Country*. He is co-editor with Mari L'Esperance of the anthology *Coming Close: 40 Essays on Philip Levine*. His poems have appeared in *Slate*, *Threepenny Review*, *Boulevard*, *New England Review*, and *Narrative*. He teaches literature and writing at Texas State University.

**Paul Muldoon** was born in 1951 in County Armagh, Northern Ireland, and educated in Armagh and at the Queen's University of Belfast. From 1973 to 1986 he worked in Belfast as a radio and television producer for the British Broadcasting Corporation. Since 1987 he has lived in the United States, where he is now Howard G.B. Clark

'21 Professor at Princeton University and Founding Chair of the Lewis Center for the Arts. Between 1999 and 2004 he was Professor of Poetry at the University of Oxford. In 2007 he was appointed poetry editor of *The New Yorker*. Paul Muldoon's main collections of poetry are *New Weather* (1973), *Mules* (1977), *Why Brownlee Left* (1980), *Quoof* (1983), *Meeting The British* (1987), *Madoc: A Mystery* (1990), *The Annals of Chile* (1994), *Hay* (1998), *Poems 1968-1998* (2001), *Moy Sand and Gravel* (2002), *Horse Latitudes* (2006), and *Maggot* (2010).

**Amanda Nadelberg** is the author of *Bright Brave Phenomena* (Coffee House Press, 2012), *Isa the Truck Named Isadore* (Slope Editions, 2006), and a chapbook, *Building Castles in Spain, Getting Married* (The Song Cave, 2009).

**Marilyn Nelson** is the author of multiple collections of poetry including the most recent, *Faster Than Light: New and Selected Poems, 1996-2011* (Louisiana State University Press, 2012). Her honors include a Guggenheim Fellowship, the Frost Medal from the Poetry Society of America, two Pushcart Prizes, two creative writing fellowships from the National Endowment for the Arts, a Fulbright Teaching Fellowship, and the 1990 Connecticut Arts Award. Nelson was the Poet Laureate of Connecticut from 2001 to 2006 and in 2013 was elected a Chancellor of the Academy of American Poets.

**Ethan Paquin** is the author of five books of poems, most recently *Cloud vs. Cloud* (Ahsahta Press, 2013). His creative writing and criticism/commentary have appeared in publications including *The Colorado Review, The Boston Review, New American Writing, Quarterly West, Verse, Esquire.com, The Wall Street Journal, Canadian Review of Books,* and *Meanjin* (Australia). Paquin is the founding editor of the longstanding online literary journal *Slope* (http://www.slope.org), and is co-founder and director of the nonprofit small poetry press, Slope Editions. He lives and teaches in his native New Hampshire.

**Richard Peabody** is a French toast addict and native Washingtonian. His latest books are *Speed Enforced by Aircraft* (Broadkill River Press) and *Blue Suburban Skies* (Mint Hill Books). He won the Beyond the Margins "Above & Beyond Award" for 2013. He has edited *Gargoyle Magazine* since back before Elvis died.

**Kiki Petrosino** is the author of *Fort Red Border* (Sarabande, 2009) and *Hymn for the Black Terrific* (Sarabande, 2013). She teaches creative writing at the University of Louisville.

**Carl Phillips** is the author of twelve books of poetry, most recently *Silverchest* (2013). He teaches at Washington University in St. Louis.

**Ezra Pound** (1885-1972) was an American expatriate poet and proponent of the Imagism movement. His best-known works include *Ripostes* (1912), *Hugh Selwyn Mauberley* (1920), and his unfinished 120-section epic *The Cantos* (1917–1969).

**Michael Quattrone** served as a curator of the KGB Monday night poetry reading series from 2007-2011. His work has appeared in the journals *Octopus, No Tell Motel,* and *Jacket,* among others, and in several anthologies, including the *Best American Erotic Poems* (Scribner, 2008). His chapbook, *Rhinoceroses* (2007), was selected by Olena

Kalytiak Davis for the New School Chapbook Award. He is a co-founder of the non-profit organization, Hearthfire, that celebrates creativity and consciousness by offering retreats in nature to deepen connections with Earth, Art & Heart. For more information, visit http://www.hearthfire.org.

**Ned Rust** wrote his first sestina at age thirty and has written approximately one every four years since then. He has co-authored two #1 *New York Times* Bestsellers and a third book that did not make #1; has been an assistant maritime investigator for a law firm, managed to complete most of a semester in a Ph.D. biochemistry program, and was briefly a rock journalist and concert photographer. He now works in a New York City office building and lives in Croton, NY, with his wife and two children.

**Carly Sachs** is a poet, fiction writer, and Kripalu yoga teacher. Her short story "Tender" was selected by Jennifer Egan as the winner of the Stella Kupfenberg Memorial Short Story Prize. "Tender" was read live at Symphony Space in New York City and appeared on "Selected Shorts" on NPR. She is the author of two collections of poetry, *the steam sequence* and *Yama Niyama*, as well as the editor of *the why and later*, a collection of poems women have written about rape and sexual assault.

**Michael Schiavo** lives in Vermont.

**Lawrence Schimel** has published over 100 books in many different genres as author or anthologist, writing in both English and Spanish. His latest poetry collection, *Deleted Names* (A Midsummer Night's Press, 2013), contains two sestinas. Earlier poetry titles include the Spanish-language collection *Desayuno en la Cama* (Egales, 2008) and *Fairy Tales for Writer* (A Midsummer Night's Press, 2007), as well as various anthologies, such as *Best Gay Poetry 2008*. His poems have appeared in numerous anthologies, including *Chicken Soup for the Horse-Lover's Soul 2, The Random House Treasury of Light Verse, The Practice of Peace*, and *Neil Gaiman's The Sandman: Book of Dreams*, as well as in a wide range of periodicals, such as *The Saturday Evening Post, Isaac Asimov's Science Fiction Magazine, The Christian Science Monitor*, and *Physics Today*. He lives in Madrid, Spain where he is a Spanish-to-English translator.

**Jason Schneiderman**, essayist and poet, is the author of *Sublimation Point* and *Striking Surface*. His poetry and essays have appeared in numerous journals and anthologies, including *American Poetry Review, The Best American Poetry, Poetry London, Grand Street, The Penguin Book of the Sonnet, Story Quarterly*, and *Tin House*. Michael Montlack included Jason's essay about Liza Minnelli in his book, *My Diva: 65 Gay Men on the Women Who Inspire Them*. Schneiderman has received fellowships from Yaddo, The Fine Arts Work Center, and The Bread Loaf Writers' Conference. He won the 2009 Richard Snyder Prize from Ashland Poetry Press. He was also the recipient of the Emily Dickinson Award from the Poetry Society of America in 2004. He is an Assistant Professor at the Borough of Manhattan Community College.

**Esther Schor**'s most recent book of poems is *Strange Nursery: Selected Poems* (Sheep Meadow Press, 2012). Schor's other books include *Emma Lazarus* (Schocken, 2006), a biography of the American poet, and *The Hills of Holland: Poems*. Schor edited *The Cambridge Companion to Mary Shelley* (2004), and co-edited *Women's Voices: Visions and*

*Perspectives* (McGraw-Hill, 1990). Her essays and reviews have appeared in *The Times Literary Supplement*, *The New York Times Book Review*, and *The New Republic*. She is Professor of English at Princeton University.

**Ravi Shankar** is the founding editor and Executive Director of *Drunken Boat* (drunkenboat.com), one of the world's oldest electronic journals of the arts. He has published or edited seven books and chapbooks of poetry, including the 2010 National Poetry Review Prize winner, *Deepening Groove*. Along with Tina Chang and Nathalie Handal, he edited W.W. Norton's *Language for a New Century: Contemporary Poetry from Asia, the Middle East & Beyond*, called "a beautiful achievement for world literature" by Nobel Laureate Nadine Gordimer. He has won a Pushcart Prize, been featured in the *New York Times* and the *Chronicle of Higher Education*, appeared as a commentator on the BBC and NPR, received fellowships from the MacDowell Colony and the Connecticut Commission on the Arts, and has performed his work around the world. He is currently Chairman of the Connecticut Young Writers Trust, on the faculty of the first international MFA Program at City University of Hong Kong, and an Associate Professor of English at CCSU.

**Peter Jay Shippy** is the author of four books. *A Spell of Songs* (Saturnalia Books, 2013) is his most recent. His work appeared in *The Best American Poetry* in 2012 and 2013. He teaches at Emerson College.

**Rachel Shukert** is the author of the critically acclaimed memoirs *Everything Is Going To Be Great* (Harper Perennial) and *Have You No Shame?* (Villard), as well as the young adult novel *Starstruck* (Delacourte Books), the first in a three-part series. She has also contributed to a variety of anthologies, including *Click: When We Knew We Were Feminists* and *Best American Erotic Poetry: 1800 to the Present*. Rachel's plays include *Bloody Mary* (NYIT nominee), *Johnny Applefucker, Everything's Coming Up Moses, The Sporting Life* and *The Nosemaker's Apprentice* (both with Nick Jones), and *The Three Gabor Sisters*. Her work has been produced and developed by Ars Nova, Soho Think Tank, the Williamstown Theater Festival, and the Ontological/Hysteric. With Julie Klausner, Rachel co-created, co-wrote, and co-starred in *Wasp Cove*, New York's favorite live prime-time 1980's soap opera. She is currently developing her first feature with Yarn Films in Los Angeles, where she lives with her husband Ben and her bipolar cat, Anjelica Huston.

**Patricia Smith** is the author of six books of poetry including the most recent collection *Shoulda Been Jimi Savannah* (Coffee House Press, 2012). She is also the author of children's book and a companion to the PBS series *Africans in America*. The winner of multiple awards including the Hurston-Wright Legacy Award in Poetry, the Carl Sandburg Literary Award, and the National Poetry Series award, Smith was inducted into the International Literary Hall of Fame for Writers of African Descent and was the recipient of both MacDowell and Yaddo fellowships. Her work has appeared in many literary journals including *Poetry, The Paris Review, Granta, Tin House*, and *TriQuarterly*. Smith has performed her work in various venues across the United States and worldwide. She is a Cave Canem faculty member, a professor of English at CUNY College of Staten Island and a faculty member of the Sierra Nevada MFA program.

**Jay Snodgrass** is the author of *Monster Zero*, poems about Godzilla, from Elixir Press. He lives in Tallahassee, FL. Author most recently of *America: A Prophecy: The Sparrow Reader*, **Sparrow** created quite a stir in 1995 when he picketed *The New Yorker* magazine, holding a placard reading, "My Poetry is as bad as yours." His poetry has since appeared in that magazine as well as *The Quarterly, The New York Times*, and other erudite journals. He was also featured in the PBS series *The United States of Poetry* and can be heard, along with his legendary band Foamola, on the poetry compilation *Poemfone: New Word Order* (Tomato). He is a gossip columnist for *The Phoenicia Times*, a contributing editor to *Chronogram*, a substitute teacher, and the author of two books: *Yes, You ARE a Revolutionary! Plus Seven Other Books* and *Republican Like Me* (both Soft Skull Press). Sparrow lives with his wife and daughter in the hamlet of Phoenicia, New York, in the Catskill Mountains.

**Heidi Lynn Staples**'s debut collection, *Guess Can Gallop*, won the 2004 New Issues Poetry Prize. She is the author of *Dog Girl* (Ahsahta Press 2006) and *Noise Event* (Ahsahta, 2013), drawn from the ecology of her native Gulf Coast. She has also published a nonfiction work, *Take Care Fake Bear Torque Cake* (Caketrain, 2012). Staples's poems have been published in such places as *Best American Poetry 2004, Chicago Review, Denver Quarterly, Green Mountains Review, Ploughshares*, and *Women's Studies Quarterly*. She is co-founder and co-editor with Amy King of Poets for Living Waters, an international poetry response to the BP oil disaster in the Gulf of Mexico, and founder of *pressing on*, a book-arts project utilizing "locally thrown" trash. An Assistant Professor of English and the Learning Center Director at Piedmont College, Heidi lives in Athens, GA with her husband, daughter, cat, and front-yard veggie patch.

**Mark Strand** is the author of numerous collections of poetry, including *Almost Invisible* (2012), *New Selected Poems* (2007), *Man and Camel* (Knopf, 2006), *Dark Harbor* (1993), *The Continuous Life* (1990), *The Story of Our Lives* (1973), and *Reasons for Moving* (1968). His 1998 collection, *Blizzard of One*, won the Pulitzer Prize. Strand has also published books of art criticism, including *The Art of the Real* (1983) and *William Bailey* (1987). His honors include the Bollingen Prize, grants from the National Endowment for the Arts, a National Institute of Arts and Letters Award, a Rockefeller Foundation award, and fellowships from The Academy of American Poets, the MacArthur Foundation, and the Ingram Merrill Foundation. Strand served as Poet Laureate of the United States and is a former Chancellor of The Academy of American Poets. He has taught at Johns Hopkins University and on the Committee on Social Thought at the University of Chicago, and currently teaches English and Comparative Literature at Columbia University.

**Chris Stroffolino** has published seven books of poetry, including *Stealer's Wheel* (Hard Press, 1999) and *Light as a Fetter* (The Argotist UK, 2007). His critical study (with David Rosenthal) of Shakespeare's *Twelfth Night* (IDG books) was published in 2001; more recent writing on contemporary media studies and ethnomusicology have appeared online at *Radio Survivor* and *The Newark Review*. A recipient of grants from NYFA and The Fund For Poetry, Stroffolino was Distinguished Poet-in-Residence at Saint Mary's College from 2001-06, and has since taught at SFAI and Laney College. As a session musician, Stroffolino worked with Silver Jews, King Khan & Gris Gris, and many others. He organized a tribute to Anne Sexton's rock band for The Poetry

Society of America, and joined Greg Ashley to perform the entire *Death Of A Ladies' Man* album for Sylvie Simmons's Leonard Cohen biography in 2012. His most recent musical project (a collaboration with filmmaker Jeff Feuerzeig) is pianovan.com. He is currently looking for work.

**Jade Sylvan** has been published in *PANK, Bayou, Basalt, BuzzFeed, The Sun, Word Riot,* and others. Jade was the winner of the 2011 Bayou Editor's Poetry Prize and was a finalist in the 2012 Basalt Bunchgrass Poetry Prize. Jade has published a book of poetry, *The Spark Singer* (Spuyten Duyvil Press, 2009), and a nonfiction novel, *Kissing Oscar Wilde* (Write Bloody Press, 2013). Jade has collaborated with some of the most groundbreaking artists in the Boston arts community in the role of creator, writer, and/or performer, in such wide-ranging genres as film (including co-writing and starring in the feature film, *TEN*), indie folk music, hip-hop, improv/sketch comedy, vaudeville, drag, visual art, playing anime theme songs on a harmonium, legitimate theatre, and rock & roll. Jade is originally from the Midwest, but now lives in Cambridge, Massachusetts among a rotating cast of geniuses, fairies, magicians, and kings.

**David Trinidad**'s most recent books are *Dear Prudence: New and Selected Poems* (2011) and *Peyton Place: A Haiku Soap Opera* (2013), both published by Turtle Point Press. He is also the editor of *A Fast Life: The Collected Poems of Tim Dlugos* (Nightboat Books, 2011). Trinidad teaches poetry at Columbia College Chicago, where he co-edits the journal *Court Green*.

**Quincy Troupe**'s most recent book of poetry is *Errançities* (Coffee House Press, 2011). *Earl The Pearl: My Story*, an autobiography of basketball legend Earl Monroe, was co-written with Troupe and was published by Rodale Press in 2013. A children's book, *Hallelujah: The Story of Ray Charles* (Disney/Hyperion, 2013), is forthcoming. Among his best-selling works are *Miles: The Autobiography of Miles Davis* and his memoir, *Miles & Me. The Pursuit of Happyness*, an autobiography he wrote with Chris Gardner, which was made into a major motion picture. His collection of poems, *The Architecture of Language*, won the Paterson Award for Sustained Literary Achievement. *Transcircularities: New and Selected Poems* won the 2003 Milt Kessler Poetry Award and was selected by *Publisher's Weekly* as one of the ten best books of poetry in 2002. He has also edited *Giant Talk: An Anthology of Third World Writing* (1975) and is a founding editor of *Confrontation: A Journal of Third World Literature* and *American Rag*. In 2010 Troupe received the American Book Award for Lifetime Literary Achievement. A professor emeritus of the University of California, San Diego, he lives in Harlem with his wife and continues to write as well as edit NYU's *Black Renaissance Noire*.

**Lewis Turco** is a contributor to the recently-published *Garnet Poems: An Anthology of Connecticut Poetry Since 1776*, edited by Dennis Barone (Wesleyan) and *Take Heart: Poems from Maine*, edited by Wesley McNair (Down East). His most recent books, all published in 2012, are *The Book of Forms: A Handbook of Poetics, Including Odd and Invented Forms, Revised and Expanded Fourth Edition* (UPNE); *Wesli Court's Epitaphs for the Poets* (BrickHouse Books); and *Dialects of the Tribe: Postmodern American Poets and Poetry* (Stephen F. Austin State University Press) his second book of critical essays.

**Laura Van Prooyen** is the author of *Inkblot* and *Altar* (Pecan Grove Press). Recent work appears in *The American Poetry Review, Boston Review*, and *The Southern Review*, among others. She is a recipient of grants from the American Association of University Women and the Barbara Deming Memorial Fund, and also was awarded a Dorothy Sargent Rosenberg prize for her poems. Van Prooyen teaches creative writing at Henry Ford Academy: Alameda School for Art + Design in San Antonio, TX.

**Martha Modena Vertreace-Doody** is Distinguished Professor of English and Poet-in-Residence at Kennedy-King College in Chicago. A National Endowment for the Arts Fellow, her several books include *Glacier Fire* (Word Press, 2004, winner of the Word Press Poetry Prize), *Dragon Lady: Tsukimi* (Riverstone Press), and *Second Mourning* (Diehard Publishers). Vertreace-Doody was twice a Fellow at the Hawthornden International Writers' Retreat in Scotland. Her work appears in *Illinois Voices: An Anthology of Twentieth-Century Poetry* (University of Illinois Press, 2001) and *Poets of the New Century* (David R. Godine Publisher, 2001). She lives in Chicago with her husband, Tim, who is a hospital chaplain, and their cats Fred and Patrick Samuel.

**Anne Waldman** is the author of more than 40 books, including the mini-classic *Fast Speaking Woman*, the collection of essays *Vow to Poetry*, and several selected poems editions including *Helping the Dreamer, Kill or Cure* and *In the Room of Never Grieve*. She has concentrated on the long poem as a cultural intervention with such projects as *Marriage: A Sentence, Structure of The World Compared to a Bubble*, and *Manatee/Humanity*, a book-length rhizomic meditation on evolution and endangered species, as well as the monumental anti-war feminist epic *The Iovis Trilogy: Colors in the Mechanism of Concealment*, a 25-year project. Waldman was one of the founders and directors of The Poetry Project at St. Marks's Church In-the-Bowery, working there for twelve years. She also co-founded, with Allen Ginsberg, the celebrated Jack Kerouac School of Disembodied Poetics at Naropa University, the first Buddhist inspired University in the western hemisphere, in 1974. Waldman is a recipient of a 2013 Guggenheim Fellowship, the Poetry Society of America's Shelley Memorial Award, and has recently been appointed a Chancellor of The Academy of American Poets. She divides her time between New York City and Boulder, Colorado.

**Miller Williams** is the author, editor, or translator of thirty-three books, including *Time and the Tilting Earth* (LSU Press, 2008), *Some Jazz a While: Collected Poems* (University of Illinois Press, 1999), and *Patterns of Poetry: An Encyclopedia of Forms*. Among his honors are the Amy Lowell Traveling Scholarship in Poetry from Harvard University, the Poets' Prize, and the Prix de Rome for Literature and the Academy Award for Literature, both from the American Academy of Arts and Letters. He was inaugural poet for Bill Clinton's second swearing-in as president. As a young man he played the clarinet and saxophone in a jazz combo. He is the father of three-time Grammy Award-winning singer and songwriter Lucinda Williams.

**Jonah Winter** is the author of two poetry volumes, *Maine* and *Amnesia*. He is also the author of many children's books, including *Gertrude Is Gertrude Is Gertrude Is Gertrude* and *Here Comes the Garbage Barge!* He has a forthcoming book on the Founding Fathers being illustrated by the New Yorker cover artist Barry Blitt, whose name Winter loves to drop whenever possible or useful.

**Louis Zukofsky** (1904-1978) was one of the founders and the primary theorist of the Objectivist group of poets and has been an important influence on subsequent generations of poets in America and abroad. He spent forty-six years writing his masterwork "*A*," and died before he could see the completed version published. Poet, translator, fiction writer, essayist, anthologist, critic, teacher, WPA worker, Zukofsky was born in New York City and lived in or near the city his whole life.

# COPYRIGHTS

# ABOUT THE EDITOR

**Daniel Nester** is a poet, essayist, editor, and teacher. His most recent
books include *How to Be Inappropriate*, a collection of nonfiction, as
well as *God Save My Queen* and *God Save My Queen II*, cross-genre
explorations on his obsession with the rock band Queen. A former
Assistant Web Editor for Sestinas for *McSweeney's Internet Tendency*,
his writing has appeared in such places as *Salon, The New York
Times, The Morning News, The Daily Beast,* and *Salon,* and has been
anthologized in *Best American Poetry, Third Rail: The Poetry of Rock and
Roll, The Best Creative Nonfiction,* and *Now Write! Nonfiction.* He lives
in Upstate New York with his wife and daughters. Find him online
at danielnester.com.

# IF YOU LIKE DANIEL NESTER,
# DANIEL NESTER LIKES...

*Everything Is Everything*
Cristin O'Keefe Aptowicz

*Scandalabra*
Derrick C. Brown

*Racing Hummingbirds*
Jeanann Verlee

*Spiking the Sucker Punch*
Robbie Q. Telfer

*Kissing Oscar Wilde*
Jade Sylvan

# WRITE BLOODY BOOKS

*After the Witch Hunt* — Megan Falley

*Aim for the Head: An Anthology of Zombie Poetry* — Rob Sturma, Editor

*Amulet* — Jason Bayani

*Any Psalm You Want* — Khary Jackson

*Birthday Girl with Possum* — Brendan Constantine

*The Bones Below* — Sierra DeMulder

*Born in the Year of the Butterfly Knife* — Derrick C. Brown

*Bring Down the Chandeliers* — Tara Hardy

*Ceremony for the Choking Ghost* — Karen Finneyfrock

*Courage: Daring Poems for Gutsy Girls* — Karen Finneyfrock, Mindy Nettifee & Rachel McKibbens, Editors

*Dear Future Boyfriend* — Cristin O'Keefe Aptowicz

*Dive: The Life and Fight of Reba Tutt* — Hannah Safren

*Drunks and Other Poems of Recovery* — Jack McCarthy

*The Elephant Engine High Dive Revival* anthology

*Everything Is Everything* — Cristin O'Keefe Aptowicz

*The Feather Room* — Anis Mojgani

*Gentleman Practice* — Buddy Wakefield

*Glitter in the Blood: A Guide to Braver Writing* — Mindy Nettifee

*Good Grief* — Stevie Edwards

*The Good Things About America* — Derrick Brown & Kevin Staniec, Editors

*Hot Teen Slut* — Cristin O'Keefe Aptowicz

*I Love Science!* — Shanny Jean Maney

*I Love You Is Back* — Derrick C. Brown

*The Importance of Being Ernest* — Ernest Cline

*In Search of Midnight* — Mike McGee

*The Incredible Sestina Anthology* — Daniel Nester, Editor

*Junkyard Ghost Revival* anthology

*Kissing Oscar Wilde* — Jade Sylvan

*The Last Time as We Are* — Taylor Mali

*Learn Then Burn* — Tim Stafford & Derrick C. Brown, Editors

*Learn Then Burn Teacher's Manual* — Tim Stafford & Molly Meacham, Editors

*Live for a Living* — Buddy Wakefield

*Love in a Time of Robot Apocalypse* — David Perez

*The Madness Vase* — Andrea Gibson

*The New Clean* — Jon Sands

*New Shoes on a Dead Horse* — Sierra DeMulder

*No Matter the Wreckage* — Sarah Kay

*Oh, Terrible Youth* — Cristin O'Keefe Aptowicz

*The Oregon Trail Is the Oregon Trail* — Gregory Sherl

*Over the Anvil We Stretch* — Anis Mojgani

*Pole Dancing to Gospel Hymns* — Andrea Gibson

*Racing Hummingbirds* — Jeanann Verlee

*Rise of the Trust Fall* — Mindy Nettifee

*Scandalabra* — Derrick C. Brown

*Slow Dance with Sasquatch* — Jeremy Radin

*The Smell of Good Mud* — Lauren Zuniga

*Songs from Under the River* — Anis Mojgani

*Spiking the Sucker Punch* — Robbie Q. Telfer

*Strange Light* — Derrick C. Brown

*These Are the Breaks* — Idris Goodwin

*Time Bomb Snooze Alarm* — Bucky Sinister

*The Undisputed Greatest Writer of All Time* — Beau Sia

*What Learning Leaves* — Taylor Mali

*What the Night Demands* — Miles Walser

*Working Class Represent* — Cristin O'Keefe Aptowicz

*Write About an Empty Birdcage* — Elaina Ellis

*Yarmulkes & Fitted Caps* — Aaron Levy Samuels

*The Year of No Mistakes* — Cristin O'Keefe Aptowicz

*Yesterday Won't Goodbye* — Brian S. Ellis

CPSIA information can be obtained at www.ICGtesting.com
Printed in the USA
LVOW13s1342300913

354648LV00003B/6/P